Intergalactic
JUDAISM

An Analysis of Torah Concepts
Based on Discoveries in
Space Exploration, Physics and Biology

Rabbi DAVID LISTER

URIM PUBLICATIONS
Jerusalem · New York

Intergalactic Judaism: An analysis of Torah concepts based on discoveries in space exploration, physics and biology
by Rabbi David Lister

Copyright © 2011 by David Lister
All rights reserved. No part of this book may be used or reproduced in any manner whatsoever without written permission from the copyright owner, except in the case of brief quotations embodied in reviews and articles.

Printed in Israel. First Edition.

Book design by Ariel Walden

ISBN-13: 978-965-524-053-5

Urim Publications
P.O. Box 52287, Jerusalem 91521 Israel

Lambda Publishers Inc.
527 Empire Blvd., Brooklyn, New York 11225 U.S.A.
Tel: 718-972-5449   Fax: 718-972-6307   mh@ejudaica.com
www.UrimPublications.com

'This thought-provoking book demonstrates how modern physics can refresh our perception of Torah and our work in the world.'

—Rabbi Dr. AKIVA TATZ

Author of *Anatomy of a Search, Living Inspired, Worldmask* and *The Thinking Jewish Teenager's Guide to Life*

Rabbi Zev Leff

הרב זאב לף

Rabbi of Moshav Matityahu
Rosh HaYeshiva—Yeshiva Gedola Matityahu

מרא דאתרא מושב מתתיהו
ראש הישיבה—ישיבה גזולה מתתיהו

D.N. Modiin 71917   Tel: 08—976—1138 טל'   Fax: 08—976—5326 פקס'   ד.נ. מודיעין 71917

Dear Friends,

    I have read the manuscript of "Intergalactic Judaism" by Rabbi David Lister. I have found it fascinating from a scientific perspective and enlightening and inspiring from a Torah perspective. Rabbi Lister has effectively conveyed how "The Heavens declare the Glory of G-d" in an informative, interesting and inspiring manner.

    May Hashem Yisborach grant Rabbi Lister the ability to continue to use his multifaceted knowledge to merit the community with further works.

           Sincerely,
           With Torah blessings

           Rabbi Zev Leff

DEDICATIONS

Dedicated by HENRY ARNOLD in memory of ARON and RENA ZABIELAK, who felt that Jewish literature is very important in order to promote the continuity of the Jewish people.

అ

The BALSAM FAMILY would like to dedicate this to the six million Jews who perished in the Holocaust. 'Please ensure that the future generations never forget!' – HARRY BALSAM, Holocaust Survivor 1929-2003.

అ

Thank you to the A & G COHN MEMORIAL TRUST for their generous support.

అ

Dedicated by ELI & ADRIENNE DWEK in memory of their fathers YITZCHAK BEN ELIAHU DWEK HA-COHEN and MOSHE MORDECHAI BEN ISRAEL SOCKET.

అ

Dedicated by RICHARD EKER in loving memory of his parents YEHOSHUA BEN MENDEL and FREIDEL BAS AVRAHAM and his brother MENDEL BEN YEHOSHUA.

అ

From the GOLDMAN FAMILY in loving memory of ARTHUR GOLDMAN – ASHER MELECH BEN ELIEZER YAACOV zt"l. As a travel journalist, he was privileged to travel widely. In his wisdom he would say 'You don't have to own the world to appreciate its beauty.'

CONTENTS

FOREWORD
Chief Rabbi Professor Jonathan Sacks

A WHILE BACK I INDUCTED A NEW RABBI INTO OFFICE. IT'S something I do often, and there is a certain predictability to the proceedings. I give the new rabbi my blessings and encouragement. He in reply thanks those who have helped him through the years, and sets out his aspirations as a spiritual leader and his vision for the future of the congregation. Imagine, therefore, my surprise when this particular rabbi took as the centerpiece of his address a poem entitled 'Ode to a Harley Davidson' (a classic motorbike, for the uninitiated). It was unexpected, eccentric, and wholly effective. It perfectly fitted his theme – as unusual as the poem itself – which was that Judaism is about celebrating the present moment, the epiphanies of everyday life.

By now you will have guessed that the rabbi was David Lister, the author of this book. He is a man of rare spirituality and deep humanity, with a radiant smile that seems to come all the way from heaven itself. This is an unusual person, and appropriately he has written an unusual book. The title itself, *Intergalactic Judaism*, is enough to make you want to open it immediately and start reading. Once you have started, you are unlikely to stop. I'm not sure that I've read anything like it before.

Here is a work that combines dazzling erudition in astronomy, theoretical physics and various other scientific disciplines, together with a fine knowledge of Jewish mysticism and biblical commentary, and – what is truly rare – an ability to combine them seamlessly into a view of the world that is both spiritual and humane. What Rabbi Lister has, and generously shares with us, is a capacity for wonder: at the majesty of creation and therefore of the Creator. Here, with examples drawn from interstellar space to lightning,

An aerial view of the San Andreas Fault, where two plates in the Earth's crust have fetched up against each other, creating an earthquake hot spot. (Ian Kluft)

earthquakes and the humble lichen, is one man's testimony to the miracles with which we are daily surrounded and which, if only we would open our eyes, testify to the awesome splendor of the universe. This is a surprising book and a moving one, and no reader will come away without having learned not only facts of which he or she was previously unaware, but also a new reverence in the face of existence itself, a sense of privilege at being alive. 'Lift your eyes and look to the heavens,' said Isaiah, 'and see who created all these.' Rabbi Lister has written, in effect, an extended commentary to that verse.

In his halachic code, the *Mishneh Torah*, Maimonides wrote that the natural sciences, along with metaphysics, are the paths to the love and awe of God. Understanding the complexity of the universe, he believed, we could not but feel the greatness of God, the smallness of mankind, and the strange and striking grace by which we are able to communicate with heaven because God has communicated with us. That is a set of ideas that suffered an eclipse with the mechanistic view of the universe that grew with the Enlightenment, and the 'blind watchmaker' of neo-Darwinism. The time is right for us to reconsider and rehabilitate the Maimonidean perspective because so much of modern science – from cosmology to the mapping of the human genome – has revealed a world far more complex and finely tuned for the emergence of life than had hitherto been suspected. Rabbi Lister's book, though not on this theme, is part of that process. Rightly he sees religious faith and science not as enemies but as potential friends.

The great nineteenth-century mystic, Rabbi Zadok ha-Cohen of Lublin, once said that in the beginning, God wrote a book. He called it the universe. Then he wrote a commentary to this book and called it the Torah. That, he added, is why there are new insights (*chiddushim*) into Torah every day. We say in our prayers that God, every day, renews the work of creation. And if the universe is new every day, then Torah – God's commentary to the universe – must also be new every day. To that lovely thought this book is testimony. It is full of new ideas, or rather ancient and classic ideas in a new context, and just as a diamond sparkles with new radiance when placed in a new setting, so do the words of Torah when reset by a jeweler, which is what our author is. Thank you, Rabbi Lister, for an unusual and delightful book which, by making us see the universe in a new light, will help us be a little different in future, more attuned to the wonders of creation, more open to the divine music of life.

"Lift your eyes and look to the heavens and see who created all these!" This picture shows the planet Venus reflected in the Pacific Ocean. (Mila Zinkova).

The universe is a complex place. In the spiral galaxy M81, the bluer colors towards the edges are made by younger stars, while the yellows and whites of the centre are made by older stars like our own Sun. Clouds of interstellar dust can also be seen in the galaxy's swirling arms. (NASA, ESA, and the Hubble Heritage Team (STScI/AURA))

ACKNOWLEDGMENTS

MANY PEOPLE HAVE HELPED TO CREATE THIS BOOK, AND without them it would not be here. My thanks are due to the Chief Rabbi Lord Jonathan Sacks, Rabbi Zev Leff, Rabbi Dr. Akiva Tatz and a blessed Jewish friend and mentor for giving me the benefit of their knowledge, insight and expertise; to Greg Chamitoff for generously sharing impressions of his experiences in space and allowing me to publish pictures of him; to Dr Paul Newham and Dr Mervyn Black for invaluable help with the science; to Louise Greenberg for her kind advice on getting the book published; to Urim Publications for nurturing this book from manuscript to completion; to Bernie Nyman of BM Nyman & Co., Publishing Lawyers, for his meticulous legal advice; to RK for careful proofreading; to the people who kindly contributed towards the cost of producing the book; to my parents and parents-in-law for their guidance and wisdom freely given over many years; to my children Moshe Chaim, Shoshana, Yishai, Leora and Akiva for making me smile, and, *acharona acharona chaviva*, to my wife Rachie for her unwavering support and encouragement.

The Space Shuttle Discovery blasts off from the Kennedy Space Centre, bringing supplies and research equipment to the crew of the International Space Station. (NASA/Ben Cooper)

INTRODUCTION

ASTRONOMY AND THE SPACE AGE HAVE IRREVOCABLY changed our perspective on our place in the universe. A thousand years ago, many people believed that we lived on a flat Earth and that the heavens were not much larger than our home planet. Since then, discoveries made by diligent astronomers and advanced space probes have shown that the Earth is a tiny speck in a huge cosmos containing wondrous phenomena and structures that are difficult for us to comprehend and visualize. During the last two hundred years, we have vastly increased and refined our understanding of the nature of planets, the composition of stars and the possibility of life on other worlds.

Alongside this drive to plumb the secrets of the most gigantic thing we know of – the entire universe – there have been remarkable advances in our comprehension of what it is made of. Scientists have formulated an understanding of the atom's structure and behavior, and moved on to define and understand the particles which make up atoms, having to cope with increasingly surreal findings which have revolutionized our understanding of the nature of matter and physical existence.

Is there a place for all these cutting-edge discoveries within the pages of the Torah?

If we remember that God is omniscient[1] – the ultimate Scientist – then we should not consider scientific discoveries as alien to the ancient text of the Torah. Facts that would only be discovered by humans thirty or forty centuries later were known to God when He vouchsafed prophetic insight to those worthy to receive it, and it would be reasonable to suppose that He included these insights as part of His message. Similarly, the traditional explanations of

---

1   Daniel 2:22.

the Bible, handed down from God to Moses and on to the sages of the Talmud and Midrash[2], were transmitted and crystallized with a divine sub-text which takes into account all the scientific principles which underpin nature.

Early Jewish sources indicate that this was the case. Around two thousand years ago in the Talmudic era, the sage Ben Bag Bag said, 'Turn [the Torah] over and over, for everything is in it.'[3]

Nachmanides made this point more clearly in the introduction to his commentary on the Torah:

> God gives wisdom without any falsehood to know how the universe came into being, the action of the constellations . . . the arrangement of the stars, the constitutions of animals, the strength of winds, the thoughts of people, how trees relate to each other and the strength of roots, everything hidden and revealed . . . All this did [King] Solomon know through the Torah, and he found everything in it.

The Gaon of Vilna expanded on this theme as well, writing:

> Everything that was, is and will be is included in the Torah . . . even the details of every animal, plant and inanimate object, with all their features.[4]

The implications of this notion are far-reaching. When God spoke of light, He was aware that it bends in a strong gravitational field, and that certain kinds of light can blast through solid rock. When He designated the Moon as the principal criterion for regulating the Jewish calendar, He knew how the Moon orbited the Earth and that, from time to time, it would eclipse the Sun. When He spoke about the cosmos, He was watching the progress of asteroids and the brief blossoming of supernovae.

This premise enables us to revisit primordial Torah ideas and attempt to reconstitute them as they may have been understood by those who had deeper insight into them. A simple Biblical reference to something from the physical world takes on startling depths

---

2 Pirkei Avot (Ethics of the Fathers), chapter 1, Mishnah 1.
3 Pirkei Avot chapter 5, Mishnah 25.
4 In his explanation of Sifra DiTzniuta chapter 5.

and dimensions when we bear in mind the knowledge offered to us by modern disciplines such as astrophysics, quantum mechanics, meteorology, geology, biology and space exploration. *Intergalactic Judaism* seeks to investigate and enhance our understanding of the Torah in the light of the revelations of modern science, using these discoveries as a commentary on Biblical imagery.

Employing knowledge of the physical world as an adjunct to spirituality does not constitute a new approach to Judaism. Maimonides emphatically encouraged people to look at the creation in order to reach a higher spiritual plane:

> How can one come to feel love and reverence for God? When one considers [God's] great and wondrous deeds and creatures, and understands through them His infinite and incomparable wisdom, immediately one is moved to love and praise God, and one yearns to know Him better . . .
>
> When one thinks about the [elements of creation] themselves, one is immediately brought up short, one is seized with awe, and one knows that one is a small, lowly and obscure creature with a limited and wayward understanding before the One who is all knowing.[5]

Many centuries later, Rabbi Samson Raphael Hirsch recommended in a similar vein that one should develop one's knowledge of the natural world in order to properly appreciate the Biblical account of creation:

> Consider how much more profound our children's understanding of the rest of the Biblical text will be if, by the time they read it, their knowledge of natural sciences and learning of Genesis will have made them aware that the whole world, down to the minutest form of matter, down to each fiber of every living thing and every component of that fiber, represents the realization of one single thought . . .
>
> Consider the new understanding with which the students who have a background in natural sciences will read such reflections on nature as the one uttered by Job[6] whose praise of God's almighty power so long ago bears such an uncanny resemblance to a Newtonian thought thousands of years later: *toleh eretz al blimah*, literally 'He keeps the Earth suspended by forces that act to limit one another.'
>
> Think of the new understanding with which they will hear the Psalms

5   Hilchot Yesodei HaTorah 2:2
6   26:7

A view of Israel and the Sinai desert from space. When God spoke to us here, He knew the science that would underpin the Modis 11 mission which created this photograph of the Promised Land. (Jacques Descloitres, MODIS Land Rapid Response Team, NASA/GSFC).

of David . . . which extol all of nature and history as one single chorus reflecting the glory of the one, sole God.[7]

In fact, Rabbi Hirsch himself did occasionally apply science to the Torah in order to explain it. We see an example of this in his science-based interpretation of the rainbow which God designated as a sign after the flood:

A rainbow is essentially one unified, complete ray of light in its purest form, broken up into seven colors. These colors range from the red ray, which is closest to the light, to the violet, which, farthest from the light, merges into darkness. Yet they are all shades of light, and, together, they form one white ray, which shines forth in full purity.

This signifies that the whole infinite variety of living things, from Adam, the 'red ("adom") one' who is closest to God, to the dullest form of life, the lowly worm; and especially the whole spectrum of humanity, from the person of the highest spiritual refinement to the one in whom there is only a faint, barely discernible glimmer of the Divine – all are

7   Rabbi Samson Raphael Hirsch, *Collected Writings Vol. VII, The Relevance of Secular Studies.*

united by God in one common bond of peace. In all of them is found a refracted ray of God's spirit, and even the dullest in spirit, who are distant from the light, are 'sons of the light'.[8]

Judaism specifically encourages us to look out into the heavens in order to develop our understanding of our mission as Jews. God said through the prophet Isaiah, 'Lift up your eyes heavenward, and see who created these!'[9] This is rendered in the paraphrastic translation of Rabbi Yonatan ben Uziel as a means to attain a sense of reverence for God: 'Lift up on high your eyes and look, that you may feel fear before the One who created these!'

We find this idea expressed more clearly in another passage in the book of Isaiah, where God rebukes Israel for not paying sufficient attention to their physical environment:

> Woe to those who get up early in the morning to chase after strong drink, and stay up late at night. Wine inflames them! The lyre and harp, the drum and the flute and wine are at their feasts, but they do not look at God's work, and they have not seen what His hands have made![10]

The clear implication is that if the people were to look at God's handiwork – the universe and its contents – they would stop to think, and mend their ways.

The Talmud presents this verse as an obligation to study the workings of the heavens:

> Rabbi Shimon ben Pazi said that Rabbi Yehoshua ben Levi said in the name of Bar Kapara, 'If someone knows how to calculate equinoxes, solstices and the passage of the stars but does not do so, Scripture says, "They do not look at God's work, and they have not seen what His hands have made!"'[11]

We should not think that this is simply laying down a requirement that the calendar be maintained in good order with reference to the seasons. If that were the case, it would be sufficient for the

---

8   Rabbi Hirsch's commentary on Genesis 9:15.
9   Isaiah 40: 26.
10   Isaiah 5: 11 – 12.
11   Shabbat 75a.

rabbinical authorities of each community to have the requisite skills and knowledge and make the appropriate calculations.

Rather, Bar Kapara might have meant that the act of observing the intricate movements of the colossal cosmic mechanism instills in one a sense of wonder at the creation, and at the same time a sense of intimate connection with its vastness and might. Both these feelings can be the first steps away from sin and towards a better connection with God.

In a similar vein, Rabbi Samson Raphael Hirsch showed that Judaism regards the wisdom of creation as a way of attaining an understanding of the Torah:

> The moral law that is to be translated into reality in the lives of men and nations is simply the universal law of God in the microcosm of the small circle of mankind and of human existence, the same law that operates in the cosmic existence of Heaven and Earth. This is a law that Heaven and Earth must obey without a will of their own, that rules all the cosmic and earthly phenomena, that is present in every drop of water . . .
>
> That same law was offered to man so that he might choose to obey it of his own free will. It did not originate from within man but was addressed to him from without by that same lawgiving God. By obeying this moral law of his own free choice, man joins the great chorus of creatures that serve God.
>
> With this philosophy as our guide, we need not fear what will happen to man's moral character if he undertakes to delve into the workings of nature. Indeed, this philosophy expressly invites us to study the heavens and the Earth so that the course of every star in the heavens and the growth of every seedling on Earth may reveal to us not only [God as] the Creator but also [God as] the Lawgiver . . .
>
> In the view of this philosophy, the seraph before God's throne and the tiny insect in the sunshine are both ruled by the same concept of divine law, and alongside, or rather, high above both of these, there is man, who is at liberty to chart his life of his own free will. This is the concept of duty, duty in the concept of mitzvah, the commandment of a higher authority.[12]

But we must proceed cautiously in analyzing Biblical texts with the help of science, because Torah and science work in different ways.

---

12 Rabbi Samson Raphael Hirsch, *Collected Writings Vol. VII, Ethical Training in the Classroom.*

The Torah itself is God-given and eternally binding[13], and the accompanying oral tradition that explains its laws and ethics is sacrosanct too. We can apply and clarify the Torah, we can derive and explain its principles and laws, but we dare not alter it, because God has given it.

Conversely, science gains its strength from its mutability. As scientists discover more about the universe, they must refine and recast what they have already learned. Ptolemy's view of the universe as a system of spheres one inside the other with the Earth at its centre was widely held to be true until the sixteenth century when Copernicus devised an alternative approach which had the Sun at the centre of the Solar System. Likewise, Newtonian physics was sacrosanct in scientific circles for centuries until Einstein and his peers showed that Newton's theories are not universally applicable, and that they break down over very large or very small scales. The same root and branch reassessment could befall the apparently conclusive scientific truths of our own time.

Thus, a science-based approach to the Torah must be undertaken with a caveat in mind – that science changes. The evaluation of Torah symbolism with the science of the twenty-first century is no exception to this. If we view the Torah through the lens of science, we will find that view changing over time, because science is continually evolving.

This means that science may be brought to bear on a Biblical metaphor in a hundred years' time with different results to our own because science, having developed over a hundred years, might mesh with the Torah in a different way. Nevertheless, we are entitled to seek after spiritual truth as we understand it now, always bearing in mind that human frailty and ignorance might mean that we must change our minds later on.

There is another caveat that needs to be mentioned. In analyzing the Torah from a scientific standpoint and attempting to deepen our understanding of its symbolism, we must be careful not to allow the scientific reframing of the ideas implied by Torah symbolism to outweigh the explicit message of the Biblical text or the

---

13 Deuteronomy 29:28.

The immensity of the cosmos is demonstrated by this picture taken by the Hubble Space telescope. Each of the patches of light is a galaxy containing billions of stars. (NASA, ESA, F Summers (STScI))

complementary, God-given Oral Tradition dating back to the time of Moses. To do so would be absurd: no author would include a symbol in their text and intend it to be interpreted in a way inconsistent with the same text's explicit message. The reverse should be the case: the broad context of received Torah knowledge and law ought to be borne in mind when we investigate a Biblical metaphor, and it must inform our understanding of God's work.

To cite a simple example: we find God compared to the Sun[14], but we would not be justified in deducing that God is physical and finite just like the Sun, since the Torah emphasizes repeatedly that God is not physical[15], and that He has no limitations[16].

Here again, the writing of Rabbi Samson Raphael Hirsch is instructive. Commenting on a Jew's engagement with science, he observed:

> Israel endeavors to penetrate into the significance and development of all interrelationships of the world and humanity in the light of revealed truths, the truth from Sinai.[17]

Our task is further complicated by the fact that a metaphor is by definition not explicit. Rather, it is a literary device employed to express near inexpressible ideas and stir our hearts. So there is bound to be a degree of choice and subjectivity in the analysis of a metaphor. It is difficult to decide exactly how far one should apply science to a commentary on a metaphor, and what aspect of the metaphor is most prominent. The analogy of the Sun is illustrative in this regard: when God is compared to the Sun, does this mean He is as powerful, as necessary for human life, as spiritually radiant or as beautiful? Or all of these things?

The Ohr HaChaim outlines the limits for interpretation of scripture in his introduction to his commentary on the Torah:

---

14 Psalms 84:12.
15 Deuteronomy 4:12.
16 Genesis 18:14.
17 Rabbi Samson Raphael Hirsch, *Collected Writings Vol. IV*, in the chapter *Shirei Hama'alos – The Fifteen Songs of Ascent.*

Permission is given to those who explore the Torah to work and sow it with the light that is sown for the righteous, and the land of life will bring up fruit for all seed that a child of the Torah sows in it. Only in matters of Jewish law should one not deviate from the direction established by predecessors. And one should not invent new things that were not regarded by the heirs of the Torah. . . . From them the children of Torah should take guidance to work and blaze a new trail to make a path through the Scriptures.

This book does not pretend to use scientific knowledge to offer definitive interpretations of Biblical texts. It merely suggests possible approaches to the melding of contemporary scientific knowledge with Biblical passages, in the hope that a further degree of spiritual enlightenment will emerge.

As we look at our ancient heritage through modern eyes, we will be moving from tiny subatomic particles to curious features of our own terrestrial environment, to the Moon, our neighboring planets, the limits of the Solar System, and beyond to the stars and the furthest reaches of the universe. We will find a wondrous and beautiful system, the magnificent handiwork of God Himself. We will encounter religious imagery which is simultaneously innovative, ancient and timeless.

Our findings will be included in the ancient and majestic corpus of Jewish tradition as long as they are firmly grounded in the truth entrusted to the leaders of our nation at Mount Sinai thousands of years ago.

A beam of electrons creates a circular pattern in a magnetic field. (Marcin Bialek)

PERFORMING UNDER PRESSURE

THE FIFTH AND FINAL BOOK OF THE TORAH CONSISTS OF Moses' final speech to the Jewish people, which he gave just before he died. Towards the end of his address, Moses reassured the Israelites that the Torah is accessible and not at all beyond their grasp:

> [The Torah] is not in the heavens, such that you might say, 'Who will go up for us into the heavens and get it for us, so that we could learn it and perform its commandments?' . . . But really, it is very close to you – in your mouth and in your heart, to do it.[1]

Rabbi Avdimi bar Hama bar Dosya, one of the sages of the Talmud, explained the implications of this speech: 'What is the meaning of "[The Torah] is not in the heavens"? That if it were in the heavens, you would need to go up after it!'[2]

This hints about the centrality of Torah in our lives.

Imagine a situation where the Torah was written in a book which just happened to be on a different planet. As Jews charged by God to observe the laws of the Torah, we would have to get up there and bring it back– an almost impossible task. But without Torah, the voice of God in our lives, our existence is flawed[3]. Torah is so precious that we would need to perform the most elaborate feats of ingenuity in order to gain access to it – even if interplanetary travel were involved.

---

1   Deuteronomy 30:11–14.
2   Eruvin 55a.
3   Deuteronomy 30:20.

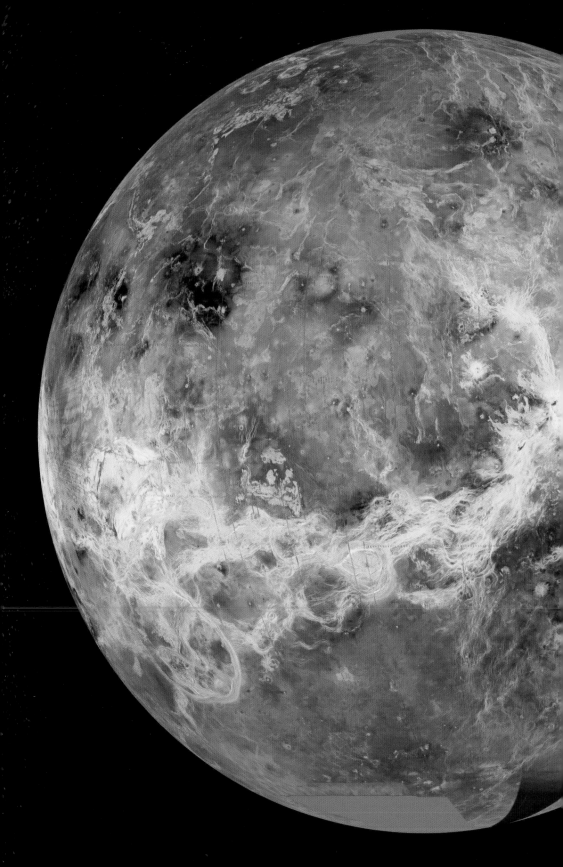

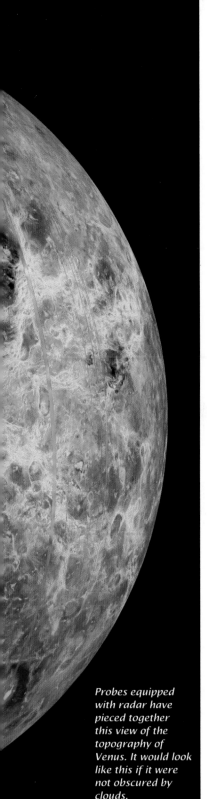

dred degrees Centigrade. To make matters worse, the atmosphere seemed to be much heavier than Earth's – possibly as much as twenty times as heavy.

In October 1967, *Venera 4* was the first Soviet probe which attempted to have a really close look at Venus. This unmanned spacecraft was to penetrate the twenty miles of cloud cover above the planet's surface and transmit information back to Earth from ground level.

All went well for an hour and a half as the metal sphere dropped gently through the alien atmosphere. The probe transmitted back to Earth ongoing reports of its altitude, together with some startling data about what it encountered. The Venusian welcome was a little too enthusiastic. Atmospheric pressure soared to eighteen times that of Earth, while temperatures were way up in the hundreds of degrees Centigrade. Abruptly, the stream of data was cut off.

Initially, there was jubilation back at mission control. The Soviet scientists assumed that the probe had touched down. Then the truth became clear: the last altimeter reading placed it some fifteen miles above the ground. *Venera 4* simply hadn't been able to cope with the enormous atmospheric pressure accumulating above it, and the pride of the Soviet Union's space exploration program had been ignominiously squeezed into a tangle of scrap metal. By the time *Venera 4* hit the ground, it had probably already begun to melt.

Probes equipped with radar have pieced together this view of the topography of Venus. It would look like this if it were not obscured by clouds.
(NASA)

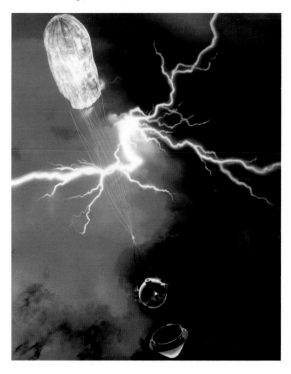

Artist's impression of a Venera lander being struck by lightning as it opens its parachute during its descent to the surface. (NASA)

The spacecraft designers at the Lavochkin Bureau in Moscow put up a brave fight. *Venera 5* followed in 1969 and, soon after, *Venera 6*. Both were built to withstand twenty-five times the terrestrial atmospheric pressure. But Venus was still too strong. Neither of them got within ten miles of ground level before they, too, succumbed to the immense weight and burning heat that engulfed them during their slow descent through the sulfurous atmosphere.

A lesser individual might have thrown in the towel. But the designer of the Venus probes, Vladimir Perminov, would not be discouraged. If Venus wanted to play tough, he'd play tough as well.

Venera 7 was a rudimentary but extremely sturdy probe shaped like half an orange. It was designed to withstand the most hostile environment that the scientists could reasonably predict. The Soviet team even decided to send up two of these powerful spacecraft to allow for malfunctions. Both the craft were encased in shells of titanium, a metal both stronger and lighter than steel, and with a melting point of eighteen hundred degrees Centigrade.

The twin *Venera 7* probes were subjected to awesome stress trials before being launched. A giant centrifuge was specially built to see whether the probes could stand the sudden deceleration they would undergo when they hit the planet's gelatinous atmosphere at twenty-five thousand miles per hour. The tests appeared to be successful.

The team also constructed a pressurized chamber and placed a probe inside it. So immense was the pressure exerted on *Venera 7* that it took a day to decompress the room enough for the door to be opened. Again, *Venera 7* seemed to make the grade.

The parachutes designed to give the probes a soft landing were reduced in size in order to hasten the descent. Care had to be taken to get things just right. If the parachute slowed the craft too much, they would be roasted or crushed before it touched down. On the other hand, if the descent were too rapid, the probes would be smashed to pieces on the ground they had travelled so far to examine.

Both probes were set to depart from Baikonur Cosmodrome in Kazakhstan in the summer of 1970. Only one – the first – successfully blasted off on August 17.

Venera 7 entered the Venusian atmosphere on December 15, 1970, having travelled twenty-six million miles. As the little metal hemisphere plummeted down to its alien destination, its radio transmissions registered blistering temperatures, and its hull began to bear the strain of the terrible atmospheric pressure.

It was at this point that the Soviet scientists back on Earth discovered that a mechanical switch on the probe was not functioning. The communications system was only able to send back a single channel of data. However, it so happened that the one reading the scientists could receive informed them about temperature, and they were able to deduce details about atmospheric pressure from the temperature figures.

As the probe was about thirty feet from the ground, it lost its parachute and crashed to the surface without anything to slow its fall. Mission control could hear nothing but the hissing of

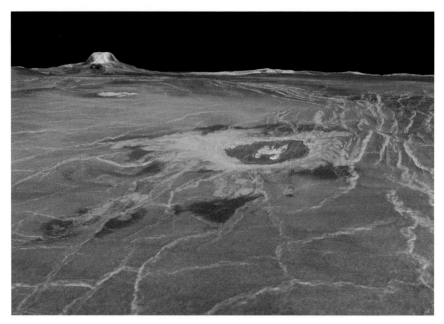

A three-dimensional image of the Eistla Regio area on Venus, derived from the Magellan probe's radar imaging. (NASA/JPL)

background radiation from distant stars. The probe was given up for lost. *Venera 7* seemed destined to join the collection of Soviet space-age rubbish on the surface of Venus.

However, there was yet another twist to the story. Experts from the Institute of Radio Electronics in Moscow analyzed a recording of the *Venera 7* transmission, and informed the Lavochkin engineers that they had been able to detect an extremely weak signal among the background noise pouring in from outer space. It seemed that the *Venera 7* probe had landed on its side with its radio antenna facing away from the Earth, but it had continued transmitting temperature data for over twenty minutes. Thereafter, it had finally surrendered to the Venusian atmosphere, which bore down on it with the weight of ninety-three Earth atmospheres, the equivalent of what would be experienced on an ocean floor on Earth at a depth of two and a half thousand feet.

So the scientists learned that the planet's surface temperature was hot enough to melt zinc, tin and lead – and that there was definitely no chance of life on Venus.

The story of the *Venera* spacecraft illustrates just how hard it can be to get down to the surface of a different world and report findings back to Earth. There were complete failures along the way as the earlier probes cracked like eggshells, fell victim to botched launch attempts or buckled beneath the enormous heat and pressure on Venus. The most painstaking research and brilliant engineering had to be accomplished as top scientists, funded by one of the most powerful governments on Earth, patiently thought their way around or picked their way through the intractable problems that arose. And all this work was only possible as a result of millennia of slow scientific progress.

The Torah is not in space or on another planet. We can take it from a bookshelf or listen to it being read in a synagogue. But we may find ourselves facing other challenges when we set ourselves to study Torah. We may feel tired, distracted, or stumped by the

This artist's impression of Venus shows what we might see if we could stand on the planet's surface. Sunlight can barely penetrate the swirling orange haze that dominates the sky, and the ground is rocky and barren. (ESA)

delicate complexities of its hermeneutics. We may feel discouraged by previous failures to comprehend or live up to the lofty ideals of the Torah.

Moses, the supreme prophet, addressed this, telling us that were the Torah in the heavens, we would need to marshal all our scientific capabilities and employ them with great tenacity and imagination in order to bring it down to Earth. This is not mere hyperbole. Rather, Moses told us that the degree of effort that we should be prepared to exert in order to study and observe the Torah is akin to the effort required for space exploration. God's word – the lifeblood of the Jewish people – is so precious that the problem of how we might acquire it should loom large over our mental horizon, becoming our principal concern.

The *Venera* team showed remarkable tenacity, patience and skill in their attempt to reach the surface of Venus, devoting years of effort to their project, thinking their way through difficult problems and adapting their approach until they achieved their goal. Like them, we should be thinking in terms of decades of work, rather than minutes or hours, when we devote ourselves to Torah. Giving up should not be an option. We must not allow any setbacks, problems or failures to obstruct our progress any more than the Venera team allowed the challenges of the Venusian environment to defeat them.

The story of *Venera 7*'s conquest of Venus has an encouraging epilogue. The next probe, *Venera 8*, which was launched on March 27, 1972, held out for fifty minutes after landing, transmitting data about how much light there was on the surface.

Venera 9 managed to send back black-and-white photographs of the surface. Soviet scientists watched with awe and jubilation as a picture of a barren, rocky landscape, its perspective distorted by the curvature of the thick pressure-resistant lens, inched its way out of a primitive fax machine. *Venera 13* transmitted color pictures as technology continued to develop.

Translating this into the realm of Torah study, we are reminded that a supreme effort, irrespective of its outcome, is not just a one-off that comes and goes. It is a learning experience. Just as the

NASA used the knowledge gained by the Russians to take a different approach to gathering information about Venus, building the Magellan *probe which mapped 98% of the surface of Venus with radar. (NASA/JPL)*

Venera team built on their mistakes and used the information that it gathered from its failed attempts to create future successes, one attempt to attain spiritual greatness paves the way for a second and a third – until we find that we have ascended to a whole new spiritual plane that is literally out of this world.

DIVINE BRILLIANCE

ONE OF THE PHENOMENA WHICH HAVE MOST INTRIGUED researchers over the last few hundred years is light. The simple task of ascertaining exactly what light is and how it travels has preoccupied and baffled some of the world's greatest scientists.

The first conclusions about light's behavior were reached long ago. It was discovered that the spectacular color schemes in rainbows, diamonds and, occasionally, common glass, were not new. Rather, they were the results of white light being split up into its constituent elements. If we take colored lights representing the main colors of the spectrum – red, orange, yellow, green, blue, indigo and violet – and shine them on to one spot, the colors will recombine, creating a splash of white light.

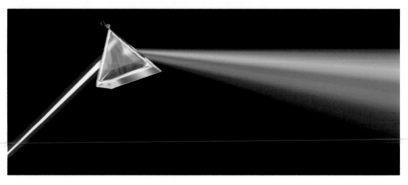

A beam of white light is broken into its constituent colors as it passes through a prism. (NASA, ESA, A Feild (STScI))

More recently, scientists have discovered that light is not actually a standalone phenomenon, but rather that it is part of a larger continuum called the electromagnetic spectrum. In the 1860s and 1870s, a Scottish physicist named James Clerk Maxwell showed

It may look like straight lines but light is in fact a series of waves travelling through space. (Zouaveman le Zouave)

that light can be described as waves of electromagnetic radiation of a certain narrow range of frequencies that are visible to the human eye. Visible light is a particular kind of electromagnetic radiation with wavelengths of between 400 to 700 nanometers (billionths of a meter). X-rays or ultraviolet light have smaller wavelengths (down to 10 picometers, or trillionths of a meter), while the wavelengths of infrared light, microwaves and radio waves are larger. (Radio waves can be up to a hundred kilometers long). Thus visible light is just a tiny part of a whole span of wavelengths of electromagnetic radiation.

Water droplets in clouds can act as prisms as well. (Mila Zinkova)

The Torah is compared to light. We can understand this to mean that it helps us to see, or that it is beautiful. (Ibrahim Iujaz)

Bearing this in mind, it is intriguing to consider a verse from the book of Proverbs: 'A commandment is a lamp, and the Torah is light.'[1]

We can understand this on a very simple level to mean that, while the performance of a divine commandment is a source of "light" or spiritual enlightenment, Torah study is like the light itself.

But, equipped with modern science, we can look at the parallel between Torah and light, and discern new connotations in this terse aphorism.

First of all, we are not to look at the Torah as having a single meaning. A ray of light is made up of a whole range of colors, and every line of the Torah has not one, but several meanings, each of which complements the others to make a multi-dimensional array

---

1   Proverbs 6:23.

of meanings. Only when we can understand a verse or precept from all these points of view will we have seen the true light of Torah.

Secondly, we should not be content with reading the most accessible parts of the Torah, such as the Five Books of Moses and the Mishnah. Just as light is part of a much broader range of frequencies which are invisible but nonetheless real and powerful, so the Torah has many layers that are parallel to its most visible one. Just as the other light frequencies can only be detected through the results of careful thought and investigation – radio sets, photographic plates, radar screens and so on – so the deeper explanations of the Torah can only be grasped with a lot of thought on our part.

But we can push this analogy further still. Modern science has produced a new kind of light – the laser – which also has a bearing on our verse. The word 'laser' is actually an acronym for *light amplification by stimulated emission of radiation*, a brief description of the principle involved in generating this new kind of light. By understanding it better, we can better appreciate the power of Torah.

Atoms from luminous substances (such as neon) release photons (tiny specks of light) in a random way. The photons are released at different times and travel in different directions. This is known as 'incoherent light.'

A laser produces coherent light. Light is shone into the appropriate medium – such as a ruby rod – with a mirror at one end and a semi-transparent mirror at the other. The beam of light excites the molecules in the rod, and bounces back and forth along the tube, building up energy with each passage. At a certain point, a chain

Infrared light (in the picture on the left) helps us see things that are normally invisible. The infrared picture (on the left) shows that one half of the coffee maker is hot and the other half is cold. In visible light (the picture on the right) this difference is not apparent. (Torsten Henning)

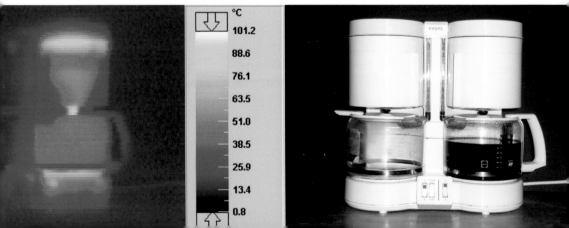

reaction of photon releases is triggered. A flood of photons travels in the same direction out through the semi-transparent mirror, creating an amazingly focused beam that will retain its size and shape over many miles.

The first laser was built in 1960. Since that time, many different kinds of laser have been developed, from the weak beam that scans products in a supermarket to rays so strong that they can punch through metal in a fraction of a second.

A laser beam is also light. What does this tell us about the Torah?

Perhaps the simplest way of understanding this is that focused Torah study and observance have mind-boggling possibilities.

There are different ways of applying oneself to the study of a passage of the Torah. One can undertake the task at hand in a desultory, disorderly way, in which case the spiritual glow from that endeavor will be bright, but similarly disorganized.

Alternatively, one can set about the job in a thorough and concentrated manner. Like the light in a laser hurtling back and forth, one can revise a text again and again, clarifying one's perception and recollection of the passage with each new reading. In fact, this is the precisely the way we are supposed to learn. The Aramaic word for 'tractate' (a section of the Talmud) is *masechta*, which also means 'fabric.' This term is chosen because Talmud study is like weaving fabric. The more often the weaver throws the shuttle back and forth through the cloth, the richer the fabric will be. Similarly, the more one studies a section of the Talmud, the richer will be one's understanding and recollection of it.

This method of spiritual self-enrichment is not confined to abstract study. One can subject one's performance of commandments to a repeated and ongoing scrutiny, reviewing the zeal and insight which one has concerning a particular ritual, and seeing where improvements can be made. Thinking about how one carries out a commandment and how to do so better is also a kind of Torah study.

Furthermore, the nature of certain commandments – daily prayer, weekly Sabbath observance, charity to be offered to those who ask for it – is such that we will perform them again and again. We can treat this repetition as an opportunity to refine and strengthen our

The Greenwich Meridian is marked after dark by a laser in Greenwich Park. (RJP)

connection with God through these observances in the same way that a musician works towards perfection by practicing a piece again and again, learning it well and exploring its possibilities.

We recall that the beam of light in a laser will ultimately burst out as an unstoppable shaft of light which can be visible for miles. Equally, this constant enrichment of one's spirituality will eventually yield amazing results. The spiritual impact of a Torah giant can be incredibly far-reaching, creating an aura of spirituality that captivates and uplifts everyone who sees it. A strong Torah community can serve as a beacon of morality to an extensive neighborhood, spreading the word of God for many miles around with its brilliant example.

And, like the laser beam, Torah can help us to punch through physical limitations.

We may feel defeated or hemmed in by human needs. We all have to eat and sleep. We all have to contend with powerful physical and psychological urges that threaten to take over our lives, and will certainly color our perceptions in countless ways. Can we teach the mouth to pray when its favorite occupation is eating cream cakes? Can the hand that grasps money learn to become as eager to grasp a *lulav*?[2] Can we really hope to operate in a truly spiritual way when we are encased in a shell of profane desires, concerns and inhibitions?

The Torah, like the laser beam, is the answer to this. Just as the laser beam can smash through solid matter in an instant, so the Torah can help us to smash through the burden of our own limitations. If we learn it and apply the fruits of our learning to our own lives in a focused, honest way, then we will discard the shell of materialism in a moment and better serve the world as a 'light unto the nations'.[3]

---

2   Leviticus 23:40.
3   Isaiah 42:6.

MOONSTRUCK!

O N AUGUST 11, 1999, THE MOST DISPARATE CULTURES and civilisations were united by an event of epic proportions. For a few hours, a coincidence of trajectories in the heavens impinged on human consciousness in a unique fashion as the Moon passed directly between the Sun and the Earth, creating a solar eclipse. The lunar shadow raced at one thousand five hundred miles per hour from the east coast of America across the Atlantic Ocean, Europe and Asia, disappearing from the face of the Earth in the Bay of Bengal.

If the sky is clear during an eclipse of the Sun, the effect is awe-inspiring. The first thing that happens as the Moon begins to creep across the face of the Sun is that a tiny notch appears in the solar orb. More and more of the Sun is obscured as the Moon progresses, creating little crescent-shaped shadows wherever sunlight is scattered. The temperature drops as the Sun's light and heat are increasingly obstructed by the Moon, and the sky darkens. Birds might begin to roost, and bats can sometimes be seen flitting around in the temporary night.

Night falls in the middle of the day during a total eclipse seen at Hacibetkaş, Turkey in March 2006.
(Cactus 26)

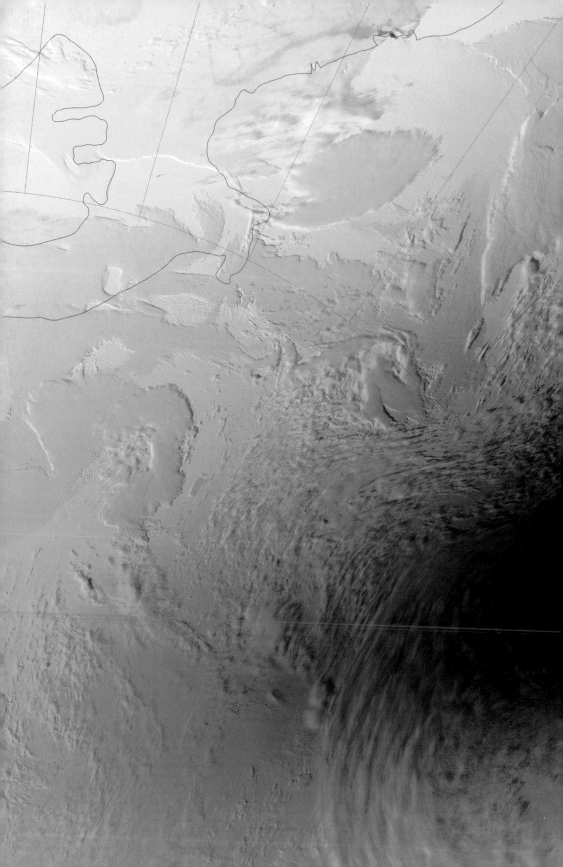

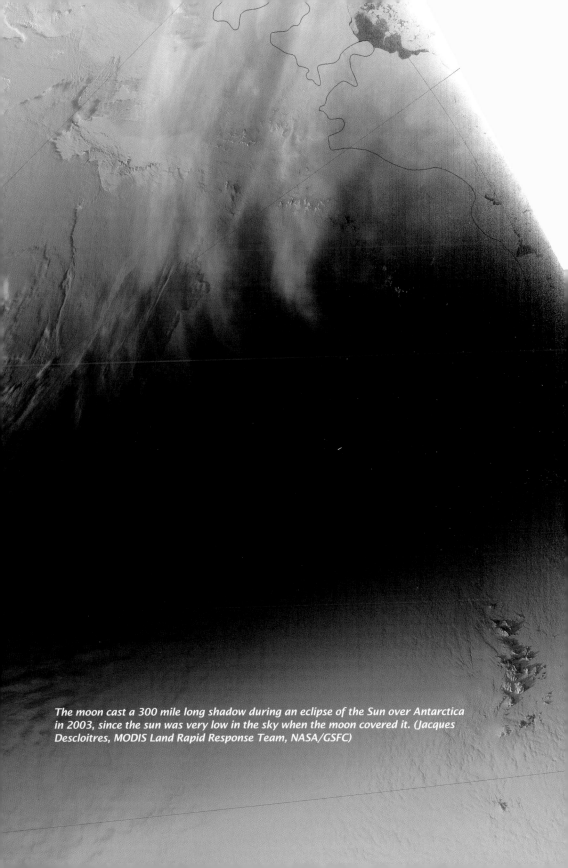

The moon cast a 300 mile long shadow during an eclipse of the Sun over Antarctica in 2003, since the sun was very low in the sky when the moon covered it. (Jacques Descloitres, MODIS Land Rapid Response Team, NASA/GSFC)

Diamond ring effect during a solar eclipse. (John Walker)

The moment when the Sun's light is almost totally obscured is known as totality. As totality draws near, the most spectacular effect becomes visible. Known as the 'diamond ring,' a burst of light flashes out at the Sun's rim before disappearing as the Moon stands for a heart-stopping minute squarely in front of the Sun. The Sun's atmosphere blazes out around the Moon in a magnificent corona of light. Neighboring stars and planets become visible in the twilight sky.

Additional specks of light are visible because of irregularities on the Moon's surface. If the Sun shines directly down a lunar canyon towards us, it will be visible on Earth as a flicker of light against the inky darkness of the Moon's disk.

It is small wonder that this spectacular phenomenon captivates us. Across the Northern Hemisphere on August 11, offices and factories emptied out as people watched the sky darken. Millions of people gathered in Cornwall, Munich, Ramnicu Valcea in Romania and Isfahan in Iran to experience the event. Court cases were ad-

A total eclipse. (John Walker)

journed so that judges and jurors (but not defendants) could witness the eclipse.

The following day, newspapers carried a full-page photograph of the eclipse on their front pages. There was no doubt about what people wanted to see.

Eclipses not only touch the imagination, but they also raise questions. What was God's purpose in making the world in such a way that it occasionally experiences them? Do eclipses have an ethical significance? Beyond the revelation of the Solar System's clockwork precision, which allows us to predict exactly when and where an eclipse will occur, can we *learn* anything from an eclipse of the Sun?

The Torah hints at an explanation. If we look carefully at biblical references to the Sun and Moon, we can discern a message from God to His people in what actually happens during an eclipse.

Rabbi Samson Raphael Hirsch investigated the relationship between the Sun and the Moon in his commentary on the Torah. His starting point was the book of Exodus[1], where God said to Moses in Egypt, 'This renewal [i.e. the new Moon] is yours as a start of months.' The traditional punctuation for these words as indicated by the way they are sung from a Torah scroll suggests that one can read the first phrase in isolation: *this renewal is yours*. The Moon, with its constant cycle of waxing, waning and rebirth, is a symbol of the Jewish people and their fluctuating fortunes. Just as the Moon's light grows, shrinks and re-emerges, so our spiritual welfare, our prominence and our capacity for survival vary over time.

This point is stated explicitly in the blessing we say every month shortly after the new Moon has appeared in the sky in the ceremony called *Kiddush Levanah* ('sanctifying the Moon'):

> Blessed are you, Lord our God, King of the universe . . . who told the Moon that it should renew itself as a crown of glory for [Israel] who are carried in the womb[2] and are destined to renew themselves like [the Moon] and honor their Creator for His glorious kingdom.

Let us recall that in the book of Psalms God is compared to the Sun: 'For the Lord is a Sun and a shield.'[3]

Rabbi Samson Raphael Hirsch analyzed this relationship between the Sun and the Moon – between God and His people – in an intriguing way,[4] basing his thesis on the fact that the Moon has no light of its own. While the Sun is an immense ball of exploding gas and an autonomous source of heat and light, the Moon is simply a ball of rock the size of Australia that orbits the Earth at a distance of two hundred and forty thousand miles. The Moon only shines on the Earth because it reflects the light of the Sun.

This phenomenon parallels the relationship between God and the Jewish people. In our pre-Messianic era, the world is in a state of spiritual darkness. The prophet Malachi depicted the advent of God's kingdom as being like the dawn of a new day: 'Behold, the

---

1   12:1.
2   The Jewish people are referred to as 'those who are carried in the womb' in Isaiah 46:3.
3   Psalms 84:12.
4   *Tishri III* in Volume 2 of his *Collected Writings*.

day is coming . . . . For you, who fear My name, a Sun of righteousness will shine with healing in its wings.'[5]

This passage indicates that until the end of time, we do not have the direct light of the 'Sun' (i.e., God), so the whole world is in a spiritual night. Just as the Moon reflects the Sun's light to brighten up the night, so Jewish people are charged with reflecting God's light – as found in the Torah – into the world. We are to bring brightness, clarity and vision to people in the grip of somber depression or who grope in spiritual darkness, lacking meaningful goals.

We can extend this metaphor slightly. By ourselves, we are like the Moon in darkness, giving out no light – an insignificant people: 'God did not desire you because you were greater than all the nations – for you are the smallest of all the nations.'[6]

But when we face up to our spiritual responsibilities, we reflect God's light just as the Moon reflects the Sun's light. We can radiate God's holiness in a way that is awe-inspiring:

> I have taught you statutes and laws ... which you should observe. Safeguard them and carry them out, for this is your wisdom and understanding in the eyes of the nations. When they hear these statutes, they will say, "Surely this great nation is wise and intelligent!"[7]

The Moon's waxing and waning express the vicissitudes in our relationship with God. Its waxing portrays our efforts to gain more of God's light. The Moon at the height of its splendor, reflecting all the light of the Sun, depicts the Jewish people receiving gifts from God and becoming empowered to pass them on to the whole of humanity. The waning Moon shows the Jewish people moving away from divine bounty, but still shining with some celestial radiance.

We should not think that this imagery is obscure or incidental to the main thrust of Judaism. So fundamental is this idea to our mission as a people that, as Rabbi Hirsch explains, it actually dictates the patterns of our calendar.

---

5   Malachi 3:19-21.
6   Deuteronomy 7:7.
7   Deuteronomy 4:5-6.

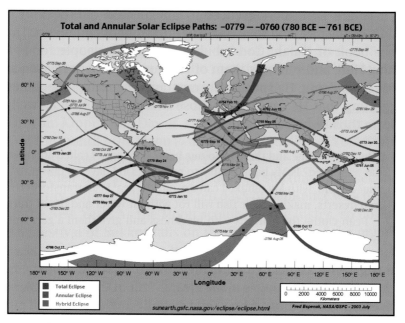

A map showing solar eclipses from around the time of the prophets. One of them may be the eclipse to which Amos referred. (Fred Espenak, NASA/GSFC)

True, the drive to be a light for the nations was planted in us at Mount Sinai, when God declared that we would be a 'kingdom of priests and a holy people.'[17] But we still have free will. It is our prerogative to decide whether and how we will fulfil this divine task. We can choose to spread sacred Torah values by keeping the Torah and leading exemplary Jewish lives. Or we can abandon the Torah and spread whatever message appeals to us.

What happens to the world if we stop receiving wisdom from God's Torah and try to invent a new Torah? What if we neglect God's light and imagine that we have a light all of our own that is better than God's Torah? What if the Moon tries to take over the Sun's task?

A solar eclipse gives us the dramatic answer. If the Moon pushes in front of the Sun instead of reflecting the Sun's light, then the Earth is plunged into darkness.

---

17 Exodus 18:6.

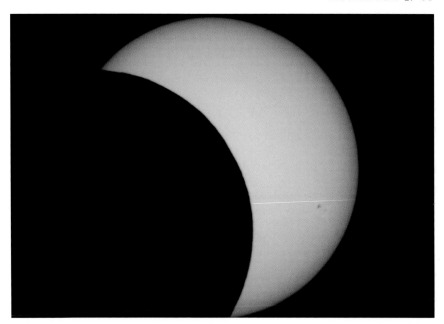

The Moon begins to obscure the Sun at the start of a solar eclipse. (John Walker)

Equally, if the Jews stop learning and observing the Torah and try to dictate a new Torah, then we will be obscuring God's light instead of spreading it. Where we should bring light, there will be darkness. Our contribution to the spiritual welfare of mankind will be much reduced.

We can understand the passages from Isaiah and Amos in this context. Isaiah castigated the people, warning that God had arrived and no-one was there to greet Him, He called and no-one answered – because instead of listening to His word, people were making up their own ethos and mission. Amos rebuked dishonest people because they had replaced God's law of justice and kindness with financial chicanery and oppression.

It seems that we need to have a reality check about this from time to time, as solar eclipses recur periodically and predictably. Perhaps God has built this device into creation as a periodic reminder to us of the need for humility in our divinely-appointed mission.

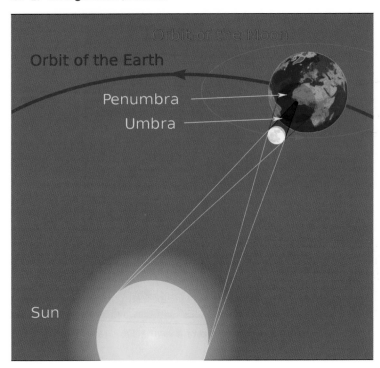

Orbit of the Moon

Orbit of the Earth

Penumbra ———

Umbra ———

Sun

The geometry of a solar eclipse. (Sagredo)

This is not to say that humanity will suffer instant spiritual annihilation should the Jewish people abandon their mission. God created human beings 'in His own image'[18], meaning that He implanted a sense of right and wrong in the human psyche. Even without Jewish guidance, there will still be an understanding of good and evil in people's hearts.

We can see a portrayal of this in the fact that even during an eclipse there is still some light. The Sun's corona flashes around the Moon's edge. Flecks of light burst out beyond the darkness, slightly augmenting the corona of the solar atmosphere. Perhaps this reassures us that in the absence of a properly functioning Jewish people, there will still be human goodness in the world. Thus, while the world does not enjoy universal peace, good health and prosperity, there are still laudable and useful efforts by govern-

___
18 Genesis 1:27.

*A total
lunar
eclipse.
(NASA)*

ments, NGOs and individuals to provide relief from famine, cures for illnesses and conflict resolution.

One would be equally justified in investigating a lunar eclipse in this vein. A lunar eclipse occurs when the Earth passes directly between the Sun and the Moon. The Earth's shadow obscures the Moon, which takes on a ghostly red tinge.

Perhaps a lunar eclipse symbolizes what happens when the nations of the Earth try to come between the Jewish people (symbolized by the Moon) and God (symbolized by the Sun), preventing us from learning about Him and serving Him. In such a situation, both the Moon and the Earth are plunged into darkness, indicating perhaps that anti-Jewish persecution harms both the Jews and those who persecute them.

This gloomy interpretation of a lunar eclipse is corroborated by a custom to fast whenever such an eclipse takes place. This prac-

Sunlight reflected off the Earth as seen by crew members on the International Space Station. (STS 129 crew, NASA)

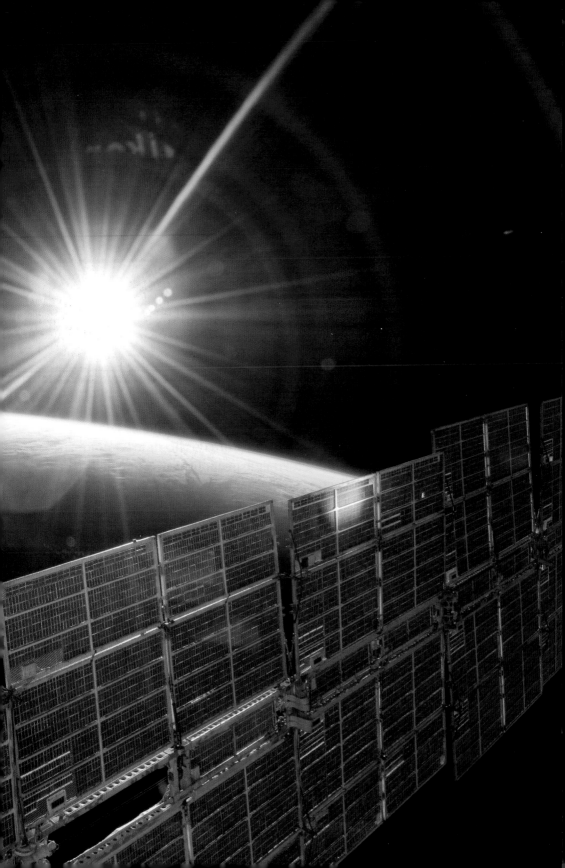

For someone standing on the Moon, earthshine would look like this. The Sun lights up the Earth and the Earth illuminates the Moon. (NASA)

between the Sun, Moon and Earth. We are to watch and learn from every human encounter, and use every experience to enhance our spiritual sensitivity. But we will shine most brightly for the benefit of our fellow humans when we turn to the Torah and share its beautiful light with everyone around us.

TO LIFE!

I N A PREVIOUS CHAPTER, WE EXAMINED THE MOON'S REFLEC-tion of sunlight onto the world and understood it as a metaphor for Jewish spirituality vis-à-vis the rest of humanity. But we can understand yet another facet of the Jewish people's ideal relationship with the world by considering a different aspect of the Moon's relationship with Earth.

Scientists have moved beyond understanding the relative trajectories of the Earth and Moon, how the Sun's light goes from one to the other and how far apart the two worlds are. Jacques Laskar, a scientist in the Paris Observatory, found in 1993 that the Moon actually plays a pivotal role in sustaining life on Earth.

If we imagine a line going through the Earth from the North to the South Pole, we can designate this as the axis around which the Earth spins once every twenty-four hours. If we draw another imaginary line tracing the Earth's movement around the Sun, then we find that the axis of the Earth's spin is actually tilted relative to its direction of travel, at an angle of about 23.5 degrees. The fact

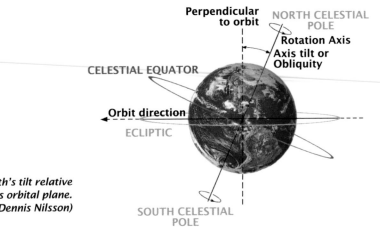

The Earth's tilt relative to its orbital plane.
(NASA, Dennis Nilsson)

In this diagram of the Solar System, the planets are shown with their relative sizes on top (left to right: Mercury, Venus, Earth, Mars, Jupiter, Saturn, Uranus, Neptune and Pluto) and the relative distances at which they orbit the Sun underneath. Each planet exerts a gravitational pull on the Earth depending on its mass and its distance from us. However, our orbit around the Sun is kept stable by our Moon. (NASA, JPL)

that we spin at a consistent angle to the plane of our trajectory around the Sun means that we have a stable climate with regular seasons. Without the Moon, the angle of the Earth's spin to its orbital plane would change dramatically over time, and our climate would be thrown into chaos.

We can see a paradigm of this devastating impact on our ecology by looking at Mars. The Martian environment is hostile to life as we experience it partly because Mars wobbles too much to have a stable climate. Mars has two moons, but they are much too small to stabilize its spin. So the seasons are chaotic, temperatures are extreme and Mars is a desolate wasteland where most living things could not survive.

A typical desolate Martian landscape photographed by Mars Exploration Rover Spirit.
(NASA/JPL)

There is actually a set of circumstances that threatens to change the angle of the Earth's spin. As other planets in our Solar System pass us on their orbits around the Sun, their gravity plucks at the Earth, and this threatens to destabilize the crucial tilt on which we depend. But the Moon's own gravity counteracts this, maintaining the angle of our own spin within a variation of one degree, and ensuring that we experience the gentle round of seasons that enable the ecology to function.

The Moon aids life on Earth in another way as well. One of the effects of the Moon's gravity on our planet is that it slows the Earth's rotation. If our Earth were spinning at the speed of Jupiter, whose day is only ten hours long, winds of one hundred miles per hour would be commonplace and hurricanes would occur much more frequently. It is questionable whether humans could survive in such a harsh environment.

But because the Moon acts as a brake on the Earth's spin, our winds travel at more manageable speeds that are normally not life-threatening, and the devastation wrought by hurricanes remains at a level from which we can recover.

Again, we can use our understanding of this to clarify the importance of the Jewish mission. We recall that the Moon symbolizes the Jewish people. Just as the Moon regulates the angle of the Earth's rotational axis and the speed of its spin, maintaining conditions for life, so our role is to promote and nurture life on Earth.

This task has many aspects. On a simple level, we can spread an awareness of the value of human life and promote exemplary standards in health care, charitable giving and social justice. We can encourage peace in the world by seeking ways to live harmoniously with other peoples and encouraging them to do the same. In our professional lives, we can work conscientiously and to the best of our ability, stimulating economic development and fostering the common good. We can nurture the home as a powerhouse of sanctity, strengthening the family as a force for stability in our society.

On a deeper level, we have a responsibility to bring the knowledge of God into the world. In Torah terms, a godless life devoted to the pursuit of wealth or fame to the exclusion of all else is no life at

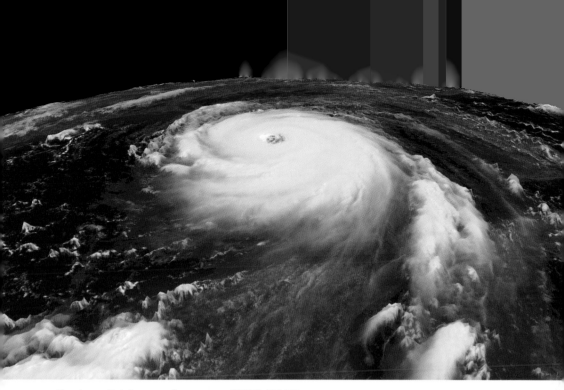

Hurricane Katrina seen from space. (GOES, NOAA)

all. Conversely, a life devoted to walking in God's ways, practising kindness and justice and observing God's law as revealed in the Torah, is the best possible outcome from our time on Earth.

Our guide to all this is the Torah. Every time we learn or practice what the Torah says, we are building our connection with God and training ourselves to act according to His divine standard. When we encounter situations that require us to make a contribution to the world – a homeless person seeking help, a business decision with wide social ramifications – we will find it easier to disregard our own needs and view the world from a divine perspective because we will be accustomed to relating to God and considering what we can do for Him instead of only what He can do for us.

Furthermore, even the most obscure and personal command-ments can provide us with insights into the standards by which we relate to wider society. The prohibition against eating meat and milk together,[1] for example, reminds us of the vast difference

---

1   Shulchan Aruch, Yoreh Deah 87-89

High winds batter palm trees during a typhoon. (FEMA/ NOAA)

between life (symbolized by milk) and death (meat from a slaughtered animal), and that life must be respected as having intrinsic value.

On a mystical level, we can say that any engagement with Torah brings life and goodness into the world. Thus, Pirkei Avot says, 'One who increases Torah increases life.'[2] Rabbi Moshe Chaim Luzzatto expands on this in his mystical work *Derech Hashem* (The Way of God):

> Among the influences sent down by [God] for the needs of His creatures, there is one influence which is higher than all others, whose quality is more precious and superior than anything else that can possibly exist ... and it is the method whereby God apportions a part of His honor and glory to His creatures.
>
> God has connected this with one of His creations – the Torah.[3]

---

2   Pirkei Avot 2:8.
3   Part 4, 2:2.

The Moon is remote from the world, and seems to have nothing to offer it. But we have seen that, for all its remoteness, it is essential to life on Earth. The same applies to us Jews, since in a way we are remote from other cultures. Our customs are distinctive, our attachment to our roots and our homeland is tenacious, and our very language, Hebrew, is grounded in our religious law and liturgy. But these factors need not prevent us from making a contribution to the world that is vastly disproportionate to our numbers. Some twenty percent of Nobel Prize winners have been of Jewish descent, although Jews only represent approximately 0.2 percent of the world population.

Were we all to observe the laws of the Torah as we ought, our contributions would not just be in the fields of medicine, the arts, economics, technology and politics. After all, God designated us as priests to the world. Our primary concern should be to care for the world's spirituality.[4] By devoting ourselves more fully to our mission of the observance and propagation of Torah, we could become a still more potent force for life and for good in the world, encouraging mankind to seek God and build a more compassionate society. We look forward to meeting this challenge, and to bringing closer the time when 'death will vanish forever and the Lord God will wipe away tears from all faces.'[5]

---

4   Exodus 19:6
5   Isaiah 25:8.

The Moon looks remote and alien, but it helps to maintain life on our planet. (Wing Chi Poon)

THE LENS OF TORAH

'**M**OSES COMMANDED US CONCERNING THE TORAH. IT IS an heirloom for the congregation of Jacob.'[1] This is one of the best-known verses in the Torah. We can understand this quite simply to mean that it is our duty to pass knowledge of the Torah on to the next generation.

But the Talmud gives an unexpected gloss to this verse. Because the Hebrew word for heirloom ('morashah') is like the Hebrew word for a betrothed woman ('meorasah'), the Talmud[2] says that the Torah is like a new bride for the Jewish people.

There seems to be an inherent contradiction here. How can something be new and yet as old and familiar as a family heirloom at the same time? We can understand how to reconcile these apparently contradictory ideas by discussing the Torah's similarity to light.

We have seen from the symbolism of the solar eclipse that it is never wise to try to come between God and those to whom He wishes to speak. But a balance must be struck here. Whereas we should not presume to replace the Torah's message with our own, we can and indeed should receive the message of Torah from our parents or teachers and then transmit it to others in a creative spirit. A phenomenon that occurs much further out in space, known as gravitational lensing, both illustrates and clarifies this task.

Albert Einstein was one of the first to analyze the effect of gravity on light. He calculated that under the influence of a massive gravitational field, light would actually bend. This later became

---

1   Deuteronomy 33:4.
2   Sanhedrin 59a.

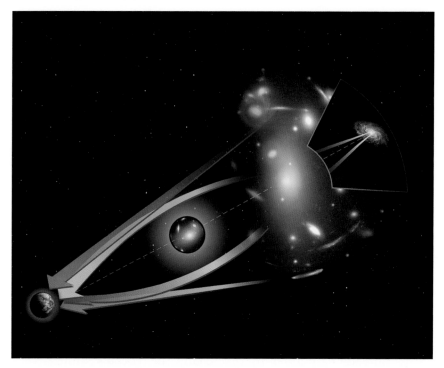

Gravitational lensing explained: Someone on Earth (bottom left) is observing a distant spiral galaxy (top right). The intervening massive cluster (center) bends the light coming from the distant galaxy, distorting its appearance for the observer. Because its light has bent en route to the observer, the observer sees images of the distant galaxy distorted and multiplied several times around the intervening galaxy cluster. Colored arcs can also be created by this effect. (NASA, ESA, Andrew Fruchter (STScI), and the ERO team (STScI + ST-ECF)

known as gravitational lensing, since the gravitational field bends light and produces magnified images like a lens.

Arthur Eddington, an English astrophysicist, confirmed Einstein's theory in 1919. He traveled to the island of Principe, off the west coast of Africa, to observe the position of the Hyades star cluster during a total solar eclipse and found that the cluster appeared to have moved just as Einstein's theory predicted. The only explanation for this was that the cluster's light had been bent by the Sun's gravitational pull, so that the cluster appeared to have moved away from its actual position.

The effects of this phenomenon can be startling. As light from a remote source – such as a distant star – encounters a massive object such as a black hole (a very dense collection of matter) or a galaxy, it will bend around the object and then reconverge on the other side like water flowing around a rock. For an observer on the far side of the intervening body, the reconverging light can create an arcing effect, helping them to see the distant star reconfigured and multiplied in a series of arcs or a ring shape around the intervening body. If the lensing mass is evenly distributed, the light from the distant star will be bent into a ring shape, known as an Einstein ring, around the intervening body. Or, if the lensing mass is unevenly distributed, the light from the distant star might bend in such a way that the distant star appears many times around the intervening body, in a formation known as an Einstein cross.

This is a counterintuitive effect. We would expect the body in the middle to obscure something behind it, whereas in fact it serves as a means of transmitting and even magnifying light from the more distant body.

Furthermore, since gravitational lensing magnifies starlight from

This picture shows examples of arcs caused by gravitational lensing. (NASA, Andrew Fruchter and the ERO Team [Sylvia Baggett (STScI), Richard Hook (ST-ECF), Zoltan Levay (STScI)] (STScI))

Starlight from different eras and distances mingles in the night sky. (Roberto Mura)

ciples underlying old ideas and setting them in different modern contexts to see how they will be applied in their own era.

Perhaps, like the Einstein cross, we will see the same idea repeated many times in different contexts and in different relationships to the issues of our own time and our own interpretations. Or, like a star inside an Einstein ring, we will create our own *chiddush* (original idea), a new Torah light of our own, ensuring that it is circumscribed and defined by the beautiful light of Jewish tradition.[4] Or, like the arced image of a galactic cluster, we will find that what looks like a linear process of thought that takes one from a starting point to an ending point can in fact be presented as a circular idea, giving new meaning, depth and beauty to the statement with which it began.

When we engage in this sacred activity, we are not just helping

---

4   The Jerusalem Talmud (*Peah* 2:6) says that even Torah ideas which are formulated now were disclosed by God to Moses at the start of the chain of Torah transmission. This is reflected by the fact that even new stars are the products of the process which began our universe. Their light is new, but was inherent in the very birth of the cosmos.

people to keep up with the demands of the present. We are transmitting ideas that might otherwise be lost because of their antiquity. Instead of allowing their light to be forgotten in the passage of time, we can magnify that light and ensure that future generations will benefit from its radiance. Just as gravitational lensing magnifies distant stars and makes them visible to people far away, so those who learn the Torah can take up the light of old ideas and pass it on, ensuring that it is not forgotten.

Like a gravitational lens showing us light emitted long ago, Torah gives us glimpses of the very earliest stages of physical existence, helping us to understand what God made, how and why. We gain a special view of the earliest reaches of time and the ancient history of our people.

Now the Talmudic exposition of the verse with which we began is much easier to understand. We have seen that the process of handing Torah over from one generation to the next is not just like bestowing an ancient heirloom on one's child.

The Torah is, in fact, neither simply old nor simply new. As we receive the Torah, we need to work with it and find new ideas within it, embarking on a relationship that both respects the inviolable and immutable tradition of Torah and also engages and works with it, building new interpretations and drawing out new inspiration from the immeasurable divine wisdom with which it was created. This is like a marriage, where the two partners respect each other's individuality but also become a single working unit, fusing their strengths and identities to create a home and a life with which to serve God.

This was the lesson of the stars for Abraham and for us. The Torah is an effortless fusion of ancient and modern, the light of the past brought forward, complemented and contextualized by the light of the present. The delicate, beautiful interplay of starlight from the past and the present, from near and from far, models for us the melding of Torah tradition with the challenges of modernity, and assures us that the darkest situations in the remotest recesses of the future will always be illuminated by the soft, timeless radiance of God's light.

THE CELESTIAL CLOCK

ONE OF THE FRAILTIES OF THE HUMAN CONDITION IS OUR inability to take the long view. Events and situations which unfold before our eyes can be distorted by our consciousness, sometimes appearing to threaten our wellbeing precisely because we are confronted by them.

With hindsight, we often come to realize that, in the grand scheme of things, they were really not so important after all. But humans tend to look at the short term. Our horizon is dominated by the bottom line of a balance sheet, a frustrating red light that threatens to make us late for work, sharp words that cut deep, or the pain of stepping barefoot on a plug. For now, it is immensely important, and we are preoccupied by it, sometimes in a way that is out of proportion and which excludes bigger issues.

No less a prophet than Moses was keenly aware of this problem. He was divinely inspired to compose the ninetieth Psalm, which includes a reflection on the transience of all things, in an effort to attain the correct perspective on time and on life:

> Before the mountains were created and the Earth was born, since the most remote past and until the most distant future, You are the Lord .... A thousand years in Your eyes are like yesterday, which is soon past ... Men are like grass that springs up in the morning, and withers in the evening .... Teach us to count our days, so that we may acquire a wise heart.[1]

Moses was not talking about the ability to reckon figures. Rather, he was praying to be lifted out of the human vantage point with its units of seconds, minutes, hours and days, so that he – and we – could judge things according to their proper importance.

---

1   Psalms 90:2-12.

Lichen growing on a rock. (Barbara Page)

It so happens that, through our increasing knowledge of our world and the fragment of space immediately beyond it, we have been able to detect a cosmic rhythm that beats much more slowly than our own. Some of the best examples of this slow, powerful beat are actually beneath our feet.

Lichen is one of the humblest members of the plant family. The Lebanese flag may sport the cedar, and the English may sing that they have a heart of oak – but no civilisation boasts that it is like the lichen. Even its dictionary definition is uninspiring: 'a plant organism of group Lichenes, composed of fungus and alga in association, usually of green, gray or yellow tint, growing on and coloring rocks, tree-trunks, roofs, walls, etc.'[2] Notwithstanding its humble form, lichen can teach everyone a lesson in perseverance.

The fastest-growing lichen species grow up to 1.2 inches in a year, and a normal specimen might grow just one inch in twenty-

---

2   *The Concise Oxford Dictionary of Current English* (seventh edition), Clarendon Press, 1982.

A footprint in the lunar dust. (NASA)

five years. This means that lichen's average rate of growth is around one ten-thousandth of a millimeter per day.

This slow growth is complemented by exceptional longevity. Lichen found in West Greenland is estimated to be four and a half thousand years old, and scientists use large specimens in the Arctic to estimate how old a particular section of the ice-cap might be.

When we look out into space, the time scales become even more striking. The dwarf planet Pluto is one of the most remote bodies in our Solar System, about three and a half billion miles from Earth. This means that its orbit around the Sun is much larger than ours, and therefore its year – the time it takes to complete one circuit around the Sun – is much longer than a year on Earth. Travelling at just under three miles per second, Pluto encircles the Sun once in two hundred and forty-eight Earth years.

It is now some forty years since Neil Armstrong and Buzz Aldrin trod the surface of the Moon. But their footprints are still as clear and sharp as the day they were made. This is because the Moon has no atmosphere. There is no wind to disturb the imprints made in the lunar dust, and no rain to wash them away. There are no living creatures to walk over them and obliterate them with their own footprints. The only thing that might obscure them is the drizzle of tiny grains of interplanetary dust – formerly mighty rocks that have gradually been worn down by repeated impact with their fellows. These gradually fall to the Moon's surface as they drift within its weak gravity, adding to the gray, powdery deposits that already blanket its surface. It is estimated that, at the present rates, the astronauts' footprints will be obscured after about a million years.

We also find very long cycles further out in our galaxy. Our Sun (and the planets around it which make up our Solar System) is not simply hanging still in space. Rather, it is revolving around the centre of the galaxy at an approximate rate of one revolution every 250 million years, traveling at a speed of about one hundred miles per second. The time it takes the Sun to make one complete revolution is called a "Galactic Year" – and it makes our year feel distinctly short.

The world of the very small also underlines the limited human scale of our perspective. In the early 1900s, scientists detected

This diagram shows our Sun orbiting the Milky Way.
(NASA, JPL-Caltech/R. Hurt (SSC))

changes in the radiation emitted by certain substances: there seemed to be a tendency for the radioactivity to decrease over time. It finally became clear that radioactive materials gradually release particles from the centers of their constituent atoms, and the rate of release decreases as time goes by. This is known as radioactive decay, and the time it takes for a substance to lose half its radioactivity is referred to as its half-life.

Different elements decay at different rates, which means that they all have different half-lives. Yet again, as we look at the time-scales, we find that a human lifetime is hardly the right criterion for measuring what is going on all around us. Radium, for instance, has a half-life of 1,600 years. A piece of radium that had a certain radioactive count in the year 400 – during the decline of the Roman Empire – would have about half as much today. The half-life of carbon-14 – a kind of radioactive carbon – is almost six thousand years, on which scale the historical analogy is almost redundant. And radioactive potassium, it has been estimated, would decay with a half-life of 1.3 billion years.

One of the larger time scales we can detect relates to the interaction of galaxies. It has been tentatively calculated that the massive Andromeda Galaxy - the nearest galaxy to our own Milky Way, and composed of about a trillion stars - is bearing down upon us at over fifty miles per second. This means that, ultimately, one would expect the Andromeda Galaxy and our own to interact and perhaps merge. It is estimated that this intergalactic merger will take place in about three billion years' time.

When we confront these huge stretches of time, we feel insignificant. Ancient monuments to human endeavor - the pyramids, the Acropolis, the Colossus of Rhodes - all seem trifling when viewed in this context, and the effort put into them suddenly looks rather pathetic. These were men's attempts to make their mark for all time. But after several thousand years, they are already badly worn, and governments scramble to preserve them. Compared to a mark in the lunar dust, the pyramids are here today, gone tomorrow.

And people? A human lifetime, which might span an entire century, is so brief as to be totally negligible. The delay caused by a missed bus or a hold-up at the supermarket check-out does not even register on the cosmic time-scale. But contemplating the vast time scales beyond our own experience makes us wish for more time and a longer view.

Here is what Greg Chamitoff, a NASA astronaut, wrote about his perception of the passage of time when he was working on the International Space Station:

> There is a timelessness to the Earth and the universe around us. Regardless of anything we do as a species, and regardless of politics or the intricate web of societal interactions on the ground, the Earth keeps turning and orbiting the Sun, the Moon keeps circling, and the natural cycles - on a scale of size and time so much greater than the experience of our lives –continue undisturbed . . . We do not have all the time in universe - our lives are very limited, and perhaps there is a sense of wishing for more, wishing that we could experience our lives and the universe in which we live on an eternal time-scale as well.[3]

Moses knew that this ability to take the long view, which is the key to spiritual maturity, can give us a special kind of serenity. If

---

3   See *An Interview with an Astronaut,* Appendix 1.

Two galaxies colliding half a billion light years away from Earth. (NASA, ESA, and the Hubble Heritage Team (STScI/AURA)·ESA/Hubble Collaboration, B. Whitmore (Space Telescope Science Institute) James Long (ESA/Hubble))

only we could look at things within the appropriate time scale – the infinite, divine one, where a millennium is as ephemeral as our twenty-four-hour day – trivial setbacks would lose some of their ability to frustrate or distract us. Our heart – our emotions – would mature, and we would be able to feel what is transient and what endures. We would instinctively try to lead more meaningful lives.

In our own time, this message takes on extra depth. The advance of human knowledge has revealed more than we ever knew about the massive time scales within which the universe operates. This can help us to measure our lives within the Creator's time frame instead of the schedules that His creatures use.

Every so often, we can focus on the stretches of time that govern our universe. As our view of time becomes longer, we can tend towards infinity, approaching the divine perspective, stepping slightly away from life's setbacks, and remembering that not everything in this life is worth getting upset about. Then, as Moses so beautifully put it, we will attain a prize of great value – a heart of wisdom.

QUICK AS A FLASH

WE TURN NOW TO A PHENOMENON THAT IS MUCH MORE familiar, but no less spectacular – lightning. There are around forty-five thousand thunderstorms on Earth every day, and six hundred bolts of lightning strike the Earth every second. Even if we were to travel to another planet to get some peace and quiet, we might not manage it. Most of the storms that rage on Jupiter are punctuated by lightning, and two of the later Russian *Venera* probes that examined the atmosphere on Venus were bombarded by streams of lightning bolts as they descended.

Many bizarre explanations have been advanced over the centuries to account for the unpredictable, eerie flashes that illuminate whole clouds or dart down to blast trees and buildings. Primitive pagan cultures believed that there was a god of thunder who roared his wrath against the Earth, driving his message home with bolts of lightning.

Modern science has revealed to us how lightning and thunder work. But this proper understanding does nothing to diminish

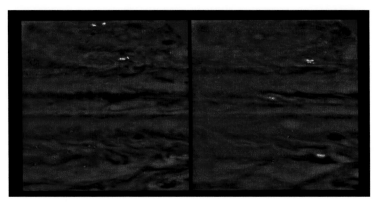

These two pictures of Jupiter were taken seventy-five minutes apart. The bright spots are huge flashes of lightning generated during storms. (GSFC, NASA)

Lightning brightens the night sky. (John R Southern)

Lightning is attracted to high metal points, as shown by this picture of a strike on the CN Tower in Toronto. (Raul Heinrich)

their awe-inspiring nature. The real story of lightning and thunder is scarcely less fantastic than the atavistic imaginings of bygone civilisations.

Despite the thundercloud's static appearance, it is one of the most dynamic phenomena in the natural world. Inside the thundercloud, there is a constant process of collision between raindrops and pellets of ice. It is thought that as a result of these collisions, an enormous electrical field (up to one million volts per meter – over four thousand times the voltage available from the socket in the wall of an average house) accumulates within the cloud, with the positive charge at the top of the cloud and the negative charge at the bottom.

Since it is part of the nature of electricity to balance out a charge,

Lightning seen from above. This picture was taken at an altitude of 30,000 feet. (350z33)

these pent-up stores of electricity will interact with a body that has an opposite charge to their own, such as the ground, discharging their own store of electricity through this interaction.

When lightning strikes the ground, the electricity in the base of the cloud will send out a negatively charged 'leader' stroke that makes its way downwards. As the negative leader comes down to within approximately three hundred feet of the ground, a positively charged leader shoots up from the ground to meet it and travels all the way along it back up to the cloud. This creates a colossal electrical spark that may be only five centimeters wide, but can be as long as twenty miles and can pack a punch of up to a trillion watts. If a rock suffered a direct hit from a bolt of lightning, it could melt. To put it another way, the electricity released in twenty-four hours of tropical storms across the world would be enough to power a small country for a year.

While all this might sound like quite a complex chain of events, it happens with incredible rapidity. The blast from the cloud base typically travels at about one thousand miles per second, while the return stroke from the ground up to the sky races back at eighty-seven thousand miles per second. If *Apollo 11* had been able to travel at that speed, it would have arrived at the Moon in less than three seconds.

Considering how quickly lightning travels, it is hardly surprising that the flash is very brief: it normally only lasts for a quarter of a second. This ought to make it very difficult to see lightning, but because it is so bright, the light from the bolt actually leaves an image on the retina that lasts longer than the flash itself.

All this takes place in total silence. To understand how thunder comes into all this, we must first consider how we perceive sound.

Every sound is actually a disturbance in the air. When we hear something, that is because it has disturbed the air around it, and this disturbance has moved along to our ears (in the same way that a ripple of water spreads out across a lake), at which point it is translated by the brain into a perception of sound. When we speak, our vocal cords vibrate, making waves in the air which are registered and decoded by the listener's brain.

We have already seen that lightning is enormously powerful. One of the side effects of the discharge of electricity is that the air immediately around it becomes extraordinarily hot, reaching thirty thousand degrees Centigrade. This burst of very intense heat causes the air to expand away from the flash at over seven hundred miles per hour, and with up to a hundred times as much pressure as normal. The air around the flash is affected in the same way as a lake which has a huge rock dropped into it. Enormous ripples of air shoot out from around the lightning bolt at the speed of sound – over a thousand feet in a second – and we perceive this wave of moving air as a huge explosion of sound. Thunder is simply an after effect of the heat generated by a flash of lightning.

All this gives us food for thought when we read Psalm 104, which describes various forces of nature. It tells us that God 'makes the winds act as His messengers, and appoints flashing fire to be His servants.'[1] Radak, one of the major Jewish biblical commentators, explains this last expression to be a reference to lightning. When we look at lightning, we are to think of it as a servant of God.

1   Psalm 104.

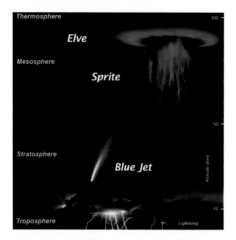

Some forms of lightning occur so high up that we rarely see them. (Abestrobi)

The simplest way to understand this is to view it as an indication of God's power. Even a bolt of lightning, with all its power, is only a servant of God.

But we can take this metaphor a stage further. Perhaps we are supposed to view it as a description of what is required of a servant of God. The only force of nature that God designates as His servant in this passage is lightning. This is the force that is a suitable example of obedience to God, and one that we should emulate.

This idea gains strength from the fact that the same word for 'service' is used in biblical passages[2] to describe Aaron the High Priest performing the sacrificial rituals in the Temple.

We should not think that only Aaron and his descendants had the privilege of ministering to God. This concept can actually pertain, in a limited way, to every Jew. The Shulchan Aruch says that on waking up in the morning, we are supposed to wash our hands in the same way that the priests washed their hands before serving in the Temple[3]. Rashba, a medieval commentator on the Talmud, interprets this ritual as a reminder that whatever we do during the course of the day is to be as sacred and pure as the rituals performed in the Temple.[4] We are all, like the High Priest, to be "servants" of God serving Him in the macro-Temple which is His world, and the image of lightning is supposed to be a positive lesson for us all.

Non-Jews can also attain this spiritual status if they deepen their understanding of their own spiritual duties. Rabbi Meir is quoted

---

2   Exodus 28:35 and 29:30, *inter alia.*
3   Shulchan Aruch, Orach Chaim 4:1.
4   Quoted in paragraph 1 of the Mishnah Berurah's commentary on Orach Chaim 4:1.

in the Talmud as saying, 'A non-Jew who studies Torah [relevant to her or him] is like the High Priest.'[5]

Lightning is often viewed as a frightening and destructive force. But if the text praises true servants of God by comparing them to lightning, there must be some positive qualities in lightning that we are to focus on and learn from. What lessons can lightning teach us?

If we simply look at the scientific workings of lightning, we can learn a lot from it. When we serve God, we are not supposed to move reluctantly and haltingly. We should not devote a tiny fraction of our physical and mental vigor to Torah study and observance, and reserve the rest of our strength for work and leisure. We should not postpone doing a worthy deed until it fits into our schedule.

Quite the reverse: like the lightning bolt, the thought that we are standing before God should motivate us to act with incredible speed and energy.

Furthermore, God's summons should be so immediate and pressing to us that we will not allow ourselves to be obstructed by trivial impediments as we respond, just as a lightning bolt will blast through anything that prevents it from returning heavenward. There is no room for lethargy or nonchalance in the service of God.

We can learn a further lesson from the areas where the lightning appears. Lightning flashes from cloud to cloud. Equally, the servant of God should live primarily 'in the heavens.' He or she should regard the heavens and the heavenly perspective as their natural standpoints for engaging with the world.

But lightning also flashes from the clouds towards the ground, from where a return stroke leaps up to join the initial flash and shoots back to the skies. This teaches us that the truly holy person – the true servant of God – only stoops towards the Earth in order to draw some element of earthly existence, or another person, up to their own heavenly perspective. When we are in the proximity of such awesome people, the effect is inexorable. Even before they have touched us, even if they have just approached, we feel drawn to them, and we catch a glimpse of an otherworldly perspective.

5   Sanhedrin 59a.

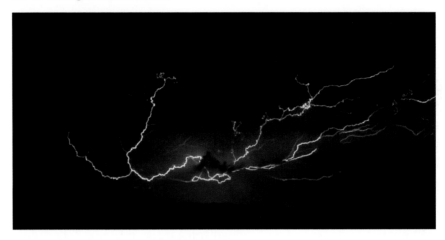

Cloud to cloud lightning. (Fir 0002/Flagstaffotos)

In the same way that a stroke of lightning is focused throughout its length along a channel of air which is only a few centimeters in diameter, so should we concentrate exclusively on what God has prescribed for us. During our prayers, our gaze and our minds should not wander from the prayer book to the newspaper.

Finally, we should not think that the servant of God needs to make efforts to broadcast the message of sanctity to the world. One can deduce this from the awesome peals of thunder generated by lightning, which follow as an automatic result of the lightning's incandescence. Similarly, holiness can make waves, thundering a message through the world, and those who bear God's name through the world will find that His word will be heard as much as necessary.

Scripture even states this explicitly. We are assured in Deuteronomy that, if we adhere to God's word, our reputation will spread across the entire world. We will be famed for being a nation of awesome spirituality: 'All the nations of the world will see that the name of God is associated with you, and they will be in awe of you.'[6]

---

6   28:10.

A tree struck by lightning. (laberis)

Perhaps, if we all resolve to move as quickly and energetically as a flash of lightning to do God's word, He will hasten His Messiah to meet us. Once again, as of old,[7] the fire of God will flash down from the heavens and blaze on the Temple altar, a tangible sign of His enduring presence in our midst.

7   Leviticus 9:24.

ALL FIRED UP

I N THE CHAPTER ON LIGHTNING, WE LEARNED SOMETHING about the characteristics of a true servant of God. There is in fact another passage in the same Psalm which gives us further insights into this, with reference to two other natural phenomena: earthquakes and volcanoes. Here is the passage at the end of the Psalm:

> The glory of the Lord will last forever: the Lord will rejoice in His creatures. He looks at the Earth and it trembles; He touches the mountains and they smoke. I will sing to the Lord while I live: I will sing praise to my God while I still exist. Let my meditation be sweet to Him: I will rejoice in the Lord. Sinners will disappear from the Earth, and the wicked will be no more. Bless the Lord, my soul! Praise the Lord![1]

Overall, we can find a balance in this Psalm. It begins with a panoramic view of the natural world, illustrating God's majesty and His care for all creatures. The Psalmist continues with some inspirational ideas about what we can do for God. Most of these concluding verses depict God glorying in His creation, but the verse about God shaking the Earth and making the mountains smoke seems out of place. It appears to belong somewhere among the preceding thirty verses that detail God's greatness!

We can guess that there is a hint here as to how God can 'rejoice in His creatures,' as mentioned in the introduction to this closing passage. Perhaps the references to the earthquake and volcano ('mountains that smoke') are meant to be metaphors, showing how our relationship with God works and how we can develop to such a point that He rejoices in us.

Of course, earthquakes and volcanoes are greatly feared by

---

1   Psalms 104:31-35.

Boiling magma erupts from Stromboli, an Italian volcano.
(Wolfgang Beyer)

humans. To this day, they can wreak massive destruction on even the most advanced civilizations. Therefore, when we look at this passage as a metaphor of the service of God such that He 'rejoices in His creatures,' we must first understand the basics of serving God as a context for this metaphor. Wanton destruction and sowing fear in people's hearts are incompatible with Torah values, since we are commanded to be kind to one another. Thus, in Isaiah we read:

> Behold, you fast for debates and strife, and strike with the fist wickedly. Do not fast as you have done until this day, crying out so as to be heard on high. Is this the fast I would choose: for a man to afflict his soul for a day? Is this it, to bend one's head like a reed, and to spread sackcloth and ashes? . . .
>
> Is not this rather the fast that I have chosen? Loosen the bands of

wickedness, undo the bundles that oppress, set free those who are broken, and break apart every burden. Give out your bread to the hungry,
and bring the needy and the homeless into your house. When you see
someone naked, cover him, and do not hide away from your own kin.
Then your light will break forth like the dawn, and your health will
speedily recover, and your justice will go before your face, and the glory
of the Lord will gather you up. Then you will call, and the Lord will hear:
you will cry out, and He will say, 'Here I am.'[2]

Rather like our understanding of the metaphor of lightning bolts,
we must therefore understand the Earth shaking and the mountains
emitting smoke only as illustrations of the raw spiritual energy of
those who serve God, not as recommendations of destruction.

With this in mind, let us understand what takes place when the
Earth shakes.

The interior of our planet is not cold, solid rock. Instead, there
are various internal sources of heat. For instance, decaying radioactive elements deep inside the Earth give off heat. Uranium-238
gradually turns into lead-206 and generates heat during this transformation. A second source of heat is the energy from meteorite
impacts, rocks that have slammed into the Earth over time. Their
kinetic energy – the energy of their motion – was converted into
heat energy which is slowly released in the same way that a bicycle
pump heats up during use. In addition, gravity draws the whole
Earth inward towards its own core, and this energy can also be
converted into heat.

The heat generated by these three processes is very intense. It
is typically around a thousand degrees Centigrade, and this means
that the rock inside the Earth is actually magma – a boiling mass of
molten rock which pushes up against the Earth's surface. There is
only a thin crust – around twenty miles thick – separating us from
it, and this crust represents just one percent of the Earth's volume.

The crust is not only very thin – it is actually broken! Geologists
have established that it consists of twelve large 'plates' and several
smaller ones. These plates drift, propelled by currents of heat that

2   58:4-9.

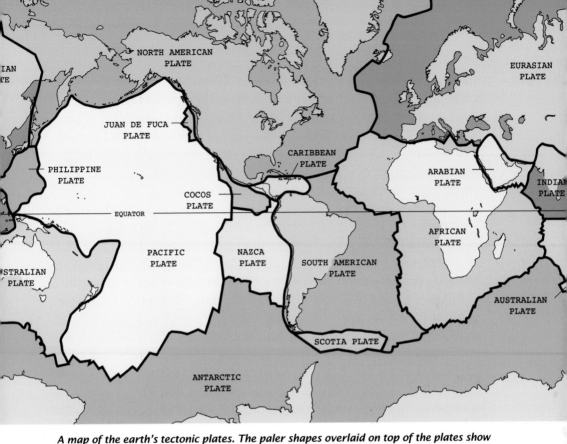

A map of the earth's tectonic plates. The paler shapes overlaid on top of the plates show the position of continents and countries, which are really protrusions on the tops of the plates which are not covered by the sea. (United States Geological Survey)

emanate from the molten depths beneath, and their motion is the root cause of most earthquakes.

There are various classifications of earthquakes, but the underlying mechanism is the same. Two plates that float along at a rate of approximately one millimeter per week might fetch up against each other if some irregularity prevents them from sliding past each other smoothly. For many years, after the initial shock of collision, nothing happens. But all the while, the arrested momentum of the plates is building up incredible pressure from both sides. Eventually, one of the plates will move, causing an earthquake.

The San Andreas Fault in California is a prime example of this. The fault is the line where the Pacific and North American plates are sliding past each other. When they jam together, pressure builds up, to be released in an earthquake. After the earthquake, they drift apart, and carry on floating about. But, since they are so close to each other, it is not long before they lock together again. Once again, the pressure builds up until another earthquake is triggered. This is why this part of the world is an earthquake hotspot.

The energy released during an earthquake is amazing. The earthquake which struck northern Chile in November 2007 released three times more energy than the biggest thermonuclear blast ever created, matching the energy which would be produced by 178 gigatonnes of TNT. (A gigatonne is 1,000,000,000 tonnes.)

Volcanoes are no less awesome than earthquakes. They can erupt at a weakness in the Earth's crust, or when plates in the crust move towards or away from each other, releasing the magma beneath.

The raw power of eruptions is spectacular. The biggest eruptions can blow the tops off mountains and fling rocks out over several miles as they hurl billions of tons of magma, known as lava once it reaches the surface, into the surrounding area. Ash and rock fragments are hurled twenty or thirty miles up into the air, and hundreds of cubic miles of ash shoot out to blanket areas up to a hundred miles or more away from the site of the eruption. The billions of tons of gases released by the lava can be hot enough to melt steel. All this energy can be complemented from above by the collision of rock particles, ash and ice particles in the air, which can generate electrical charges and create hundreds of bolts of lightning.

Another fearsome feature of volcanic eruptions is pyroclastic flow. These billowing clouds of boiling dust, rock and gas, with a temperature over a thousand degrees Centigrade, are swept along at hundreds of miles per hour by the force of the volcano's blast, devastating everything in their way. Water provides no escape from these lethal clouds. Such is their heat that when they billow out over water, a cushion of superheated steam is formed on which they can float across.

However awesome all this may seem, it is actually dwarfed by the power of extraterrestrial volcanoes. Although the volcanoes on Mars are not currently active, their size gives us an indication of just how enormous their eruptions must once have been. The largest Martian volcano, Olympus Mons, is over sixteen miles high,

Mount St Helens the day before the 1980 eruption. (Harry Glicken/USGS)

Mount St Helens after the eruption. The top of the mountain has been blown away, and the plume rises 3,000 feet above the rim of the crater. (Lyn Topinka/USGS)

Pyroclastic flow sweeps down the side of Mount St Helens. This flow, one of seventeen that swept down the mountainside during the May 1980 eruption, extended from the crater down to the valley floor. (Peter W Lipman/USGS)

Lightning generated by an eruption on Mount Rinjani, Indonesia, in 1995. (Oliver Spalt)

Olympus Mons, the largest known volcano and mountain in the Solar System, seen from above, swathed in carbon dioxide clouds. (Mariner 9/NASA/ JPL/Caltech)

making it three times the height of Mount Everest. Its base is bigger than the whole of England, and its crater could hold a city twice the size of London.

Io, one of Jupiter's moons, hit the headlines in 1979, when it was discovered to be volcanically active. *Voyager 1* and *Voyager 2* both spotted plumes of sulfur being thrown two hundred miles up into the atmosphere from eight volcanoes, and the surface of the little moon showed solidified rivers of liquid sulfur. There are now over three hundred known volcanoes on Io, and more may well be born or discovered as time goes by.

It is thought that Jupiter's huge gravitational field actually creates boiling tides of rock within Io. Europa and Ganymede – two other moons orbiting Jupiter – exert a pull on Io, keeping it in an elliptical orbit around Jupiter. This means that Io's distance from Jupiter changes during its circuit around the planet, and it is being subjected to different

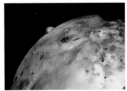

A volcanic eruption on Io photographed by Voyager 1. (NASA/JPL)

gravitational pulls at different times during its forty-two hour orbit. Just as the Moon pulls our own seas back and forth in a tidal cycle, so Io is being plucked at by Jupiter, with great tides of rock surging ceaselessly to and fro beneath the surface, creating a bulge in its surface that can be up to a hundred meters high. The enormous amount of friction generated by the internal chaos on Io actually

The San Francisco earthquake of 1906 ripped the ground apart. (GK Gilbert, USGS)

melts the moon's interior, creating an underground ocean of liquid sulfur which occasionally bursts through the moon's crust as a volcano.

Enceladus, one of the moons orbiting Saturn, also has volcanoes, possibly heated by a gravity-powered mechanism similar to Io's. Gas, dust and ice gush some nine hundred miles up from vents near the South Pole on Enceladus' surface, creating a plume three times as large as the diameter of the moon itself. It has been estimated that over a hundred kilograms of ice per second are bursting forth from this volcanic system at eight hundred miles per hour.

Pictures from the Cassini space probe suggest that Enceladus might be orbiting Saturn in a ring generated by its own volcanoes.

God looks at the Earth and it quakes. He touches the mountains and they belch forth smoke. We have seen that these are analogies for service of God, as the context indicates.

Perhaps there is a hidden message here as well, nested in this passage from Psalms to teach us a special lesson with our twentieth – and twenty-first-century science. Both earthquakes and volcanoes show us nature poised for action, ready to give vent to awesome power which we can barely withstand. So it is, wrote the Psalmist, with human beings. By virtue of being God's creatures, we have tremendous power. Sometimes, God will 'look at us' or 'touch us' and that power will burst forth with irresistible force.

A massive smoke plume from Mount St Helens dominates the sky. (Matt Logan, USGS)

How does God do this?

The Talmud[3] gives us an insight into this, quoting Rava, who says that if we are overcome by trouble, we should examine our behavior and make changes for the better.

It can perhaps be shown that our verse refers to this kind of divine intervention through the exact choice of words. The Hebrew for 'He touches the mountains' is '*yiga*' ['he will touch'] *be-harim* [literally '*in* the mountains'].' When the Torah talks about touching *in* something rather than just touching something, this normally refers to a punitive or painful contact as opposed to a gentle or pleasant touch. Thus, when Jacob wrestled with a mysterious 'man' who dislocated Jacob's thigh, the Torah relates this by saying, 'He touched *in* the hollow of his thigh.'[4]

Difficulties are, perhaps, one of God's ways of looking at us or touching us. When life becomes difficult, we are jolted out of our routine existence to confront the big questions of direction, goals and lifestyle. This is a time when we are in direct contact with our Maker and we can do something profound and life-changing.

Our passage from the Psalms shows us what immense power God can unleash within us by giving us a glance or tapping us on the

3   Berachot 5a.
4   Genesis 32:26. See Rabbi Samson Raphael Hirsch's commentary there.

An ash cloud from Mount Cleveland, Alaska, USA, photographed from space. (NASA)

shoulder. Just as the Earth can shudder and quake, altering land-scapes and crushing man-made structures as if they were paper, so we can change things in our lives that seemed irrevocable and permanent, wiping out the obstacles in our way. Just as a volcano can show astonishing power as it erupts, so we can do incredible things in our service of God, changing ourselves and influencing others in response to His touch. The earthquake and the volcano are images of the power of human response to God's call.

Modern science has granted us a better understanding of these phenomena and a glimpse of how these metaphors are writ still larger in the further reaches of our Solar System. As we discover volcanic eruptions that are taller than the entire body from which they erupt, as we understand the massive power latent within an earthquake, we have a clearer and more spectacular view of this parable of the human response to the divine call.

We can derive a second message from these metaphors as well. The power in the volcano and in the earthquake is latent, held in check until the time is ripe. This also tells us something about ourselves. It is not even as if God creates within us the power of our response when He judges it to be the right time. Rather, that amazing power is within us already, straining and seething like grinding tectonic plates or the magma beneath the Earth's crust, behind the limits that we place on our own souls. Even in quiet, easy times when it is easy to slip into mediocrity and complacency, that spiritual power still lives within us, ready to be unleashed at any moment. Even when we act weak, immense energy lies beneath the surface in every one of us. We need only feel God's glance or His touch to set it free.

This understanding of the references to earthquakes and volcanoes helps us to recast our understanding of the Psalm's conclusion. Here it is again:

> The glory of the Lord will last forever: the Lord will rejoice in his creatures. He looks at the Earth and it trembles; He touches the mountains and they smoke. I will sing to the Lord while I live: I will sing praise to my God while I still exist. Let my meditation be sweet for Him: I will rejoice in the Lord. Sinners will disappear off the Earth, and the wicked will be no more. Bless the Lord, my soul! Praise the Lord!

The awareness that we have such astonishing spiritual strength

The trees around Obscurity Lake were flattened when Mount Saint Helens erupted ten miles away in 1980. (Rick Hoblitt, USGS)

A view down on to Mount St Helens in 2004. (John Pallister/USGS)

within ourselves can be uplifting and encouraging. The Psalmist is moved by this new understanding of himself to devote his whole life to the praise of the Almighty. He anticipates the time when, through this kind of fiery dedication to all that is good, evil will be removed from the world, crushed and swept away by the earth-shattering, fiery power of a return to God.

WEIGHT LOSS

CERTAIN ROOT WORDS IN BIBLICAL HEBREW CAN BE TRAN-
slated in various ways depending on their context. The root
word *b-g-d*, for instance, can mean 'garment'[1] or 'betrayal.'[2]
Rabbi Samson Raphael Hirsch is one of many commentators who
have searched for an underlying, common meaning that unites
words' various translations. In the case of *b-g-d*, for instance, the
underlying meaning is that of covering or presenting an appearance, something that both a garment and a traitor do.

Sometimes the different meanings can actually explain one
another. For instance, the root of the word meaning 'to forgive' in
Hebrew is *n-s-'*[3]. The same root can also mean 'to carry.'[4]

The idea behind this is easy to understand. Our sins are like a
burden. We remember the bad things that we have done to God, to
others or to ourselves, and we feel guilt, shame and inadequacy.
Troubled by the prickings of our conscience, we find it difficult to
look ourselves and God in the eye. Our sins weigh us down and
impede our progress.

Indeed, the prophet Isaiah cries out, 'Woe, you sinful nation, you
people who are heavy with sin!'[5] And again later, 'Woe to those who
draw iniquity with cords of falsehood, and wickedness as with a
cart rope!'[6] God depicts our sin as a ball and chain, an irksome
burden that hampers us and from which we cannot escape.

The Hebrew word for forgiveness fits into this idea. Its alternative meaning, 'to carry,' indicates that God will carry our guilt for
us, liberating us from the crushing weight of our burden of sin.
Forgiveness brings a sense of relief akin to putting down a heavy
load.

---

1 Genesis 28:20.   2 Jeremiah 5:11.   3 Exodus 34:7.
4 Leviticus 11:25.   5 Isaiah 1:4.   6 Isaiah 5:18.

Thus, it is said that we can sense if we have been forgiven at the end of Yom Kippur because it feels as if a great burden has been lifted from our shoulders. We feel lighter, freer, liberated from our shortcomings.

Recent developments in technology give us a better understanding of this concept of sin as a crushing weight that we can cast off.

For years, NASA and the Soviet space program trained astronauts for the rigors of a zero-gravity environment by taking them up in airplanes and then flying them in parabolas or arcs. At the top of each parabola, there is a period of about thirty seconds during which the aircraft is not subject to gravity. The occupants can float about in a real zero-gravity environment, and discover whether they are suited for space travel.

Nowadays, it is possible to do this for fun. Companies in the United States and Russia offer individuals the opportunity to fly in specially adapted aircraft, with several thirty-second periods of weightlessness.

It can be an exhilarating and mind-blowing experience. The passengers delight in doing the impossible, throwing their fellow travelers effortlessly across the cabin, catapulting themselves towards the ceiling with the twitch of one hand against the floor, and swallowing water as it hovers as a spinning ball in mid-air. They become amazingly athletic, turning somersaults between the ceiling and the floor or doing press-ups with several people piled on top of them. Or they can sit cross-legged and serene in empty space, savouring a sense of freedom that is like no other.

Here is how the Zero Gravity Corporation, based in Las Vegas, describe their flights:

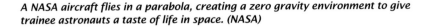

A NASA aircraft flies in a parabola, creating a zero gravity environment to give trainee astronauts a taste of life in space. (NASA)

It is an experience that few have tried, but those who have call it amazing and life-changing. It's a feeling of true freedom, a place where the impossible becomes real ... Fly like Superman; enjoy 25 times more hang-time than the best basketball player, and be more acrobatic than any Olympic gold medalist ... For once, you are in a realm where the law of gravity has lost its throne.

Another fascinating feature of the zero gravity environment is the lack of 'up' and 'down' as we know them. Our perception of 'up' and 'down' is generated by gravity pulling us towards the Earth's surface. In the absence of gravity there is no longer such a notion, enabling one to walk up a wall and across a ceiling as easily as one might walk across a floor on Earth. If 'down' is defined by where our feet are, then 'down' changes all the time. Therefore, the increase in personal power offered by zero gravity is coupled with the gift of a flexible perspective.

The return to life with gravity after a sustained period of weightlessness is difficult. Greg Chamitoff wrote movingly about his return to living with gravity after months in the zero-gravity environment of the International Space Station:

> The strength of gravity on Earth felt enormous when I returned. I couldn't believe how persistent and forceful it was for quite some time. On my first night back I recall feeling like I couldn't get all my body parts against the ground firmly enough to satisfy the Earth's gravity. I fell down even while crawling on all fours. I could lean my head to the side and feel the wash of acceleration through my head as if I was making a steep turn in an aircraft.[7]

Now that we understand the link between forgiveness and freedom from gravity, this phenomenon takes on new meaning. We recall that in Judaism, sin is for the soul what weight is for the body. The zero-gravity experience shows how exhilarating it is to be physically weightless. God's absolution, totally effective and delivered in love, offers us a parallel gift in spiritual terms, allowing us to resist and even defy the retrograde pulls of laziness, self-doubt, guilt and temptation.

A soul that has been freed and cleansed by God can do things

---

7   See *An Interview with an Astronaut,* Appendix 1.

Greg Chamitoff floats in mid-air and ponders his next move in a long-distance chess match organised by NASA and the United States Chess Federation. The chess pieces were held down with Velcro. (NASA)

that would be impossible under normal circumstances. One can pray with new depth and fervor, perform amazing acts of generosity, and attain fresh insights into the stories and rituals of the Torah, accomplishing feats of spiritual greatness that may seem totally out of character and beyond all expectation.

But then, life after divine forgiveness is not a reasonable thing. It is a context where we are set free from all restrictions, and where we can set ourselves challenges and goals that might have been unimaginable just a few minutes earlier.

The personal liberation that repentance offers is illustrated by the amazing ease with which one can alter one's perspective in a zero-gravity environment. *Teshuva*, the Hebrew word for 'repentance,' also means 'to change direction.' In the world of repentance, we can look at everything from a new slant and revolutionize our take on life: up is down, right is wrong, highlights become low points, rock bottom becomes a new zenith, and the highest priority suddenly becomes the lowest.

NASA astronaut Greg Chamitoff carries a huge experiment rack with ease in the weightless environment of the International Space Station. (NASA)

Since zero-gravity flights cost thousands of dollars, many people may feel that they cannot afford them. But the spiritual possibilities that God offers to us are free. In fact, He presses them upon us:

> Return, Israel, to the Lord your God, for you have stumbled in your sin. Take words with you and return to the Lord. Say to Him, 'Bear all our sins!' . . . [God replies] 'I will heal their backsliding; I will give them my love as a gift, for My anger has turned away from [Israel]. I will be like dew for Israel, he will blossom like a rose and his roots will strike [deeply] down like [cedars in] Lebanon.'[8]

It is God Himself who offers to every human being a breathtaking, cleansed new world where the present is no longer a prisoner of the past and we can accomplish things beyond our wildest dreams.

---

8   Hosea 14:2-6. See also Jonah chapter 3, where God sends Jonah to warn the non-Jewish inhabitants of Nineveh to repent. They repent, and God forgives them.

OUR MASTER'S VOICE

THERE ARE ASPECTS OF RELIGIOUS THOUGHT THAT ARE difficult to comprehend simply because they involve attributes of divinity that are beyond our frame of reference. Judaism does not give us an easy ride in this regard. From the very beginning of the Torah, we find that God does things that we can barely comprehend. Thus, in the opening paragraph of Genesis, God said 'Let there be light' – and there was light.[1]

This is one of the less comprehensible phenomena related in the Torah. How does God's word, an expression of infinite intelligence and profundity, translate itself into physical form? And why does God do it this way? What are we to learn from the fact that everything in this world is a palpable reverberation of God's primordial speech?

We may only approach this subject with great trepidation and circumspection, since we are touching on some of the most sacred and least understood aspects of God's might and His relationship to the world. Anything that we deduce about His *modus operandi* must be qualified as being highly speculative, clouded by our mortal perspective and open to question. But although we cannot grasp the wonder of divine speech becoming matter, this narrative can teach us about God's power and how He invites us to share it.

In this spirit, we can refer to an aspect of nuclear physics that might help us to learn something from this enigmatic phenomenon of God's word turning into solid matter.

In 1905, Albert Einstein posited mass-energy equivalence, meaning that all matter is simply the concentration of a huge amount of energy in one place. With the right techniques, matter can be

---

1   Genesis 1:3.

This is trinitite. It is thought that sand from the desert floor was swept up into the fireball produced by the first ever nuclear explosion (codenamed 'Trinity') then rained down as a liquid before solidifying into a greenish glassy residue. (Shaddack)

converted into energy, resulting in a mighty explosion. The first nuclear bomb was developed and tested towards the end of World War II at a secret research facility in Los Alamos in the United States. The bomb's devastating shockwave, dazzling flash of light and seething mushroom cloud were the first man-made demonstration of the most famous equation in the history of science: $E = mc^2$, meaning that the energy (E) latent in a body is equivalent to its mass (m) multiplied by the speed of light (c='celeritas', the Latin for "speed") squared.

The reverse is also true. If we compress a vast amount of energy into a tiny space, we can create matter out of energy. This actually happens on a very small scale in particle accelerators, where protons accelerate to speeds approaching the speed of light and then hit a target. The energy contained in the protons is converted into short-lived particles. But we are nowhere near making an appreciable, durable quantity of matter out of pure energy.

It would be presumptuous to say that this was how God's word made things in the world, as we are dealing with mystical matters that we cannot comprehend. And it would be wrong for us to ascribe any physical quantity, however large, to the energy inherent in God's voice, since God's power is limitless.

Nevertheless, we can at least reflect on this idea as a device to help us imagine, in our own little way, just how powerful an experience it might be to hear God's voice. Perhaps the Torah is portraying the creation *as if* the energy of God's voice had been condensed and concentrated into matter, so that we can have some conception of the power of His voice.

We have already seen that a sound is actually a pulse of energy that travels through space. As it hits the listener's eardrum, the listener's brain translates the vibrations of the eardrum into sound.

Perhaps God's voice is being portrayed to us as if it were an audible wave of energy travelling through the primeval 'emptiness and waste'.[2] Maybe it was as if an infinitesimal, incalculably small

---

2   Genesis 1:2.

To assess the effect of a nuclear explosion, this house was built over half a mile away from one of the Upshot-Knothole detonations. When the blast reached the house, destruction occurred within a few seconds. (Courtesy of National Nuclear Security Administration / Nevada Site Office)

dazzling fireball blossoms after the detonation
a nuclear device in Operation Teapot.
hoto courtesy of National Nuclear Security
dministration / Nevada Site Office)

This characteristic mushroom cloud rose to a
height of 40,000 feet two minutes after the Ivy
Mike detonation. (Photo courtesy of National
Nuclear Security Administration / Nevada Site
Office)

fragment of the infinite power of God's voice was so condensed and concentrated under God's guidance that it became visible light energy on the first day of creation. In this paradigm, the energy of God's word on the second day was condensed to make a sky, an atmosphere that cocooned our planet and made it habitable. And on the fourth day of creation, God condensed the energy of His word to form the heavenly bodies in the sky around our own planet. The creation of the Sun, Moon and stars certainly could be understood as happening in this way, as we see from the account of the fourth day of creation, where there is a direct transition from God's utterance to the act of creation:

> And God said, 'Let there be lights in the vault of the heavens, to distin-
> guish between day and night .... And let them serve as lights in the
> vault of the heavens to shine on the Earth.' And it was so.[3]

However hesitantly and tentatively we dare to grasp at this hazy idea, we can use it as an illustration of the power of God's word. We are, perhaps, to think about the relationship between a colossal nuclear blast and the tiny ball of matter that created it. We can

---

3   Genesis 14-15.

then infer from this by degrees how much energy God's voice is depicted as containing.

Little Boy was the bomb that the American army dropped on the Japanese city of Hiroshima on August 6, 1945. It contained 64 kilograms of uranium-235, of which one kilogram underwent nuclear fission. Just 0.6 of a gram of uranium was actually transformed into pure energy, in accordance with Einstein's equation.

This gives us the insight that we were looking for. The energy latent in that tiny speck of matter weighing less than a gram was enough to create a fireball 1,200 feet in diameter. People close to where the bomb fell were vaporized, flammable materials burst into flames, and sand flowed as molten glass. Inside the blast zone, which was two miles across, all buildings were destroyed. The many fires started by the heat combined to create a firestorm that consumed other flammable materials exposed by the initial blast.

To reiterate: if we were to take all this energy and somehow compress it into matter, we would have a yield weighing just three fifths of a gram. How much energy would be required to create a whole planet? Or a whole solar system? How much to make an entire galaxy, with its millions of solar systems? And how much energy, how many trillions of nuclear blasts, would one need to condense to make an entire universe?

Here, as we have seen, our analogy breaks down, because we dare not ascribe quantities to the infinite and omnipotent God. But let us imagine an immense conflagration whose dimensions dwarf the entire universe and whose energy could be condensed into enough matter to make a universe. Let us then recall that this is *nothing* compared to the power of God's voice. We then have some trifling, indistinct notion of God's omnipotence.

We have now answered our second question. Why did God choose to create the world through speech? Perhaps He wanted us, the people of our own time, to have a new understanding, albeit an inadequate one, of the power of His word.

It so happens that one of the Psalms gives us a description of God's voice, which is reminiscent of a nuclear blast:

> God's voice thunders out more than mighty waters. God's voice is full of strength and splendor. God's voice breaks down cedars . . . God's voice

The mushroom cloud from the Ivy Mike nuclear test rose to a height of twenty-five miles and broadened until it measured a hundred miles across. (Photo courtesy of National Nuclear Security Administration / Nevada Site Office)

hews flashes of fire. God's voice makes the desert quake . . . and strips the forests.

(Psalms 29:3-9)

The rabbis teach that this Psalm depicts God addressing the Jewish people at Mount Sinai in the desert when He uttered the Ten Commandments. Inasmuch as the Psalm depicts the giving of the

The mighty Lebanese cedar can grow up to 40 meters in height. (Peripitus)

Torah, it also, indirectly, depicts creation. We can understand this in the light of the statement of the Talmudic sage Resh Lakish,[4] who said that the viability of creation depended on the Jewish people receiving the Torah. Thus, in a certain way, the Torah was the final act of creation. It is, perhaps, not entirely wrong to say that the voice of God at Mount Sinai was the nearest we could get to the voice of God at the birth of the universe.

There is a deep message in this. God's word is passed on from one generation to the next like a precious heirloom. We have already seen the verse from the Torah which says that 'Moses commanded us concerning the Torah. It is an inheritance for the congregation of Jacob.'[5]

This may mean that when we transmit God's word to the next generation, or help it to be transmitted, we share in some small way in that tremendous, supra-thermonuclear power with which God gave the Torah and formed the whole world.

What a tremendous privilege it is for us to learn Torah and to teach it! Inestimable raw spiritual energy is hidden in every phrase, in every letter. By studying the Torah and passing on our knowledge, we have the privilege of joining with God's own mighty voice. However weak and insignificant we may feel, we are actually wielding incredible spiritual power. Our role is to live up to the sacred mission that God has entrusted to us, and to make His voice reverberate through the world.

---

4   Shabbat 88a.
5   Deuteronomy 33:4.

A SUNNY DISPOSITION

I N RECENT TIMES, ASTRONOMERS, SCIENTISTS AND SPACE probes have discovered that the Sun is much more than a warm, bright light in the sky. Nowadays we have a good idea of what exactly it is and how it works.

We have already seen Einstein's famous equation – $E=mc^2$ – and learned that tiny amounts of matter can be converted into huge amounts of energy. This helps us to understand how the Sun works. In 1920, the British astronomer Arthur Eddington suggested that something like this might account for the Sun's remarkable longevity and power.

Picture two atoms of hydrogen gas in the middle of the Sun. Under the right conditions – including immense pressure and heat – the nuclei, minuscule collections of matter right at the centre of the atoms, will fuse together, changing into a different element – helium. During this process of nuclear fusion, a small proportion of the two atoms will not change into helium, but will actually be transformed into gamma rays, a form of high-energy electromagnetic radiation. This process, repeated countless times per second, is what powers the Sun.

The more we find out about the Sun, the more staggering the figures become. Six hundred million tons of hydrogen fuse every second, creating five hundred and ninety-six million tons of helium. The remaining four million tons of hydrogen are converted into 400,000,000,000,000,000,000,000,000 joules of energy. This means that every second the Sun releases a million times as much energy as is consumed in the whole world in a year. All this energy generates a solar surface temperature of around five and a half thousand degrees Centigrade, hot enough to vaporize every substance we know. At the Sun's heart, temperatures soar to fifteen million degrees Centigrade.

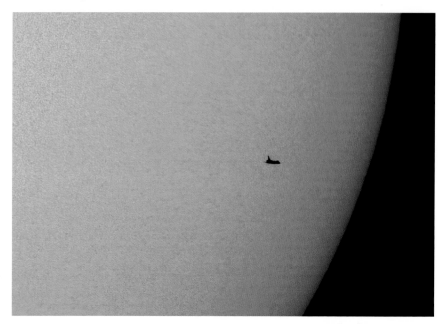

NASA's space shuttle Atlantis silhouetted against the Sun. This picture gives us an inkling of how enormous the Sun is. (Thierry Legault)

Despite this stupendous output, it is thought that the Sun's core, which measures two hundred thousand miles across, has enough hydrogen to sustain this process for another ten billion years, since it is so big. In fact, its mass accounts for all but one five hundredth of everything in our Solar System. The showers of comets and meteorites that bombard the Solar System, the mighty planets with their retinues of moons, the vast asteroid belt held in a gravitational limbo between Mars and Jupiter, are all just tiny specks in comparison with the enormous star at their center.

One would expect a beam of radiation to travel from the center of the Sun to its surface in a matter of seconds. But conditions within the Sun mean that this practically never happens. The center of the Sun is so dense that a gamma ray would not typically travel more than one centimeter before colliding with subatomic particles that prevent it from continuing. This process of collision can continue for centuries before the rays, which might have been converted into x-rays along the way, break out of the core and begin to make their way to the Sun's periphery. The rays travel via tunnels of searing gas, and some of them decay en route, losing energy and turning from x-rays into ultraviolet light. Finally, at the Sun's rim, a portion of the ultraviolet rays becomes downgraded again, this time falling within the narrow spectrum of radiation that is visible to the human eye as sunlight.

Only at this point do the Sun's rays actually become visible, since up till now the rays have been of too high a frequency for us to be able to see them. If we could look right into the middle of the Sun, it would appear black to us.

Once a ray has arrived at the Sun's surface, it streaks off into the Solar System at the speed of light – one hundred and eighty-six thousand miles per second. After the huge traffic jam inside the Sun, the rest of the journey is very straightforward. Sunlight reaches the Earth in just eight minutes, and is out at Jupiter half an hour later. Within eight hours of leaving the surface of the Sun, it has passed Pluto and its moons, three billion miles away at the outer limits of the Solar System. It will never return.

The colossal quantities of gas involved in the ongoing nuclear reactions inside the Sun help us to understand why it does not simply tear itself apart and disappear, like a nuclear explosion that only lasts for a few seconds. There is so much gas around the Sun that its sheer weight counterbalances the furious nuclear inferno raging within it, and clamps down on it like a lid on a pot of boiling water. The Sun is held in check by its own fuel reserves.

One way of appreciating the Sun's heat is to look at our own planet. Even our tiny planet, trailing humbly around this mighty giant at a distance of ninety-three million miles, absorbs four trillion kilowatt hours of energy every day. A hundred litres of oil burning on every square meter of the Earth's surface would only generate as much heat as the Earth receives from the Sun in a single year.

But this is only part of the story. During the nineteenth century, astronomers developed special telescopes that enabled them to watch the area immediately around the Sun without damaging their eyes or being dazzled by its radiance. They discovered that the Sun is not the smooth disk which it appears to be. All around the Sun, there are plumes of gas which explode from the surface, flaring for about ten minutes before they die down. A typical one would be a thousand miles across and ten thousand miles high – about the distance from the United Kingdom to New Zealand.

Observers also noted a grainy effect on the surface of the Sun, as if it was bubbling. This effect is produced by huge pockets of gas, each over six hundred miles across – about the same size as France. The gas pockets erupt from the depths of the Sun at speeds approaching two thousand miles per hour, then cool off and sink back towards the center.

Some two thousand years ago, the Chinese had noticed that dark spots would come and go from time to time on the surface of the Sun. Between 1829 and 1843, Heinrich Schwabe, a German astronomer, plotted the appearance and disappearance of these sunspots, and established that the Sun has an eleven-year cycle of activity, during which a number of dark spots gradually appear and then fade out again towards the end of the cycle. What is the cause of this phenomenon?

It was only during the twentieth century that a hypothesis was worked out to explain it. Studies of sunlight indicated that there was a strong element of magnetic distortion acting within the Sun. During the early 1900s, George Ellery Hale, an astronomer working at an observatory in Los Angeles, calculated that there are points in the Sun's magnetic field that are six thousand times as strong as the Earth's own magnetic field.

It has been suggested that this magnetic field becomes increasingly complicated and twisted as time goes by because parts of the Sun move at different speeds. The electrical charge from the gas in the Sun's interior pulls the magnetic lines of force around each other and occasionally out to the surface, where they can be seen as slightly cooler areas – sunspots, which measure 'only' four thousand degrees Centigrade. After eleven years, the magnetic force field resumes its original formation, the sunspots disappear, and the whole process begins again.

We know of hundreds of magnetic field lines that run through the outer section of the Sun in an overlapping jumble of power, drawing out loops of fire and manifesting themselves as sunspots

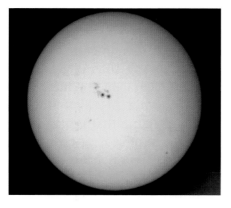

Sunspots.
(SiriusB)

This ultra-violet Hubble telescope picture of Saturn proves the range of the Sun's influence. The bright patches at the top and bottom are where charged particles streaming in from the Sun (nearly a billion miles away) burn up near the planet's poles, creating aurora similar to the ones seen at the North and South Poles on Earth. (JT Trauger (JPL) and NASA)

which can be as big as Jupiter. The Sun is not only unimaginably hot, but is also a gigantic magnet.

This discovery helped to explain another phenomenon that was first witnessed fleetingly during solar eclipses – the red gleams at the edge of the Sun, which were sometimes visible to the naked eye, and described by an Italian astronomer in 1231. He had noticed a solar prominence – a tongue of flame that erupts from the surface of the Sun and lunges out for hundreds of thousands of miles before disappearing back into the fiery heart of the Sun. It is thought that these bursts of activity follow the Sun's magnetic field, shooting out into space along one of the magnetic lines and then following it back below the surface.

The Sun bursts out beyond its visible limits in other ways as well. It frequently functions like a volcano, with huge tongues of plasma (superheated, electrically charged gas) actually erupting off the surface of the Sun and racing away into space. Here again,

A spectacular view of comet P1 McNaught with its tail being blown behind it by the solar wind. (Fir0002/Flagstaffotos)

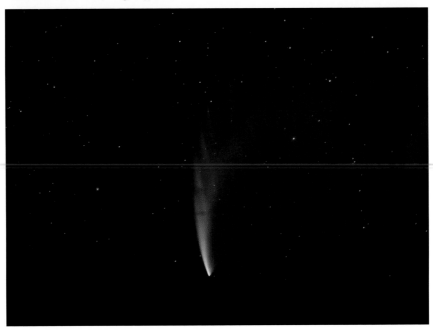

the figures are beyond human imagination. In 1973, the crew of NASA's *Skylab* watched a ball of plasma expanding out of the Sun at the rate of one and a half million miles per hour. When it finally burst, it hurled tens of billions of tonnes of plasma off through the Solar System.

In 1958, Eugene Parker, a researcher in Chicago, tried to work out why comets' tails always point away from the Sun. He proposed that the Sun is pouring out a vast quantity of charged hydrogen and helium particles which bombard the comets – and everything else – in the vicinity, blowing the comets' tails away from it, just as a gust of wind blows the steam from a ship's funnel. In 1962, the instruments on *Mariner 2*, an American space probe on its way to Venus, proved conclusively that Parker's theory was correct. The solar wind, a blast of charged particles surging out from the Sun at a million miles per hour, became part of the modern astronomical inventory.

How far does this wind blow? In 1998, when the American *Voyager* probes were hundreds of millions of miles away from the Sun, there was a period of great activity on the Sun, with the equivalent of a solar gale blasting out into space. A few months after this intense solar activity was recorded, the *Voyager* probes registered the gale and reported it back to Earth. This told scientists that the Sun's 'atmosphere' reaches out far beyond the Earth, into the depths of our Solar System.

A year later, the probes detected an 'echo' of that same gust of wind in the form of radio waves bouncing back towards the Sun. Scientists theorize that this emanated from the point where the Sun's influence is halted by the wind from other stars. This means that our Sun's wind has a range of some fourteen billion miles – fifteen thousand times the distance from the Sun to the Earth.

Let us try to bear all this incredible power in mind while we think about a verse in the book of Judges. Barak and the prophet Deborah sang it after they defeated Sisera, the commander of the Canaanite army: 'Those who love God are like the Sun emerging in all its strength.'[1]

---

1   Judges 5:31.

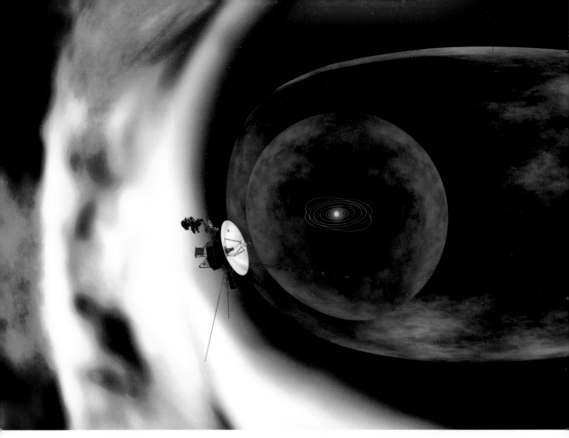

An artist's impression of Voyager 2 studying the extent of the Sun's influence. This picture shows that the Sun's power reaches far beyond the Solar System (the white concentric rings around the Sun). The light blue sphere around the Sun shows the immediate reach of the solar wind, while the larger and darker shape extending to the right shows the solar wind's range of interaction with winds from other stars. (Walt Feimer, NASA)

The Talmud[2] applies this verse to a particular characteristic: the ability to hear a taunt and not respond. If someone attempts to compromise our reputation or our dignity and we restrain our inclination to strike back, calm in the knowledge that everything comes from God and that He can look after us better than we can look after ourselves, then we exhibit the finest strength of all: self-restraint.

It is enormously difficult not to respond to taunts or character assassination. Anyone who can withstand this temptation and rise above the petty trials of backbiting and slander is a paragon of

---

2   Shabbat 88b

spiritual vitality and self-discipline. Such strength is so magnificent that its comparison to the Sun is a worthy metaphor.

If we could see such a person's soul, it would look like the Sun – enormous, awe-inspiring, powerful, and dominating all else. Just as the Sun dwarfs all the other bodies in the Solar System, so the average human being is spiritually unimportant relative to someone who is strong enough to bear insults with equanimity.

A further lesson that might be drawn from our modern knowledge of the Sun is that of influence. We have seen that the solar wind spreads far beyond the Solar System, checked only by the whisper of wind from other stars elsewhere in the galaxy. Here we find another dimension in the simile of Deborah's song.

It is tempting to think that quiet, forgiving people are socially

In this view of the Sun, a large solar flare extends across nearly half a million miles. The picture also shows the eruption of huge bubbles measuring hundreds of miles across (solar granulation) on the rest of the Sun's surface. (Skylab 4, NASA)

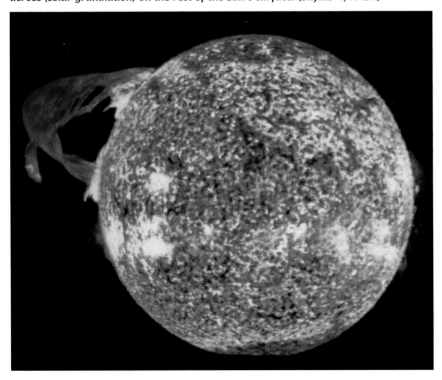

peripheral. J. Paul Getty, one of the world's first billionaires, once said that the meek would inherit the Earth, but not the mineral rights. Surely the loudest mouth, the keenest vigilance regarding one's own dignity, the most vigorous response to an insult should enable one to carry the day and 'make one's way in the world.' Not a bit, says the song of Deborah. The quiet greatness of someone who is impervious to slander makes a greater, more lasting and more honorable impact. One who does not stoop to trade insults broadcasts a potent and invincible message of quiet dignity and self-possession. Their moral legacy to humanity will endure far beyond the loud-mouthed selfishness of those who seek the lime-light.

Perhaps the finest quality of someone who can withstand the temptation to hit back is their independence. In modern Western culture, one is frequently encouraged to follow the crowd. Eccentricity is a risky business, while wearing trendy designer labels is much safer.

And what of someone who can rise above an insult? Like the Sun, they have no need of outside forces to keep them going and assure them that they are still worthy human beings. They are so aware of their own value that they have no need for their peers' admiration. Just as the Sun derives all its awesome power from within itself, so the subject of Deborah's song stands above the herd mentality that threatens individual spiritual growth.

Self-restraint is a difficult virtue to cultivate. To resist springing to one's own defense is much harder than to demolish an adversary with a witty aphorism or a solid right hook. But this is the Jewish route to stardom.

MANPOWER?

ONE OF THE THINGS THAT WE HAVE DISCOVERED OVER the last fifty years of space exploration is the range of enormous forces that exist beyond our planet. We can look at planetary features as archaeologists, piecing together events from the past. We can also examine things that are going on now. Either way, it becomes clear that the universe was, and still is, a violent place, exhibiting forces way beyond anything that we could create or manage.

One of our nearest neighbors – the planet Mercury – is rather a quiet place nowadays. Because it is so near the Sun (only thirty-six million miles away, compared to the Earth, which is ninety-three million miles away), it is subjected to a huge amount of solar radiation, and life as we know it cannot survive there. But Mercury shows signs of a tumultuous past.

When the American space probe *Mariner 10* approached Mercury in 1974, it sent back the first photographs of the planet's surface. There were several military commanders at mission control when the pictures came in, and when they saw the incredible array of craters on the little planet's surface, they were reminded of the punishment meted out by American B-52 bombers here on Earth.

It is thought that these craters were made by huge rocks floating through space. As they drifted within Mercury's gravitational field, they were drawn into orbit around it, eventually slamming down into the surface at great speed.

The force of these collisions cannot be overestimated. *Mariner 10* detected a core of iron and nickel in the middle of Mercury that is much larger, relative to the rest of the planet, than the cores of other planets. This, together with Mercury's small size (its volume is only six percent of Earth's), has prompted speculation that, at some point, an enormous meteorite crashed into the planet with

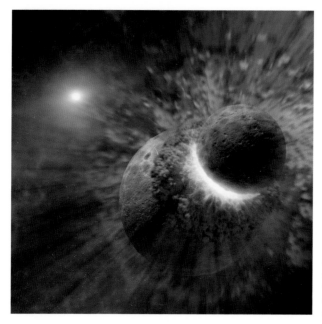

A smash like this is thought to have created the Caloris Basin on Mercury. (T Pyle, SSC)

such force that it blasted much of the planet's exterior into space. What we see nowadays might be just a fragment of the original Mercury.

Another piece of evidence on Mercury suggests that the planet has withstood a great deal. The Caloris Basin is a crater on Mercury some eight hundred miles across. Mountain ranges measuring two thousand meters in height emanate from the basin in concentric rings – like the ripples around a stone dropped into water – indicating that the surface of the planet was subjected to enormous shock waves, presumably because of a huge rock crashing into it. What is more, a range of hills on precisely the opposite side of the planet is thought to have been formed by the same impact. Shock waves from the impact are thought to have travelled around both sides of the planet's rim and met on the opposite side, throwing up the hills as they converged.

Mars also boasts its fair share of spectacular geology, bespeaking huge natural forces at play. The *Mariner 9* probe settled into an orbit around Mars in 1971 and began to map the whole planet. In the course of its photographic tour, it discovered the Tharsis region, a range of immense volcanoes perched on top of a five-thousand-mile bulge where lava had bubbled up to the surface, seeking an exit. The formation of these enormous mountains exerted such stress on the planet's crust that they cracked the surface nearby, creating Valles Marineris, a huge canyon a hundred miles wide, five miles deep and long enough to stretch across North America.

Even the atmospheres on other planets make us think twice about how tough we are. Winds on Earth can gust to over two hundred miles per hour, and such extreme events can have devastating effects. An enormous American naval force encountered a tropical storm that blew up off the Philippines in December 1944. Within a few hours, the tornado sank three destroyers, crippled a cruiser and eight aircraft carriers, and wrecked nearly two hundred aircraft. Seven hundred and fifty-nine sailors lost their lives in the storm.

But the winds on Neptune make our worst storms look like gentle breezes. *Voyager 2* found that this remote blue planet had

The Valhalla Crater on Callisto, one of the moons orbiting Jupiter. The crater was formed by a meteor smash so great that it convulsed a large part of the moon's surface, creating a ripple formation emanating from the site of the impact, similar to the Caloris Basin on Mercury. (NASA, JPL)

The dark scar across the centre of Mars is Valles Marineris, a canyon some 2500 miles long, a hundred miles wide and five miles deep. (NASA)

The nucleus of Halley's Comet. It is thought that the Tunguska event was caused by something similar smashing into the Earth. (Halley Multicolor Camera Team, Giotto Project, ESA)

clouds that formed and disappeared over several minutes, and it was calculated that winds on Neptune can blow at one thousand two hundred miles per hour, almost twice the speed of sound. If such a wind were to blow across the Earth, the effect would be akin to a nuclear explosion, and the damage would be so cataclysmic that it would probably mean the end of life on our planet.

Another remarkable demonstration of power is found between Io, one of Jupiter's moons, and Jupiter itself. Io functions as a massive electrical generator as it moves through Jupiter's magnetic field, creating an electrical current between itself and Jupiter that generates some two trillion watts of power.

One of the most devastating illustrations of our own weakness vis-à-vis the raw power of the extraterrestrial environment occurred on June 30th, 1908. An enormous explosion that could be heard from a distance of five hundred miles thundered across the region near the Tunguska River in Siberia, flattening twenty-five square miles of forest. A nomadic herdsman who escaped with minor burns reported that his herd of fifteen hundred reindeer, which

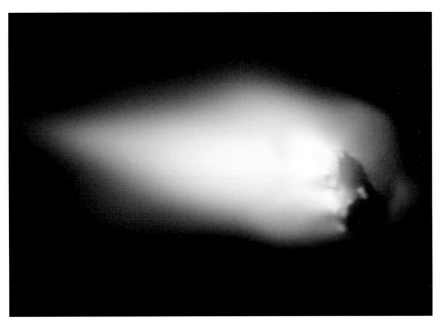

were grazing nearer the blast, had disappeared without trace. More than fifty miles from the mysterious detonation, buildings rocked and people were thrown to the ground. The shock waves halted a Trans-Siberian railway train travelling nearly four hundred miles away to the south. Seismic detectors as far away as London and New York registered a 'major earthquake.'

The exact cause of the Tunguska Event has never been established, but it is thought that the huge explosion was caused by a fragment from a comet – probably measuring less than two hundred feet across – entering the Earth's atmosphere.

This relatively minuscule chip of rock – less than one two hundred thousandth of the Earth's diameter – caused such mayhem because of the speed with which it entered our atmosphere. It is common for such a fragment to travel at more than five hundred thousand miles per hour. At this incredible speed, the friction generated by its moving through the atmosphere would create enormous heat, which would cause the rock to explode into a ball of fire.

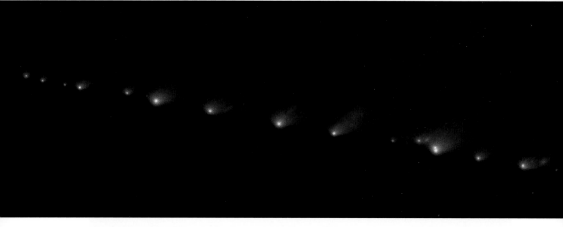

The fragments of Shoemaker-Levy 9 on their collision course with Jupiter. (NASA, ESA, and H. Weaver and E. Smith (STScI))

The size of the explosion can scarcely be imagined. It is estimated that the Tunguska Fragment exploded just three miles above the Earth, unleashing the equivalent of thirty million tonnes of conventional high explosives. Tunguska showed that, in a showdown between humans and extraterrestrial forces, we would stand no chance.

But this was nothing compared to an impact on Jupiter observed in July 1994. Shoemaker-Levy 9 was a comet that had broken up, and was travelling towards Jupiter in the form of twenty-one fragments varying in size from a few hundred meters to about a mile across.

When the first fragment ploughed into Jupiter's atmosphere at forty miles per second, it created a fireball over two thousand miles high, a dark spot as big as the whole Earth and seismic waves

This view of Jupiter shows brown marks where fragments of the Shoemaker Levy comet ripped into the planet's atmosphere. (Hubble Space Telescope Comet Team/NASA)

that careered across the planet at nearly three hundred miles per second.

The largest fragment, G, struck with such force that it created a dark spot nearly four times the size of our planet, tantamount to a detonation of six million megatons of TNT, or about six hundred times as much energy as could be released by humanity's entire nuclear arsenal. Such an impact on Earth would lead to the immediate mass extinction of all life.

When we look far out into space, we also find forces that surpass anything that our little Solar System has to offer. Some time ago, Frank Tipler, an American mathematician, designed a time machine. He operated on the principle (based on Einstein's theory of relativity) that a sufficiently strong gravitational field will warp space-time, and imagined a cylinder measuring a hundred kilometers in length and ten kilometers across. If this cylinder had as much matter as our Sun packed into it, and if it were spinning twice every millisecond, it would pull the fabric of space-time around with it, and time in its vicinity would behave very differently from the way in which we experience it.

This may sound like something out of science fiction; but something very much like it actually exists. In 1982, astronomers discovered a 'millisecond pulsar.' A pulsar is a rotating neutron star that emits a beam of electromagnetic radiation in the form of a radio wave, similar to the way in which a lighthouse sends out a rotating beam of light. The astronomers picked up a pattern of radiation bursts from this particular pulsar that indicated that it was turning very rapidly. They concluded that this body has the same mass as our Sun, the same density as the nucleus in the middle of an atom, and that it spins at a third of the speed of Tipler's time machine: once every 1.5 milliseconds. It is to be expected that the gravitational force exerted by this body is so immense that anyone venturing close enough to it would experience a distortion of time itself.

Wherever we look, we are confronted by our own weakness and fragility. Does it not, therefore, seem a little presumptuous for us to claim a special relationship with the *borei olam*, the Creator of the Universe? God made this immensely powerful mechanism. How

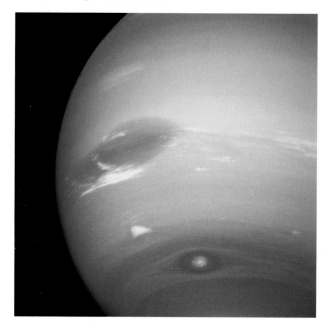

The white marks on this picture of Neptune are clouds, blown by winds travelling at over 700 miles per hour. (NASA)

can we hope that He should take an interest in a feeble species that dares not venture beyond its galactic neighborhood for fear of instant death?

This question was asked long ago by King David, in one of the most famous verses in the Psalms:

> When I look at Your actions and the work of Your fingers, what is Man that You should remember him, the son of Adam that You should consider him?
> But You made him a little lower than the angels, and crowned him with glory and majesty.[1]

It is particularly noteworthy that the word for 'man' in this text is the comparatively rare term, *enosh*, which occurs fewer than fifty times in the Bible.[2] The word *enosh* has strong connotations

---

1 Psalms 8:4–6.
2 The more common term *ish* occurs well over a thousand times.

of mortality, recalling the term *anush* – 'dangerously ill' – which is used in the later prophetic works.[3]

We can conclude that the Psalmist is evoking an image of a human race that is insignificant almost to the point of non-existence. Yet even though we are so fragile, he says, we have been granted a special relationship with the Creator of the universe, who has made us masters of the Earth. Why did God give human beings such an exalted status? In what way can we be crowned with glory and majesty?

Perhaps the Psalmist reflects in his answer on one unique aspect of the human condition – our spiritual freedom. A comet, a wind ripping through Neptune's atmosphere, a tiny photon hurtling through space – all have tremendous power, but they cannot make choices. They simply exist, performing their allotted tasks as ordained by their Creator.

But human beings can decide between right and wrong. We may be unable to survive the impact of a meteorite, and we certainly could not survive the crushing gravitational pull of a massive planet, but we can say 'no' to ourselves.

Even angels have no evil inclination – and consequently no spiritual challenge to overcome – when they do their Maker's bidding. Only a human can heed the sudden prick of conscience, look at a course of action from a divine perspective, and decide not to follow it through. In this, we are 'a little lower than the angels,' poised to do God's will. If we listen to the words of His Torah and the promptings of the soul that He breathed into us, then we will actually be the holiest and most exalted of God's creatures.

---

3   See, for instance, Isaiah 17:11 and 16; Jeremiah 15:18; Job 34:6; Micah 1:9; 2 Samuel 12:15.

HUMAN GREATNESS

W E HAVE HAD A LOOK AT THE ENORMOUS FORCES THAT function in our Solar System and beyond. But even if we just think about how big things are, we can feel marginalized. When we look at some of the universe's larger objects, we encounter sizes that inspire awe by virtue of their sheer magnitude.

In October 2009, NASA's Spitzer Space Telescope found evidence of a colossal ring around Saturn. The ring is very faint, consisting of dust particles just a hundredth of a millimeter across. The ring is so diaphanous that there are only about twenty particles for every cubic kilometer of space, and someone standing inside the ring would not even be able to see it. But while this ring may be short on substance, it is big on reach. It starts over three million miles from Saturn and extends outwards another seven million miles, making a total diameter of over twenty million miles. We can put it in a human perspective by comparing it with the size of our own planet. Twenty million miles is over two thousand times the diameter of Earth at the equator.

This huge body is dwarfed by our Solar System as a whole. It is difficult to define our Solar System precisely. If we define it as the space bounded by Pluto's orbit, the Solar System measures up at over three billion miles across. In fact, there is thought to be a cloud of billions of comets known as the Oort Cloud beyond all the planets that orbit our Sun. If we consider this to be part of the Solar System, then the Solar System is suddenly a thousand times larger still.

As we look further out into space, we encounter sizes that cannot be expressed easily in miles simply because they are so large. The Eagle Nebula (in the Serpens constellation) was photographed by the Hubble Space Telescope, which discerned columns of cool molecular hydrogen gas reminiscent of stalactites or windswept

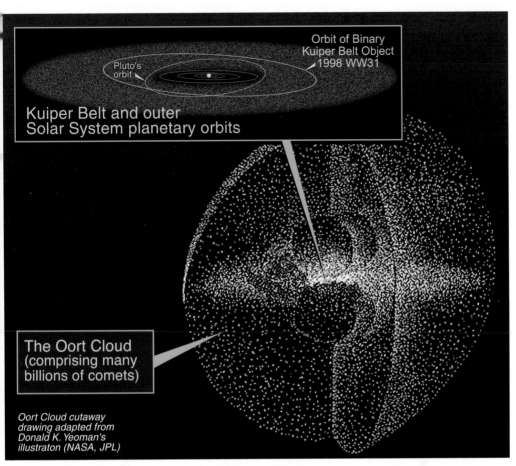

Orbit of Binary
Kuiper Belt Object
1998 WW31

Pluto's
orbit

Kuiper Belt and outer
Solar System planetary orbits

The Oort Cloud
(comprising many
billions of comets)

*Oort Cloud cutaway
drawing adapted from
Donald K. Yeoman's
illustraton (NASA, JPL)*

This diagram shows the relative sizes of the Kuiper belt (a region of icy bodies and dwarf planets beyond Neptune) and the Oort Cloud. (Donald K Yeomans, NASA and A. Feild (Space Telescope Science Institute))

rocks in the desert. Scientists concluded that these columns, because of their density, have temporarily resisted the onslaught of ultraviolet light from nearby newborn stars, creating eerie shapes that hang in space. The columns are all judged to measure around a light year from top to bottom. To put this another way: light travels about 5,878,630,000,000 miles in a year. Thus the Eagle Nebula columns are over five trillion miles high.

This figure itself feels infinitesimal when compared with the size of the Milky Way, the galaxy of which our Sun is just one star. There are estimated to be over two hundred billion stars in our galaxy, and it is thought to have a mass equivalent to three trillion

The Carina Nebula has pillars of gas and dust similar to those of the Eagle Nebula, only three times as high. (NASA, ESA, M Livio and the Hubble Twentieth Anniversary Team)

of our suns. It has been estimated that it takes light one hundred thousand years to travel from one side of our galaxy to the other. Using a human criterion, we can express this as a distance of 587,863,000,000,000,000 miles.

We can try to visualize this a little by imagining the Milky Way

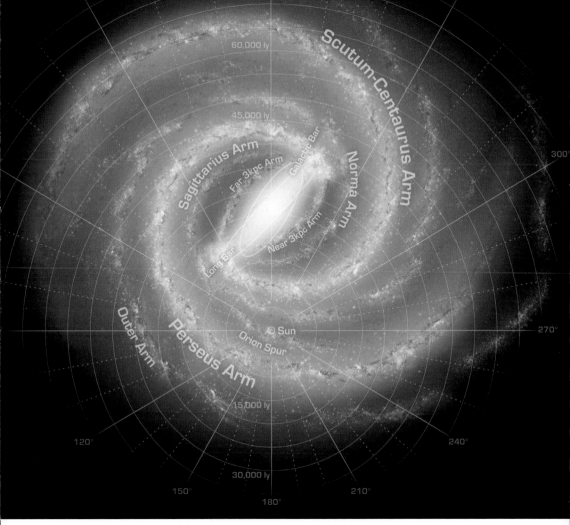

Artist's impression of the Milky Way, with measures of galactic longitude centered on our own Sun. The abbreviation "ly" stands for "light year". (NASA/JPL-Caltech)

reproduced as a scale model ten meters across. Within this model, our own Solar System would be just one tenth of a millimeter wide.

We even find ripples in space on a galactic scale. The Cartwheel Galaxy in the Sculptor Constellation, half a billion light years away from us, shows the aftermath of an impact between two galaxies.

Omega Centauri is a collection of some ten million stars orbiting the Milky Way. A large galaxy may contain as many as five hundred such formations, so a cluster of thousands of galaxies can contain trillions of stars. (ESO)

A small galaxy has crashed through the centre of a large one. The impact has created a ripple effect, a gigantic ring of energy shooting out at two hundred thousand miles per hour sweeping up gas and dust in its path, and crushing them to the point that nuclear fusion has taken place, creating a ring of new stars some 150,000 light years across.

And we can take this further. Galaxies tend to congregate in clusters. A cluster can contain thousands of galaxies, and is so large that it is cumbersome to express its size in light years. Instead, scientists use the megaparsec, equivalent to about 3,262,000 light years. A cluster can measure up to ten megaparsecs across.

There are still larger structures in the universe. Clusters themselves congregate into superclusters. A supercluster is the largest known structure in the universe, stretching over hundreds of millions of light years.

On the universal scale, human beings are like a tiny bacterial growth, too small to be noticed and unable to make any physical changes of note to their environment. Notwithstanding, the ongoing inner battle that we wage against external threats and our own weaknesses is not a trifling footnote to the unfolding drama of the cosmos, with all its incredibly powerful collisions, eruptions, hurricanes, explosions, implosions and distortions of time and space. As he continues his meditation on the significance of humans in the cosmos, the Psalmist points out that we govern creation: 'You appointed [man] as a governor over the works of your hands, and set everything beneath his feet.'[1]

This suggests that what we do in our spiritual odyssey has the most far-reaching implications for the nature of the entire universe. If a human being does indeed transcend the animal side of life and become a super-angel, this is not just a personal triumph. It is a fundamental elevation of the whole universe. Every star and planet, every cubic millimeter of interstellar vacuum, is now part of a universe where a precious human being on Earth has just made another stride forward in the fulfillment of the divine plan.

Rabbi Moshe Chaim Luzzatto's *Mesillat Yesharim* makes a similar point:

> The universe was created to serve humans, and it hangs in the balance. If one is attracted by physical things and distances oneself from one's Creator, then one becomes degraded and the universe becomes degraded with one. But if one can rule over oneself and cleave to one's Maker, and only use the universe to serve one's Maker, then one elevates oneself and the universe itself is elevated with one. Behold! It is

---

1   Psalms 8:6.

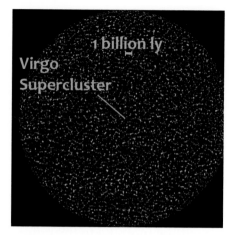

A map of the universe centred on the Virgo supercluster, in which we live. (Richard Powell)

a tremendous elevation for all created things if they serve the complete person who is sanctified by God's holiness.[2]

The whole universe is at our feet, waiting for us, its custodians, to decide what to do next. We wield enormous power, deciding whether all those indescribably huge objects and forces will operate in a hallowed or desecrated universe. With a single act of will, we can transform billions of stars and their attendant planets and asteroids, making them into a forum for the glorious realization of God's plan through human choice and human goodness.

This is the majesty attendant on us. It is for us to rule over ourselves, and to reign over God's creation by using it to do homage to Him.

---

2   Mesillat Yesharim chapter 1.

THE GREAT VARIETY SHOW

MANY PEOPLE HAVE GAZED UP AT A CLEAR NIGHT SKY and felt awed by the enormous number of specks of light that punctuate the darkness of space. But it was only with the dawn of the space age that it became possible for us to have a good idea of what is actually out there.

As probes orbited and landed on planet after planet, it became clear that there is a huge diversity of environments in space. Just as one can come across many different kinds of decor by visiting people's homes, so each planet boasts its own peculiar features. Let us take a quick armchair tour of some of our neighbors and see what they are like close up.

Our first stop is Mercury, a small planet just over three thousand miles across. We must not stay too long because we are perilously close to the Sun. The temperature here shoots up to three hundred and fifty degrees Centigrade during the day.

And watch your step! As Mercury formed, it became very hot from the energy of the rocks that crashed into it, and when it cooled down, the surface shrank and cracked, leaving huge rifts everywhere. Much of Mercury is a gigantic maze of chasms, each over a mile deep.

Mercury has wrinkles as well as cracks. As its metallic core cooled, it contracted by two or three miles, retreating inward from the planet's crust. As a result, the crust buckled, producing characteristic folds and wrinkles, such as the Discovery Rupes ridge, a scar more than a mile deep and some two hundred and fifty miles long in the surface of the southern hemisphere.

Now we will move on to Mars, which is completely different. It has an atmosphere of sorts, though it is very thin – a hundred times as thin as our own – and made out of carbon dioxide. We cannot breathe it.

The decor is interesting here as well. Together with the extinct volcanoes, there are signs that mighty rivers used to flow over the surface of Mars. The dimensions of the enormous channels suggest that there used to be gigantic flash floods on Mars, spewing out half a billion tonnes of water every second – about one thousand times the amount of water flowing out of the great Mississippi River.

The sun sets on Mars. The carbon dioxide clouds are coloured salmon pink by oxidized iron – rust – in the Martian atmosphere. (IMP/NASA/JPL)

The presence of water is also indicated by the planet's color. As you look around, you will see that the Martian plains are a rich, rusty red. This is because there is a lot of oxidized iron – rust – on Mars. It is thought that water flowing over the soil reacted with the iron inside it, resulting in this shade. There are even red dust particles suspended in the atmosphere, giving Mars a pink sky and rosy sunsets.

Since Mars is nearly half as big as Earth and has similar gravity, you might be tempted to go for a stroll. But whatever you do, keep your shoes on. The diaphanous Martian atmosphere allows the Sun's ultraviolet light to bake the soil, making it extremely corrosive. Walking barefoot here would take off your skin in seconds.

If you care to stay for a while longer, you will notice the two Martian moons, Phobos and Deimos, both shaped rather like potatoes. Deimos takes approximately thirty hours to orbit Mars, while Phobos orbits once every seven hours and forty minutes, far less time than the Martian day of twenty-four hours and forty-one minutes. This means that if we lived on Mars, we would have our choice of two lunar calendars. Depending on which moon one chooses to follow, a Martian month lasts either for one and a quarter Martian days or just less than a third of a day.

As we move on, we encounter the asteroid belt. This is a band of free-floating rocks of various shapes and sizes, drifting in an area some three hundred and fifty thousand miles wide. But what the asteroids lack in grandeur, they make up for in curiosity value.

Asteroids come in all kinds of shapes – some beyond our vocabulary, others strangely familiar. The large asteroid, 216 Kleopatra, looks very much like a dog's bone in a cartoon. Psyche is a lump of almost pure iron 150 miles long. The Ida asteroid even boasts its own tiny moon, Dactyl, which is trapped in its weak gravitational field.

Now we come to Jupiter.

To say that Jupiter is the largest planet in the Solar System is to do it less than justice. Its dimensions dwarf most of the other planets to such an extent that it is difficult to imagine the relationship between them. At its equator, Jupiter measures ninety thousand miles across; it could contain more than a thousand Earths within its surface. Jupiter's gravitational pull is more than twice as strong as the Earth's, which means that everything weighs twice as much here as it does on Earth.

Deimos, one of the two moons that orbit Mars, measures less than ten miles across and is one of the smallest moons in the Solar System. (NASA, JPL Viking Project)

Another of Jupiter's superlative features is its magnetic field – generated by a swirling mass of liquefied hydrogen near the heart of the planet – which almost destroyed the American *Pioneer 10* probe in 1973. The field is twenty thousand times as strong as the Earth's and over a thousand times as large. The solar wind, a constant blast of charged particles that hurtle across the Solar System from the Sun at a million miles per hour, strikes this field, stretching it into a tail that runs past Saturn, hundreds of millions of miles away. The interaction between the two generates a huge amount of energy – as much as a billion bolts of lightning rolled into one.

We are used to thinking of a planet as a ball of rock. But we cannot land on Jupiter's surface. In the 1930s, a chemist called Rupert Wildt analyzed the light coming from Jupiter and concluded that the planet is composed principally of two gases: hydrogen and helium. Jupiter – along with Uranus, Saturn and Neptune – is generally referred to as a 'gas giant,' since it consists almost entirely of gas.

Almost, but not quite. Wildt calculated the pressure that must be exerted on the centre of the planet by the huge mantle of gas surrounding it. He deduced that the planet's centre must be crushed by a weight that is tens of millions of times as heavy as the air pressure that we experience on Earth.

Under such conditions, gases freeze. This does not happen because they are cold and the atoms lose the energy to move. In fact, the core of Jupiter is very hot, with temperatures estimated at approximately thirty-five thousand degrees Centigrade. But the atoms in the core are packed so tightly together that they cannot drift apart to form a gas. Hydrogen-based molecules are ground down into their constituent atoms, and a metallic 'soup' of hydrogen atoms, which looks like mercury, is formed. All this occurs right in the middle of Jupiter, existing as a core of petrified gas fifteen times as big as the Earth.

While we're up here, we can enjoy the Jovian weather, which is a treat in its own right. You can see a weaving mass of gassy wraiths – red, brown, creamy white and orange – curling in fantastic patterns around the planet. A band of cloud travelling in one direction wrenches off cloud from a nearby band going the opposite way, and storms are constantly being created in this way, only subsiding when the central forces of the two streams simply rip them apart after a day or two. Larger storms simply allow the currents to spin them around. Jupiter's famous Great Red Spot – first observed three hundred years previously, and thought to be a mountain – has been proven to be a huge storm, still raging unabated since the time of the Great Fire of London, and large enough to swallow up the entire Earth twice over.

The swirling tangle of streaming colors hints at an incredibly complex mixture of weather systems. At any given time, Jupiter has over one thousand whirlwinds raging over its surface, each one shot through with huge bolts of lightning. *Voyager 1* scientists reviewing the data admitted frankly that, in the light of their close-up pictures, all the previous models for predicting the workings of an atmosphere were simply useless.

Not everything on Jupiter is big and bright. Just before we set off, have a close look at the planet's equator. You might just be able

A montage comparing the relative sizes of Jupiter and Earth. This view of Jupiter also shows the Great Red Spot, a storm twice the size as Earth that has been raging for over three hundred years. (NASA/Herbee/Brian0918)

to make out an exceptionally fine dark ring hovering in space and surrounding the planet at a distance. It consists of dust grains the size of smoke particles, and it is so fine that it was only discovered by *Voyager 1* during its 1979 encounter with Jupiter.

But there is still much more to see. Our next stop is Saturn, whose multicolored ring is one of the most distinctive features of the Solar System. What is less well known is that it is actually made up of thousands of concentric rings. Some of the rings are plaited around each other like a braid of hair. One of the rings is so thin that it should have dissipated long ago. But there are two tiny moons – the 'shepherd moons,' known as Prometheus and Pandora – that orbit Saturn on either side of this particular ring, each one going twice around the whole planet in just over twenty-four hours. The one on the inside pushes the ring out, and the one on the outside pushes it in. Between them, they maintain it intact, like painters constantly engaged in the renovation of a massive bridge. There are even dark stripes that go across the rings at one

Saturn photographed by NASA's Voyager 1 space probe. The bright dots nearby are Saturn's moons. (NASA)

point, thought to be clouds of fine dust held in place above the rings by a field of electricity.

The planet itself is large, with a diameter of more than seventy-five thousand miles. It has few features except for a small red spot known as 'Anne's Spot' because it was discovered by Anne Bunker, a scientist on the *Voyager* team. But for all its size, Saturn has the lightest touch in the Solar System. It is the least dense of all the planets, so much so that, were it to be placed on an enormous sea, it would float.

There are plenty of other curiosities to be found among Saturn's large array of moons. Both Tethys and Mimas have craters that cover an entire hemisphere. Iapetus is half white and half black. Janus and Epimetheus are two halves of a moon that cracked in half. They still orbit together with only twenty miles separating them. Titan, the largest of Saturn's moons, is clad in a foggy orange atmosphere of methane. Hyperion is so porous that it is estimated that nearly half of it is empty space. Not only that – it is covered with deep sharp-edged craters that actually make it look like a sponge.

Our next stop is Uranus, another planet that is full of surprises. A quiet gas giant, it is a pale blue ball of hydrogen, helium, ammonia and methane surrounded by a system of eleven narrow rings. But if the planet looks nondescript at first glance, it has plenty of oddities to interest the planet-hopping connoisseur.

Consider a spinning planet. We can imagine a line which goes through the middle of the planet at the centre of the spin. The two ends of the line are the planet's poles, and the line is normally roughly perpendicular to the planet's trajectory around the Sun. But Uranus is different in that its poles are not perpendicular to the plane in which the planet orbits the Sun. Instead, they are aligned with the orbital plane. This is probably the result of a meteor impact that tipped the whole planet upon its back.

To complicate matters further, the magnetic fields on Uranus and Neptune completely ignore the poles (instead of converging on them as is usually the case). The Uranian magnetic field runs diagonally around the planet at an angle of sixty degrees. If Earth's magnetic field were to work like this, our North Pole would be in Morocco.

The skewed aspect of this planet does not stop here. Even its moons – all twenty-seven of them – orbit 'the wrong way.' When viewed from the vantage point of the Sun, the planets do not disappear behind the planet and reappear on the other side. Instead,

The delicate beauty of the planet Uranus. (Voyager 2, NASA)

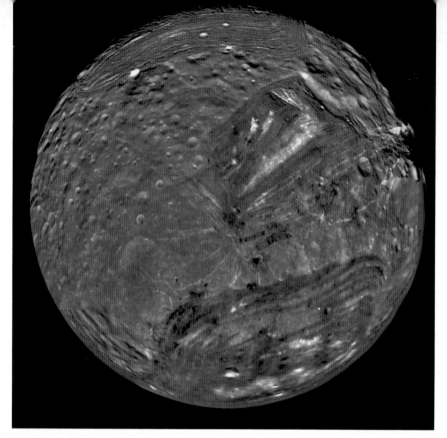

Huge canyons scar Miranda, one of the moons orbiting Uranus. It is possible that Miranda was repeatedly shattered and reassembled, creating this strange topography. (NASA)

they go over the top of Uranus, down the side, underneath and up the other side, like a giant fairground wheel.

Scientists have theorised that the magnetic fields on Uranus and Neptune have been skewed by the presence of carbon which has melted under high temperature and atmospheric pressure, forming oceans of liquid carbon. It is thought that some of the carbon might have crystallised to form icebergs made out of diamonds. Anyone hardy enough to get close in to Uranus or Neptune might

They are a precious commodity on Earth, but diamonds may be floating around for the taking on Uranus and Neptune. (Steve Jurvetson)

A close-up picture of Comet Hale Bopp: its two tails (the white tail of dust and the blue tail of gas) are clearly visible. (Hans Bernhard)

well find that they can recoup their travel expenses with what they find there.

As we move on into the recesses of the Solar System, Neptune is our next port of call. It has some of the most ferocious winds anywhere in the Solar System and a set of four uneven rings. Triton, by far the largest of Neptune's moons and the coldest object that we know of – two hundred and thirty-five degrees below zero – has an ice cap of frozen nitrogen, and geysers sending plumes of nitrogen gas several miles above the surface.

If we are lucky, we might meet a comet at some point during our travels. Comets are 'dirty snowballs' – irregular blocks of dust and ice that orbit the Sun. A comet's heart is small – the block of ice that comprises Halley's Comet is only nine miles across. But comets generally have two tails, one made of dust, and the other made of ionized gas from which certain electrons have been stripped away by the solar wind. These tails are remarkable in their own right. The tail of the Great Comet of 1843 was about two hundred and five thousand miles long – the same as the combined diameters of Jupiter, Saturn, Uranus, Earth and Pluto. The ion tail, glowing blue as carbon monoxide molecules reacquire electrons, can stretch out for millions of miles from the comet, always facing away from the Sun because the solar wind bombards it and pushes it away.

Although the tails are long on range, they are short on substance. Each of the dust grains measures about a thousandth of a millimeter across, and they are so diaphanous that there is more matter in a cubic millimeter of our air than in a cubic kilometre of the dust tail of a comet.

At this point, we are almost beyond the reach of cameras. No spacecraft has ever gotten as far as Pluto, three and a half billion miles from the Sun. The best information currently available is a set of fuzzy pictures taken by the Hubble Space Telescope. Computer enhancement has revealed a few tantalizing details of the Plutonian surface, but we are still a long way from the spectacular and precise detail that we have of planets such as Mars and Mercury. NASA's *New Horizons* space probe, which blasted off for Pluto in January 2006, is expected to reach Pluto on July 14, 2015.

We do know, however, that Pluto is fourteen hundred miles

across, and that it has a moon, Charon, that is nearly half its size. Charon orbits Pluto at a distance of only twelve thousand miles, a twentieth of the distance between us and our Moon. It must dominate the Plutonian sky in a way that we would find unearthly.

How far we have come from the simple view of the night sky as a homogenous mass of little lights! There is incredible diversity out there in space, an abundance of colors, shapes and designs. Why would God want to put such a huge range of different systems into His universe?

Perhaps we can gain a tentative understanding of this idea by looking at the very first letter in the Torah. It would be natural to assume that the Torah opens with the first letter of the Hebrew alphabet, *aleph*. Instead, it begins with the *bet* of *Bereshit* – '**In the beginning.**' There are many explanations for this unexpected opening, but one particularly concerns us as we reflect on the huge variety of planets, moons, atmospheres and the other intergalactic tourist attractions that we encountered in space.

There is a well-established ancient tradition that each Hebrew letter has its own numerical value. *Aleph* is one, *bet* is two, and so on. The Torah begins with the letter that signifies the number two instead of the letter that signifies the number one. This is the first step to solving our mystery.

Jewish tradition[1] explains that God created the universe as a place where human beings could earn closeness to God and develop a relationship of love with Him. We can build a connection with God by choosing to obey His commandments.

It follows from this rudimentary account of God's grand design that in order for the universe to be meaningful, there must be free will. If we had no choice but to do what God says, there would be no sense of our having earned reward from Him, and the universe would be redundant.

Consequently, right from the start of spiritual humankind – Adam and Eve – we have had rules to follow and the freedom to decide whether and how to follow them. We have always encountered the challenge of choosing among various attitudes and behaviors. In

---

1   Derech Hashem 1:2:1-5.

the Garden of Eden, Adam and Eve had to decide for themselves whether to listen to the snake or stand firm in the service of God.[2] Noah had to tear himself away from the corruption of his generation and obey God's command.[3] The Jewish people as a nation had to decide whether they wanted to accept the Torah.[4] Spiritual life in this world is predicated on 'yes' or 'no' – and, of course, 'maybe.'

The abundance of spiritual options available to every human being dazzles us to this day. National leaders must decide their policies in the fields of health, social welfare, foreign policy, national security or education. Individuals must wrestle with their consciences when it comes to taking time off work or betraying the trust of a loved one.

Even such a simple matter as choosing an outfit to wear presents one with spiritual decisions. Should one wear a modest outfit in order to call less attention to oneself, or should one go for something a bit more daring if doing so will make one happier and better able to face the day? Will other people feel inferior if one wears something expensive, or will they feel pleased that one has made an effort to look good for them? What if an outfit is inexpensive and chic, but was made with slave labor?

Whichever way one turns, one must make choices. Plurality lends meaning to the human condition. The challenge of resolving doubts and conflicts correctly – the test posed by the word of God – is the whole reason why our souls were placed inside our bodies in the first place.

This explains why the Torah begins with the letter *bet*. Midrash Mei ha-Shiloach observes that the numerical value of *bet* is two, suggesting plurality. The whole purpose of creation is summed up in the Torah's opening letter. As soon as we begin reading the Torah, the letter *bet* reminds us that we live in a world of choices, and that it is our privilege to decide whether we will consecrate or profane each second of our lives.

Maybe we can extend this idea a little further into the physical

---

2   Genesis 3:1-6.
3   Genesis 6:9-22.
4   Exodus 19:3-8.

creation. A well-known mystical concept teaches that God did not write the Torah in order to remedy the problems of the world that He had created. God's word is not just a response to history. On the contrary, the Midrash says that God wrote the Torah and modeled the world on it:

> It is normal that when a king of flesh and blood builds a palace, he does not build it according to his own ideas. Rather, he consults an artisan. And the artisan does not build it according to his own ideas. Rather, he has blueprints and plans to know how to make the rooms and the gates. Similarly, the Holy One, blessed be He, looked in the Torah and created the world.[5]

Thus, we should not conclude that the Torah forbids murder[6] because wholesale murder would jeopardize our future as a species. Rather, it is because the Torah forbids murder that it is so prejudicial to our survival.

If the keynote of creation is plurality, if it is the theme of the whole of physical existence, would we not expect to find echoes of this theme wherever we looked? If the plurality that the Torah indicates is so fundamental, would we not expect to find echoes of it in a physical world based on the spiritual blueprint that is Torah?

Perhaps the huge variety of colors, shapes, systems and entities within the universe is an inevitable result of a divine plan for humans predicated on the existence of options. The enormous spectrum of possibilities that confronts the thinking human being at every step is mirrored by the spectrum of possibilities in the visible universe. When we look into space, we see a spectacular depiction of the human condition – our own life experience painted on a canvas the size of the cosmos.

Intriguingly, the first letter that God spoke directly to us at Mount Sinai was *aleph*, the first letter of *anochi* ('I am').[7] On that day, God's presence was evident and accessible, and the plurality and ambiguity of choice in our world were temporarily suspended.

---

5   Beraishit Rabbah 1:1
6   Exodus 20:12.
7   Exodus 20:2.

This picture of LL Pegasi illustrates the profusion of shapes and colours in space: a glowing spiral hovers near a bright star, with galaxies of various shapes in the background. (ESA, Hubble, R. Sahai (JPL), NASA)

We had a taste of the End of Days, when our work will be done and God's presence will be clear to everyone.

It is up to us to bring an end to the plurality of the world by making choices, returning the world from *bet* to a state of oneness, a state where God's presence is apparent and all acknowledge Him as the one God.

If we do this, as individuals and as a community, we will hasten the arrival of the day when God's presence on Earth will be a tangible reality, as He promised us in the Torah.[8] On that day, spirituality will be seen by everyone for what it is – an axiom rather than an accessory. There will be no more doubt and no more double standards. We will have returned to *aleph*. 'On that day, God shall be One and His name shall be One.'[9]

---

8   Leviticus 26:12.
9   Zechariah 14:9.

SOLID FACTS?

THE HEBREW WORD FOR 'UNIVERSE' – *OLAM* – IS LINKED TO the word for 'concealment.'[1] Jewish mysticism accounts for this by depicting the universe as an unreal façade that conceals God from us. Were God's presence to be completely visible, it would swamp our perception and it would be impossible for us to choose to do wrong. So the universe can be understood as a facade behind which God's presence is hidden. The nature of our world vis-à-vis the divine realm (which we sometimes call 'heaven') prompts the sages to refer to them respectively as 'the world of falsehood' and 'the world of truth.'[2]

But what is so false about our reality? As we look around, we become accustomed to the concrete nature of its various elements. There seems to be no room for metaphysical speculation when one is faced with something as tangible and uncompromising as a meteor hurtling through space. Astronauts have stood upon the Moon and brought back rock samples, and we know what the planets are made of. Intricate analysis of the Sun has given us an idea of the composition of stars. It all seems quite tangible.

However, physicists in the twentieth century discovered that matter itself was by no means as straightforward as had been thought. The realm of quantum mechanics – the study of how things behave on a very small scale – gradually yielded the most puzzling and frustrating information about the universe, prompting Niels Bohr – the man who worked out the precise structure of the atom – to comment, 'Anyone who is not shocked by quantum theory has not understood it.'

---

1 The Hebrew word meaning 'hide' in the phrase 'You may not hide away' (Deuteronomy 22:3) is *lehit'alem.*
2 Vayikra Rabbah 26:7.

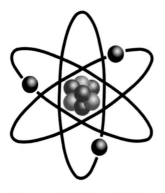

Diagram of a lithium-7 atom: the orbiting black dots are electrons, and the nucleus is made up of protons (red dots) and neutrons (blue dots). (Halfdan)

One of the first shocks to come out of the study of very small particles came from Ernest Rutherford, a New Zealander who studied radioactivity at the turn of the twentieth century. He discovered that every atom consists of a nucleus (a bundle of different particles called protons and neutrons) with electrons orbiting the nucleus in fixed paths. This in itself was something of a revolution. But it went further.

Through various experiments, Rutherford was able to determine the average size of an atom, and also the size of the nucleus at its heart.

An atom is fantastically small. The electron cloud around an atom is normally about 0.000000001 of a centimeter across, while the average nucleus, buried within the electron cloud, is 0.0000000000001 of a centimeter across. We can understand this better by translating the figures into an example. If one were to remove one atom every second from an ounce of carbon until there was none left, the process would take fifteen million billion years.

This implies that a solid is not quite solid. Imagine a lump of coal – a form of carbon – that weighs one gram. Each of the carbon atoms that comprise it contains six electrons, all of which orbit around their respective nuclei. In that tiny block that seems so inert are approximately 3,600,000,000,000,000,000,000,000 electrons, all constantly in motion. Suddenly, our perception of the world seems a little awry. This inert form is actually extremely active. The

Coal in a fireplace. (Stahlkocher)

notion of concrete reality has taken something of a blow, and the label *olam* is a bit more comprehensible. Even something as straightforward as a lump of coal contains remarkable secrets.

But there are more surprises in store. Let us look again at the relative sizes of the electron, the electron orbit and the nucleus. It has been calculated that a complete atom is 1,000,000,000,000,000 times as big as the nucleus within it. Again, we can understand this more clearly by translating the example into figures that we can understand. Imagine an enormous concert hall that is one hundred meters high. If you depicted the nucleus of the atom by putting a pinhead on the floor of the hall, the electrons would be represented by microscopic specks of dust floating around near the ceiling. The rest of the hall would be empty. Or, to put it another way: if the nucleus in the middle of an atom were a foot across, its electrons would be orbiting it at a distance of about eleven miles from the centre, giving the atom a diameter of approximate twenty-two miles.

The implications of this model are very disturbing. Each atom of the page you are reading – and of your own body – consists almost entirely of empty space. The whole observable universe is almost entirely (99.999 percent) absent, at least in the conventional sense of containing nothing durable.

If we could take all the spaces out of the atoms that make up the Eiffel Tower, it would fit in a matchbox! (Btibbets)

If the nucleus of an atom was the size of a pea, the whole atom would be the size of a tower block, and most of it would be empty space. (Simon Grubb)

But this is just the start. The more we study our world, the less clear it becomes.

We are used to thinking of the whole world as an objective reality that exists independently of us, but even this positivist creed has now fallen by the wayside.

The basis for this revolution in our understanding of the world is a fascinating experiment explained by Nobel laureate Richard Feynman at the beginning of his three-volume *Feynman Lectures on Physics.* He describes it as 'a phenomenon which is impossible, *absolutely* impossible, to explain in any classical way, and which has in it the heart of quantum mechanics. In reality, it contains the *only* mystery . . . the basic peculiarities of all quantum mechanics.'

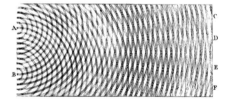

Thomas Young's sketch of an interference pattern in water.

Thomas Young, an English polymath, performed experiments in the early 1800s in order to determine the nature of light. He found that light shone through two slits on to a screen produces a pattern of light and shade known as an *interference pattern*. Each beam of light spreads out after it has passed through one of the slits, and where the two waves of light cross, there is an overlapping pattern of troughs and crests. Where two wave troughs coincide, a deeper trough is formed. Where two wave crests coincide, a higher crest is formed. And where a trough and a crest meet, they cancel each other out. This is what forms the pattern of light and shade on the screen.

We would expect that if only one beam of light were to be shone through one slit, there would be no such interference. This is indeed the case.

The experiment that Feynman described works very much like Young's, except that it deals with individual electrons being fired through one or other of the slits at random, with a detector on the far side of the screen monitoring where the electrons go after they have come through the screen. Such particles behave like waves,

This picture shows a simple pattern of light traveling through a single slit (top picture) and the interference pattern generated by light traveling through two slits, when light waves from each slit interfere with light waves from the other slit to create an interference pattern (bottom picture). (Patrick Edwin Moran)

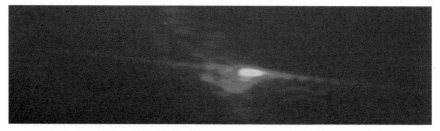

Pattern produced from a single slit.

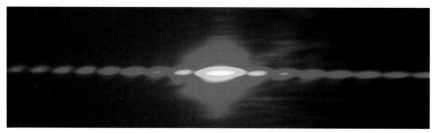

Pattern produced from a double slit.

exhibiting peaks and troughs of intensity, exactly as light does.

Let us suppose that the electrons are being fired through one or other of the slits at random with time lapses – an interval of ten seconds between each firing – to ensure that there can be no interference between one electron and the next. We would have thought that as individual electrons go through the slits, they would land somewhere near the slits on the far side, without any evidence of high peaks or low troughs. After all, nothing else is going through at the same time to interfere with the electron. But this is not the case.

It has been found – and proven countless times since – that even when electrons are fired through the slits one at a time, *a wave interference pattern is formed.* It is as if the electron passing through one of the slits has to contend with a ghostly second electron passing through the other slit, even though we know for sure that there is no second electron going through at that moment.

What makes it stranger still is that, if one of the slits is closed while the electron travels through, this phenomenon no longer occurs. The fact that the electron could not have gone through the other slit is reason enough for the 'ghost' electron to disappear.

Best of all is what happens when we try to cheat. If a detector is placed at each of the two slits so that we can see which slit the electron chooses, the wave interference also collapses. The 'ghost' electron only affects the experiment when there is a genuine chance that the real electron could have gone through either slit without being observed.

To sum up: the experiment proves that the possible path that the electron could take is actually as real as the one that it actually took, as long as neither path is being observed, and both are possible as far as we are concerned.

This experiment has profound implications for the way we view the world.

Feynman's experiment tells us that when something is not being looked at, the various possible states in which it could exist actually impinge upon one another, affecting each other in a material way. Each is as real as the other until we look, at which point one of them will turn out to be true and the other will disappear.

This is another affirmation of the *olam*-nature of the world. The theory suggests that the world may only exist in the way that we know it for our benefit, and only when we take the trouble to look. Until we look, it is an indeterminate, formless limbo. On a microscopic level at least, it is a world of illusion, hastily snapping back into 'reality' whenever it catches us looking at it.

Feynman and his colleagues found another baffling principle of electron behavior that takes a still more devastating swipe at the nature of the universe: time travel. Scrutiny of interactions between subatomic particles has led scientists to hypothesize that, as much as we talk about particles moving forward in time, we can talk equally about them moving backwards in time. The models representing the dancing particles are mathematically identical, irrespective of whether we construe the interactions as going forward or backward through time.

Technically speaking, this allows the possibility of one electron being in two places at once. An electron could move forwards in time and space away from place A, and then go back in time and be in place B at the same time as it was in place A.

Feynman and one of his colleagues, John Wheeler, extrapolated this idea further still. They suggested that an entire universe could be made out of just one electron going backwards and forwards through time, existing simultaneously at every point in the universe where there might be matter. A whole cosmos could consist of just one tiny subatomic particle.

At the moment, it seems unlikely that our universe is made in this way. But the concept has been shown to be valid in theory, and it may yet turn out to be uncomfortably relevant to us.

Even this is not the last word in weirdness. As we have seen, Albert Einstein showed that the universe consists entirely of a huge field of energy. The particles which make up all matter are simply local condensations of this energy. Everything we see and feel, including our bodies, is actually raw energy. It just happens to have been packed into such a small space that it has congealed into matter of various kinds.

Physicist Hermann Weyl took this idea further. He pointed out that if a particle is simply a wave of energy in a force field, this means that it is constantly made of different things. This can be understood by imagining a wave travelling along a flag that is flapping in the wind. The wave is not an isolated piece of flag moving along. Rather, it is a moving spot of energy which lifts successive

sections of the flag as it passes through them. Similarly, Weyl reasoned, a moving particle is simply a wave moving through the all-pervading energy field that makes up everything. As it moves, its composition changes constantly, condensing and releasing different parts of the field through which it travels. Even the most basic building blocks of matter are no more than shifting ripples in a sea of energy.

A flag flaps as waves of energy move along it. (Per Palmkvist Knudsen)

The world as we know it, then, is a fantasy. Our physical habitat, which seems so necessary and solid and whose demands dictate our lifestyle and values, is fuzzy, shifting and diaphanous, an insubstantial entity that looks real only when we see it. All our material possessions have this disappointing secret lurking within them; they are less than they seem; they are barely there.

Why did God set up His universe in such a puzzling and incomprehensible way? We can find an answer in Psalm 49:

> [Fools think] that their money will help them, and they boast about their wealth. But no one can ransom their brother [from death]; the redemption is too much, and must be forfeit forever.
>
> Does one not see that wise people die together with the fools and the boorish, and they all leave their wealth for others?[3]

People chase after the things of this world. Economies and civilizations are predicated on the drive for wealth. But, as Psalm 49 states, it slips through our fingers as our lives draw to a close. A

---

3   Psalms 49:6–11.

A gold bar weighing 12.5 kg. Such wealth has no correlation with spiritual goodness. (Szaaman)

life devoted to the pursuit of worldly gain is a life squandered on the insubstantial and illusory.

This message is inscribed in divine handwriting, discovered by atomic and quantum physicists, written for all to see across the whole of the physical world, reminding us that things of this world are not so solid or trustworthy. A lifetime devoted to owning the fastest car, the most luxurious home or the most fashionable clothing is likely to end in disappointment, as these goals are as ephemeral as the atoms they are made of.

But there is an alternative: Torah observance. By immersing ourselves in the life of the spirit, we are able to lift the veil of this world and reach behind it for something real and lasting. God and the mission that He has entrusted to us are the only real things in a subjective and deceptive universe.

The Torah makes this point explicitly. Moses explained to the people that the Jewish people were led out of Egypt and through the desert so that they would have a folk memory of being sustained by God rather than by physical means:

> Ensure that you observe all the commandments which I am commanding you today so that you may live and multiply and come and inherit the land which the Lord promised to your ancestors. Remember all the journey which the Lord took you on for forty years in the desert . . . He afflicted you and made you hungry, and He fed you with manna which

It looks tasty, but people cannot live on bread alone. (Yoninah)

you and your ancestors had not known in order that he might make you know that people cannot live on bread alone. Rather, people live on all that comes out of God's mouth![4]

The choice that we face is not just between good and bad, but between reality and falsehood. In real terms, it is hardly a choice at all.

---

4   Deuteronomy 8:1-3.

NOTHING DOING

WE HAVE SEEN A WAY IN WHICH THE PHYSICAL UNIVERSE proclaims a spiritual truth, that material possessions are intrinsically deceptive and dissatisfying. But this time, we are not going to examine any specific object in the universe. Our search will focus more closely on the gaps in between objects – the nature of nothingness.

There are six hundred and thirteen commandments in the Torah, and we are enjoined to keep as many of them as we can. They regulate and punctuate the day, the month and the year. They dictate how we dress, how we eat, how we look at things and what we listen to. For someone standing back and thinking about hundreds of rules, it can be a little awkward to pin down one principle that says it all. Is it possible to distill some essential concept and understand how everything flows from it? Does such a law exist?

Many different rabbis have grappled with this problem and answered it in different ways. One approach is quoted by one of the Hasidic masters, the Slonimer Rebbe. Here is his summary of the core value in Judaism:

> The ultimate zenith in the service of God is the attainment of *devekut* [the closest possible connection][1] to Him . . . This is what the Maharal[2] wrote . . . 'All the commandments are [given] so that a person might accomplish *devekut* with the Almighty.' The whole Torah and all its commandments are ways to attain *devekut* with God, and *devekut* with

---

1   This is a loose translation of the Hebrew *devekut*, which means 'the closest possible connection.' Because the Hebrew is a terse word for which there is no single English equivalent, I have used the Hebrew term subsequently.

2   Rabbi Yehuda Loew (1525-1609), a famous central European thinker and mystic, known by the acronym *Maharal* which stands for 'Moreinu Ha-Rav Loew.'

God is the very soul of the service of God . . . and an all-encompassing principle."[3]

This does not mean that we simply have to feel a certain affection for God. The Slonimer Rebbe continued:

The fulfillment of this commandment is the most difficult of all the aspects of the service of God, since one cannot even approach the periphery of *devekut* unless one nullifies one's entire substance in favor of [God] and feels as absolutely nothing before Him.

But by performing the [six hundred and thirteen] positive and negative commandments, one can progressively purify one's material substance to such a point that one is subsumed in the Holy One, blessed be He, and can attain the level of *devekut*.

Devekut entails allowing God into one's life, and allowing Him to shape one's life as much as possible. Those who attain *devekut* are totally preoccupied with God and only attend to their own needs inasmuch as this helps them to serve Him. They tend to nothingness, and that void is filled with the most powerful thing imaginable – God Himself. It follows that, far from being an indication of weakness, the Jewish kind of nothingness is the strongest weapon in a human being's spiritual armory. It is a nothingness seething with Godly power.

Although this concept is expressed in Hasidic thought, it actually predates Hasidism by thousands of years. In fact, there is a biblical exhortation to tend towards nothingness in one's approach, implying that self-realization, encountering and developing the image of God[4] within ourselves, paradoxically entails a kind of self-negation:

And you will know today and you will bring back to your heart that the Lord is God in the heavens above and on the Earth below. There is nothing else.[5]

As we embed in our hearts the truth that there is nothing beyond

---

3   Netivot Shalom, volume 1, Netivei Yesodei ha-Torah, section 5.
4   Genesis 1:27.
5   Deuteronomy 4:39.

God, we must conclude that the more we exist beyond Him, the less we exist!

Let us recall that the universe is made according to the Torah. It is a mirror in which we should see the Torah reflected. If we look around the cosmos, we will find plenty of nothingness. But it seems inert and impotent. How does this link up with the huge potential of spiritual nothingness as the foundation of a sacred union with our Creator?

This question has only recently been answered. A brief look at quantum physics will help us understand the universe – and our own potential – a little better. We must first recall that there is not really such thing as a solid object in the way that we understand it.

We have already seen that Ernest Rutherford found that the vast majority of every atom consists of empty space, each being made of electrons orbiting a small central nucleus at some distance. Later scientists investigated further and found that the nucleus itself consists of two different kinds of particles: protons, which have a positive electrical charge, and neutrons, which have no charge at all.

The discovery of protons and neutrons inside the atomic nucleus

An overview of subatomic particles. (Gaetan Landry)

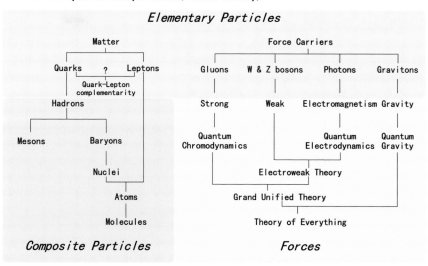

was not just a neat resolution to the quest for knowledge. It was actually a gateway to a deeper understanding of the nature of matter.

In 1935, Hideki Yukawa, a physics lecturer from Osaka University, posited the existence of 'mesons,' subatomic particles that flit to and fro between the various components of the nucleus and bind them together with a special force. This scenario was later proven correct.

Here we come to one of the most remarkable and incomprehensible features of the quantum physical world. The strange thing about this phenomenon is the origin of the particles that carry this force. It has been established that on a tiny scale, there are energy fluctuations which come out of nothing. This 'free' energy is converted into ephemeral particles, existing for a tiny amount of time (0.000,000,000,000,01 of a second, or one hundred-trillionth of a second), increasing the total energy in the atom by one part in a billion, then disappearing again. Each conventional subatomic particle is surrounded by a seething mass of even smaller particles that constantly pop in and out of existence.

The science behind this interaction can be extrapolated further to an even more bizarre scenario. Just as a particle can materialize out of nothing to jump between two other ones, so a particle should be able to appear in a vacuum, where there is nothing at all. In fact, according to this a vacuum should be a seething mass of virtual particles, all appearing and disappearing in fractions of a second, violating the accepted principle that you cannot get something for nothing.

There are many proofs of the existence of vacuum fluctuations. One such proof is the Casimir effect. Henk Casimir predicted that two plates placed close together in a vacuum would gradually pull towards each other even though their mass is too small for them to do so through gravity. Put very simply, this is because particles behave like waves and only certain wavelengths will fit into a restricted space. This means that there is less happening between the plates than around them. Now we have a situation where the vacuum fluctuations outside the plates are exerting greater pressure inwards than those between the plates are exerting outwards. So the

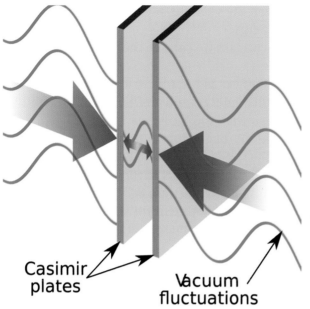

A diagram of the Casimir effect. Since there are more vacuum fluctuations outside the plates than between them, the plates are pushed together. (Emok)

Casimir plates

Vacuum fluctuations

pressure from the greater number of particles outside the plates gradually overcomes the pressure of the vacuum fluctuations be-tween the plates, and the plates are pushed together from outside. The Casimir effect was demonstrated in 1996 by Steve Lamoreaux of the Los Alamos National Laboratory.

We have found that there is no such thing as literally empty

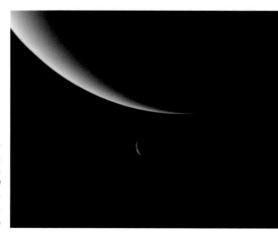

Neptune and Triton photographed by the Voyager space probe. The apparently empty black void of space in which they hang is actually seething with virtual particles. (NASA/JPL)

space in the universe. Even the vacuum beyond planets is actually bubbling with creative energy.

And here, perhaps, once again we can see the universe reflecting a spiritual reality.

Just as apparent nothingness is the only truly creative environment in the universe, with energy and matter being created *ex nihilo*, so the nothingness that the Slonimer Rebbe advocates is not actually emptiness at all, but a connection with the ultimate creative force – God Himself. Whereas solid matter disappoints us by how little it has to offer, nothingness surprises us with its gift of something for nothing. Just as a vacuum is full of energy, so the emptiness we create in our own soul will fill with God's dynamic presence, uniting us with Him and energizing us to accomplish great things in His name.

There is a further hint to this in one of the Psalms. The first verse of Psalm 121 is normally translated as, 'I lift up my eyes to the mountains. From where will my help come?'

The Hebrew word for 'From where?' is *me-ayin*, which can be taken to mean 'from nothing.' Thus, creation *ex nihilo* is referred to in Jewish thought as *yesh me-ayin*, 'something from nothing.' We can then understand the Psalm's opening verse not as a question but as a statement, with the following verse as a clarification. 'From nothing my help will come. My help is from God, Maker of Heaven and Earth.'

The idea here is simply that by admitting some nothingness into one's life, one is actually making room for God who will grant His life-giving energy to help us through difficulties.

Although the spiritual energy that we have might come from God Himself, it is up to us to make room for Him. If we can rise above our preoccupations and create a bit of space in our lives for God and His word, we will feel how Torah observance creates new energy in our souls. As we make that first little bit of room for God in our lives, it is filled by the power of the Divine Presence. The power of *devekut* is available to everyone – for nothing.

MAKING THE WORLD GO ROUND

S INCE BIBLICAL TIMES, HUMANS HAVE REFLECTED ON THE possibility of an apocalyptic end to our time on Earth. Plagues, earthquakes and international conflicts have provided plenty of material for people trying to imagine circumstances in which we would be wiped out.

In fact, some of the scenarios concocted in film studios look positively benign next to the global threats that science has shown us. While it is uncomfortable for us to consider just how hostile our immediate environment is, there are lessons to be learned from them, so let us investigate.

The more aware we are of the nature of our planet and the galaxy at large, the more remarkable it seems that we are around to look at them. Our survival hangs constantly in a delicate balance, and a small change in our galactic neighborhood would be sufficient to tip us over the edge into extinction. We have already seen how we depend on the Moon to keep our seasons and winds temperate. But that is just a tiny part of the whole story.

The Sun, the source of light and life for our entire ecology, is also a potential threat to us. It sends out cosmic rays, streams of charged particles that can cause cancer, cataracts and neurological disorders. Furthermore, by rights our atmosphere should gradually be eroded away by the barrage of particles from the Sun, starving us and all animal life of the oxygen we need to survive for more than a few minutes. Our world should become a barren, airless desert like Mercury.

One of the main things that allow us to survive so close to the Sun is a peculiar kind of envelope around our planet. This envelope is a magnetic field, known as the magnetosphere, that stretches from the Earth's core far out into space. As charged particles from the Sun zoom in at thirty-five miles per second to hit our planet and irradiate us, they encounter a magnetic force field that captures them in mid-flight and guides them towards the poles. (This is the process which generates the *aurora borealis* ("Northern Lights") and *aurora australis* ("Southern Lights"), spectacular shimmering and shifting banks of color that swirl around the sky at the North and South Poles.)

If any radiation happens to get past this defence, there is a second, inner magnetosphere that does the same job.

This mighty magnetic field arching far out into the heavens owes its existence to the spinning liquid metal near the Earth's core. If the planet were to cool or slow down just a little, its core would no longer be able to perform this vital function.

The Aurora Australis or Southern Lights seen from space. These amazing displays in the polar skies are caused by particles from the Sun burning up in our atmosphere. (STS-39 crew/NASA)

Our magnetic field would disappear, we would be more vulnerable to deadly diseases, our atmosphere would be ripped away and life on Earth would become a thing of the past.

But there is more than this. The density of the Earth's atmosphere may also be crucial in maintaining a weather system that supports life. This point is vividly made by the weather on Mars, where the atmosphere is somewhat thinner than our own and the weather is extreme.

To understand this, let us trace a typical Martian weather pattern. Although temperatures on Mars sink much lower than our own, the equator can reach a pleasant twenty-two degrees Centigrade at the peak of the Martian summer.

Because the atmosphere is very thin, it is easy for warm Martian 'air' (carbon dioxide and argon) at the equator to rise, leaving a zone of low pressure near ground level. This area of low pressure

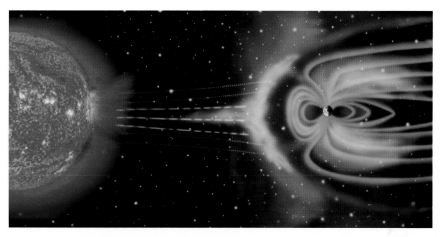

The solar wind and the Earth's magnetosphere are actually invisible. This diagram shows the direction of the solar wind blowing from the Sun (left) towards the Earth and the shape of the magnetosphere surrounding the Earth. (NASA)

sucks cold air down from the Martian Polar Regions. Air is pulled in as hurricane-force winds that tear along at hundreds of miles per hour across the entire planet. When these winds reach the equator, they are warmed by the Sun and rise in their turn to perpetuate the cycle.

This nightmare scenario is compounded by red dust whipped up by the winds from the planet's desolate surface. When the polar air reaches the equator and rises, it lifts its cargo of dust with it. Because dust can retain the Sun's heat better, the equatorial zone becomes hotter, the air rises more quickly, and the winds from the poles become stronger, throwing up even more dust. The cycle becomes increasingly frantic until, after a week, the whole planet may be engulfed in a red dust cloud.

This is where the system breaks down. Eventually, the dust becomes so thick that the Sun's heat can no longer penetrate to the equator, and the atmosphere beneath cools off. The air at the equator no longer rises because it is not being heated. The winds from the poles slow down because there is no equatorial vacuum to pull the air along. Gradually, the dust falls again, the air clears, and quiet reigns.

Our own atmosphere is about one hundred times as heavy as

A dust storm about to engulf houses in Kansas in 1935. On Mars, such storms can engulf the whole planet. (NWS, NOAA)

the Martian one. When it is heated, it rises less readily, and, while weather systems do traverse the Earth, they do not cause the same kind of global chaos as on Mars. If they did – if our atmosphere were a little thinner – we would have to endure choking dust storms and murky twilight for days at a time. The ecology would be devastated by the combined onslaught of darkness, hurricanes and dust, and humans would have to be extraordinarily well organized to survive this global mayhem even for a short time.

But an atmosphere that is too rich can also be problematic. The level of carbon dioxide in our air is crucial to the continuation of life on Earth.

When sunlight hits a planet, the planet heats up, but whether or not that heat is retained depends on the composition of the planet's atmosphere. A lack of carbon dioxide in our atmosphere would allow the heat at the Earth's surface to leak out into space, and our planet would be some fifty degrees centigrade cooler, meaning that most life would no longer be viable. Since we have the right amount of carbon dioxide in our atmosphere, it bounces some of this heat back down to Earth, warming our planet like a blanket.

If there were too much carbon dioxide in our atmosphere, a runaway heating process would kick in. As the atmosphere retained more heat, water at ground level would turn into steam, itself an insulating material that would accelerate the heating process. More carbon dioxide might be released by rocks and shells. Ultimately, temperatures would soar, plant and animal life would be annihilated, and mass extinction would be a certainty.

Venus shows us the end point of this scenario. Although cloud cover on Venus means that the planet's surface only receives a sixth of the sunlight that we receive, the massive concentration of carbon dioxide in the Venusian atmosphere – about sixty thousand times as much as in our own atmosphere – means that most of the heat reflected by the planet's surface is trapped. As we have seen, it is hard enough for a machine to survive on Venus without melting or being crushed. Human beings would have even less of a chance.

And there is still more bad news just around the corner. The asteroid belt between Mars and Jupiter consists of millions of rocks that are more than a kilometer wide. Occasionally, a rock flips out of the belt and shoots in toward the Sun. Sometimes, these fragments swing within reach of our own atmosphere, usually burning up long before they actually hit the ground, but occasionally making it down in one piece.

We have already seen from the Tunguska event that a small rock entering our atmosphere can cause huge damage. Imagine what would happen if a large asteroid – such as Ceres, which is five hundred miles across and nearly a quarter the size of our Moon - were to break out of the gravity lock and crash into the Earth at a speed of one hundred miles per second.

The impact would be cataclysmic. As well as the initial blast – which would be powerful enough to level a large town - a huge mushroom cloud would envelop the planet, blocking out the Sun's heat and light. For as long as the dust drifted in the air, there would be winter. In the absence of the Sun's heat, there would be no rain. Plants and animals would die of drought and cold, and the ecology would collapse. Humankind's future would be bleak indeed.

Measuring approximately 12 miles X 7.5 miles X 7 miles, Asteroid Gaspra, orbiting on the inner edge of the asteroid belt, would wipe out all life on Earth if it broke out and hit our planet. (Galileo Orbiter/NASA/JPL/USGS)

The more we find out about our universe, the more we learn that there are several swords of Damocles over our heads, each of them able to wipe us out. Only a few special, delicately balanced forces – lunar gravity slowing and steadying the Earth's rotation, the density of our atmosphere, the complex interplay between the gravitational fields of Mars and Jupiter that holds the asteroids away from us – enable us to survive.

Why did God set up the world in this way?

We can perhaps understand this with reference to a famous verse from Jeremiah: 'If it were not for My covenant by day and by night, I would not maintain the laws of Heaven and Earth.'[1]

The 'covenant' in question is Israel's relationship with God, expressed and bound by the Torah. Moses himself associated the Torah with a covenant between God and the Jewish people:

---

1 Jeremiah 33:25.

Then [Moses] took the book of the covenant and he read it in the hearing of the people. And they said, 'We will obey and listen to all that the Lord has spoken.' Then Moses took the blood and sprinkled it on the people, and he said, 'Behold the blood of the covenant which the Lord has sealed with you concerning all these things.'[2]

The notion of the Torah as a covenant between God and us is reiterated in Deuteronomy: 'These are the words of the covenant which the Lord commanded Moses to seal with the Jewish people, in addition to the covenant which he sealed with them at Horeb [Sinai].'[3]

God tells His people that were it not for Jewish people's engagement with the Torah, the 'laws of Heaven and Earth' would not last.

This point is made quite explicitly in Jewish tradition. In chapter 5 of Seder Eliyahu Zuta, a mystical Midrash referred to in the Talmud, we are told:

Every day, destructive angels go from before the Holy One, blessed be He, to destroy the entire world, and were it not for synagogues and places of Torah study, they would destroy the world immediately.

Rabbi Chaim Volozhin expanded on this idea in stirring words in his *Nefesh HaChaim*:

If the world were to be entirely free even for one moment of Jewish people working and reflecting on the holy Torah, instantly all the worlds would be destroyed. Conversely, one person of great strength has it within their power to maintain all

Artist's impression of a meteorite striking Earth (NASA/Don Davis)

the worlds and the entire creation through their work and reflection on the holy Torah. . . . This is what the Mishnah in Pirkei Avot meant when it said "The entire world is worthwhile for one person [who engages in Torah study]."[4] This is Torah and this is its great and inestimable reward.

---

2   Exodus 24:7–8.
3   Deuteronomy 28:69.
4   Pirkei Avot 6:1

Meteor Crater in Arizona has a diameter of nearly three quarters of a mile, and is estimated to have been created by a meteorite just fifty yards wide – about one four hundredth of the width of Gaspra. (Dave Roddy/ USGS)

Such a person will be rewarded for everyone's sake, since they have maintained all the worlds through their great strength.[5]

Jeremiah adds urgency to the Jewish mission to the world. God's love for mankind is so strong that He warns the Jews, as bearers of His message of sanctity and love, to work constantly in His service, the better to share that message with humanity. Even momentary national neglect of this awesome task can have grave consequences.

Alternatively, we can embrace our task with courage and enthusiasm, working for the good of ourselves and the whole world. We can enrich our souls through Torah study and set an example to the nations of the Earth. If we do this, then we will be partners with God. Our spiritual vitality will engage God's mercy, and He will continue to protect us in the midst of the threats that encircle us.

We have already seen that the physical universe reflects spiritual reality. Perhaps we find another instance of this here. The advance of science has opened our eyes to the threats facing us from without, and the hazards posed by the exquisite extraterrestrial equilibrium around our planet are an expression and reminder of the ongoing divine judgement to which humanity is subject. The laws of our own little world and the tiny scrap of heavens beyond us

---

5   Nefesh HaChayim 4:25.

chide that our life here is not a given, that we are not here as of right, and that the responsibility on our shoulders is great indeed.

But we need not be downcast by the enormity of the challenge facing us. We can look back over history and celebrate the fact that we *have* got this far. After all that might have befallen our planet, we can see our continued existence here as a divine assurance that we are not actually so bad after all. Perhaps there has been an admixture of divine mercy, perhaps not. At any rate, the threats around us seem to be held in check for now and for the foreseeable future. Even if we do not have faith in our own spiritual development, God continues to believe in us, and demonstrates His faith and love by shielding us from the dangers that surround us. Perhaps, alongside the stern appearance of God's justice, there glows the radiance of His love.

EXPANDING OUR HORIZONS

I F WE LOOK AT THE BIBLICAL ACCOUNTS OF GOD'S ELECTION of the Jewish people, one fact cannot escape our notice. Great stress is laid on the fact that the Torah was given to the Jewish people *from the heavens.*

This is made clear during God's instructions to Moses concerning the great revelation on Mount Sinai.

> They should be ready for the third day, for on the third day, God will come down in front of the people on to Mount Sinai . . . .
>
> The entire mountain of Sinai was smoking as God came down on it in fire . . . .
>
> God came down on to the top of Mount Sinai . . .[1]

Immediately after the Ten Commandments have been pronounced, God repeats this idea: 'You have seen that I have spoken to you from the heavens.'"[2]

In Deuteronomy, when Moses reminds the people of the momentous revelation at Mount Sinai, the point is made a second time: '[God] allowed you to hear His voice from the heavens in order to chasten you.'[3]

To this day, Jewish people refer to the Torah as *Torah min ha-shamayim* – 'Torah from the heavens.'

This analogy seems anomalous. Why should God – a trans-dimensional and trans-spatial Being – be depicted as appearing and descending from the sky? If indeed this perception was imprinted on the minds of the millions of witnesses at the foot of a mountain in the Sinai desert, *why* did God wish it to be so? This metaphor

---

1 Exodus 19:11-20.
2 Exodus 20:19.
3 Deuteronomy 4:36.

Mercury: a still, dead world without clouds, wind or rain. (NASA/ JPL)

may seem appropriate in the pagan world, which was populated by various gods of the sky – thunder and lightning, the Sun and Moon, wind and rain. But would a revelation of pure monotheism really need to pander to this polytheist cliché?

Perhaps we can look at the phrase from a slightly different perspective. The first thing that strikes us about the world beyond our own is, surely, the very fact that it is otherworldly. From the time of the Bible to the most ambitious space-age projects of the modern era, the alien character of extra-terrestrial bodies has always fascinated us.

The more we have learned about the worlds beyond our own, the clearer it has become that they are very different from our own. To appreciate this, let us first take a brief look at extraterrestrial weather.

Some of our nearest planetary neighbors have literally no weather at all. Mercury has the slightest trace of an atmosphere, composed mainly of helium, oxygen and sodium. But it is so small – only one quadrillionth of the volume of the Earth's atmosphere – that it has no palpable effect on the planet. This planet pursues its orbit as a silent, barren wasteland. It never rains or snows, the wind never blows, the sky never has a single cloud. There is no fog, mist, hail or snow.

Mars, on the other hand, does have weather: not only wind but also frost and snow of sorts. The atmosphere on Mars is composed mainly of carbon dioxide and argon, and winter temperatures plummet to less than a hundred degrees centigrade below zero – enough to freeze the carbon dioxide in the meager atmosphere. An astronaut wintering on Mars could try building a snowman out of carbon dioxide snow.

It might seem odd to encounter carbon dioxide – the gas that makes our drinks fizzy – as a solid substance; but this is just the start of what the planets can show us in terms of strange weather.

Venus is the opposite of Mars, with a very heavy atmosphere, and surface temperatures of around 460 degrees centigrade. The miles of cloud cover on Venus consist largely of sulfur dioxide, which falls down through the atmosphere as a lethal rain of sulfuric acid.

Carbon dioxide frost on the surface of Mars. (NASA)

But there is no chance of this rain actually hitting the ground. The Venusian atmosphere is so hot that the acid boils long before it reaches the surface.

Like Mars, Venus also has snow, but of a very different order. The *Magellan* probe – an American spacecraft that mapped the Venusian surface with radar in order to 'see' through the thick atmosphere – discerned metallic caps on some of the Venusian mountain ranges, and it is thought that these might be snow made of metal. The surface of Venus is so hot that any metal deposits on the Venusian lowlands could easily melt and evaporate, only to fall in the cooler mountainous areas as snow. Researchers at Washington University in St Louis have surmised that the metal in question is lead in the form of lead sulfide.

Titan, one of Saturn's moons, also boasts a strange alternative to our own weather. The atmosphere is made up predominantly of nitrogen, which means that the clouds there are not a fluffy white, but a hazy orange. It is so cold there that another of our

gases – methane – exists as a liquid, and falls to the ground as rain. Because Titan is so small – only three thousand miles across – its gravity is only a sixth as strong as our own. This means that the methane showers fall much more slowly than our own rain, and the droplets would probably be twice as large as the raindrops we encounter, measuring nearly an inch across.

The Venusian sky has a secret that has not been unraveled to this day. In 1985, the Russian probes *Vega 1* and *Vega 2* landed on Venus and sent helium balloons up through the atmosphere to find out more about the weather. They discovered that although the wind at ground level is gentle – little more than a breeze in our terms – higher up in the atmosphere it develops into a tempest

Just dropping in: artist's impression of the landing sequence of the Huygens lander arriving on Titan's surface next to a methane lake. (NASA/JPL/ESA)

Triton's pink nitrogen ice cap. (NASA/JPL)

that blasts out at hundreds of miles per hour. Why this happens over such a sluggish planet that takes two hundred and forty-three of our days to rotate once on its axis, is not known.

Some of the more exotic moons in our Solar System also display some interesting features. Triton, which orbits Neptune, has a delicate pink ice cap on its south pole, which is thought to be made of frozen nitrogen.

Io, one of Jupiter's moons, is swathed in a cloud of sodium, which produces a yellow aura when hit by sunlight. There is also chlorine in Io's atmosphere alongside the sodium. A chemical reaction between them would produce sodium chloride – table salt – which might be present in the sky and on the surface.

Strange weather has also been detected beyond our Solar System. Like our own Sun, the star Tau Bootis works as a focal point for an orbiting planet. But this planet, which is totally different from anything we know, calls into question the current theories about how planets form. Its size is colossal, nearly four times that of Jupiter. And it is so close to its sun that one orbit – one of its 'years' – lasts for a mere three days and seven hours.

This has radical implications for the nature of the planet's surface environment. Its proximity to its sun must make it so incredibly hot that it probably has a cloud of vaporized rock as an atmosphere.

Even the mechanisms behind extraterrestrial weather can be alien. Our weather is driven mainly by the Sun, which causes water at ground level to warm up and evaporate, at which point it rises to form clouds. Air circulates around our planet as wind because there is a temperature imbalance across various parts of the world. This is also due to the Sun's heat, combined with the Earth's spin. If our Sun were to go out, much of our weather would simply stop.

Jupiter works differently altogether. In 1973, infrared detectors aboard the American *Pioneer 10* probe detected that more heat was coming from Jupiter than it received from the Sun. In 1979, *Voyager* found that Jupiter is almost as warm at its poles as it is at its equator. If Jupiter depended on the Sun for heat, as we do, there should have been a substantial difference in the temperatures of the two zones. But it seems that Jupiter has its own version of

under-floor heating, with warmth emanating from within to drive its weather systems.

Subsequent studies of Uranus and Neptune proved that planets do not need a sun to have weather. Their own internal heat sources keep their weather going. So efficient is this system that Neptune – which is nearly three thousand million miles from the Sun, so remote that it only receives a thousandth of the solar heat – has some of the strongest winds in the entire Solar System.

Artist's impression of a triple sunset viewed from a hypothetical moon orbiting HD 188753 Ab (the big red planet in the top left hand corner). One sun has already set, and is shining behind the mountain range on the right. Another two suns are still in the sky and approaching the horizon. (NASA/JPL)

Looking beyond this range of bizarre meteorological curiosities, there might be different surprises beyond our Solar System as well. Dr Maciej Konacki, a Polish astronomer working in the United States, claims to have detected a planet orbiting a triple star system known as HD 188753A in the constellation of Cygnus. (Others have questioned his discovery, but Konacki has refuted their assertions, questioning the accuracy of their measurements and planning further observations and calculations to support his contention.) The planet, dubbed HD 188753 Ab, is thought to resemble Jupiter, and it flies around the three stars in just eighty hours. Because the stars at the heart of its orbit are so close together, it is thought that at the end of its day, the planet experiences triple sunsets!

The nature of the stars, however, is by far the most radically different thing that we can hope to encounter. Because the temperature inside a star is so high, the atomic structure that we are used to on Earth has no chance of forming, and the building blocks of matter – atoms composed of a nucleus with electrons orbiting around it – do not exist. Einstein deduced in his theory of relativity that the intense gravity around a star actually twists the fabric of time in its vicinity. Not only the scenery, not only matter, but time itself takes on unfamiliar forms when we venture beyond our own environment.

As we look around our Solar System and beyond, we find more and more surprises. As the frontiers of science are slowly pushed back, experts must rework their theories to accommodate new data and discoveries. This might be the key that we are looking for. Like the heavens, the Torah is supposed to challenge our prejudices.

In fact, Rabbi Samson Raphael Hirsch interprets the whole circumstance of the Mount Sinai revelation as an emphatic proclamation that the Torah – our spiritual *modus operandi* – is theocratic rather than democratic.

This concept is derived from a passage in Exodus, in which God instructs Moses:

> Sanctify the people today and tomorrow, and instruct them to wash their clothes. Let them be ready for the third day, for on the third day, God will come down in front of the people on Mount Sinai. Make a boundary around the people, saying, 'Be careful about going up on to the mountain or even touching its border. Anyone who touches the mountain will surely die. Let no hand touch it!'[4]

Why were such elaborate preparations necessary? In his commentary on this narrative, Rabbi Samson Raphael Hirsch wrote that it had to be absolutely clear right from the start that the Torah – the Law – did not emanate from the people. It had to be viewed as something that came from *outside* the people in order to challenge and mold them. From the outset, the people were to see the Torah as the ultimate, conclusive definition of Jewish identity.

The three days of purification were necessary to impress upon the people the fact that they were receiving a Law that was not intended to be an expression of their standard of behavior. They had to understand that the Torah transcended their current way of life. Our ancestors only deserved it by deciding there and then to abandon preconceptions, open their minds and learn. The same applies to us.

This message was reinforced by the rules surrounding Mount Sinai. The mountain was so far removed from the realm of human activity that no ordinary person could survive on it for a second.

---

4   Exodus 19:10-13.

*A Torah scroll,
bearing words from
beyond our world.
(Willy Horsch)*

Since the Torah came from a place that was off-limits for most human beings, it was seen as being fashioned without human intervention. Coming as it did from a different dimension, the Torah was presented as a God-given Law which is, by definition, alien to our way of life.

Perhaps we can understand the recurrent metaphor of the Torah 'coming from heaven' in the same way. The Torah is presented as coming from heaven because – like the heavens – it is alien to our way of life, beginning where our own thought processes end. Its commandments may seem outlandish or out of tune with life, just as metal snow and a warm north pole differ drastically from our day-to-day assumptions. But this is not a reason to reject or change them. On the contrary: we are to view ourselves as being out of step with the Torah, and it is our responsibility to change ourselves, bending and elevating our desires to conform to the divine blueprint.

Once again, we see that modern science has deepened an ancient Jewish parable. Discoveries of solid versions of what we normally encounter as gases, falls of alien snow and rain, weather systems that work independently of the Sun and the absence of time and matter as we know them in stars – all these things overturn our assumptions about how things are. Torah should do to our soul what alien environments do to our imagination. It should stimulate, challenge, confront – and, above all, uplift.

GO WITH THE FLOW

LET US TAKE A BREAK FROM THE ALIEN REALM OF SPACE AND look at something a little closer to home – water. One is tempted to think that here, at last, we are dealing with something mundane. But a peep into the world of meteorology will show us that water has a surprising capacity all of its own. It is one of nature's shape-shifters, assuming many different textures, shapes and consistencies, depending on what happens to it. It can change from one guise to another, and yet another, indefinitely.

We can begin by considering water in one of its most common forms – rain. The Sun's heat evaporates water from seas, lakes and trees. Hot air currents carry drops of water vapor upward into the atmosphere. As the vapor rises, it cools and condenses to form water droplets that coalesce into bigger drops and accumulate as clouds. The clouds develop until they are too heavy to be kept up by the air currents. When the clouds reach this critical weight, they fall as rain.

A large hailstone. (NWS, NOAA)

This theme has many variations. Imagine that the air currents rising from the ground are very strong, and the cloud keeps accumulating more and more water droplets. At the cloud's summit, the air is so cold that the water droplets actually freeze, becoming ice pellets. These tumble down through the cloud, but if the updraft from below is strong enough, they are propelled upward once again, adhering to other ice particles all the while and gathering them along with it. If this cycle occurs many times, the ice pellets can become larger and larger, forming hailstones that can measure several centimeters across.

This understanding of how hailstones are formed is supported by the fact that a cross section of a hailstone will normally show concentric rings of ice chunks. The number of rings gives an indication of how many times the hailstone hurtled up and down inside the cloud. Specimens with twenty such layers have been found, and the damage inflicted by severe hailstorms can be immense. A hailstone that fell in Nebraska on July 6, 1928 weighed nearly two pounds and had a circumference of seventeen inches – twice as big as a bowling ball. So water need not necessarily be wet, and it can shape itself into an effective weapon.

Even the clouds themselves come in various forms. At ground level, we experience them as mist or fog. The cloud formations that we see in the sky have many shapes, and names to go with them. Starting from forty-six thousand feet above ground level and working our way downward through the atmosphere, we might encounter cumulonimbus, cirrostratus, cirrocumulus, altocumulus, altostratus, cumulonimbus, nimbostratus, stratocumulus, cumulus and stratus. If we were very lucky, we might even spot a lenticular cloud, which is often mistaken for a UFO.

This is not the end of the story. If water vapor condenses at a temperature below freezing, it forms snow. Each snow crystal has its own unique shape, and the crystals accrete to form snowflakes. A snowflake can consist of up to forty crystals and measure several inches across.

The most well-known form of snow-crystal is the six-sided variety. But beyond this, there is a bewildering array of basic shapes of snow-crystal, depending on the temperature at which they are formed.

From twenty-five to thirty-two degrees Fahrenheit, the crystals form as thin hexagonal plates. From twenty-one to twenty-five degrees, they make needles. From fourteen to twenty-one degrees

A storm cloud gathers over Chaparral, New Mexico. (Greg Lundeen/NOAA)

Snowflakes under a microscope.
(Wilson Bentley)

and below minus eight degrees, they make hollow hexagonal columns. From ten degrees to fourteen degrees and from minus eight degrees to three degrees, they form 'sector plates' which resemble thick, six-pointed stars. And from three degrees to ten degrees, they form beautiful filigree dendrites – jagged crystals that branch off into repeated smaller sections.

Sometimes, water vapor undergoes not condensation but sublimation – it metamorphoses directly from a vapor into a solid. This forms deposits of ice crystals on solid objects, which are known as hoarfrost. A much harder version of hoarfrost – rime – appears when supercooled water hits something solid at a temperature below freezing point. This is commonly found on aircraft.

Water can even take on different colors. Sunlight hitting a water droplet is split up into its constituent colors of red, yellow, green, blue, indigo and violet – the colors of the spectrum. As the different colors travel on through the water, they reach the back of the drop,

A microscopic image of a snowflake in a column shape. Rime has formed on the ends of the column. (Erbe, Pooley: USDA, ARS, EMU)

1337
300 μm

A mist of water droplets helps us to trace the paths of sunbeams through the air.
(Mila Zinkova)

which acts like a mirror, bouncing the beams out and refracting them further so that each beam follows its own path.

There are normally several million raindrops at any given altitude during a period of rainfall, and if the Sun shines on them, each of these sends out colors in exactly the same way. The end result is that all the red beams are sent out in the same direction, all the orange ones in a slightly different one, and so on. An observer standing at a distance will see this as a rainbow.

Minuscule ice crystals at very high altitude can cause the same effect around the Sun or the moon. The crystals refract the light to create a spectacular multicolored halo that can dominate the sky.

There is more. Water forms steam, foaming waterfalls, crashing waves, stagnant ponds, whirlpools and glaciers, mighty rivers of ice that flow inexorably down mountainsides and hew valleys out of solid rock, sweeping away everything in their path and refracting sunlight to create a bluish tinge in their frigid depths. In zero gravity, it forms a sphere and, when air is blown into it, a wave travels along it.

Wall cloud with tail cloud on the Oklahoma-Texas border. (NOAA Photo Library, NOAA Central Library; OAR/ERL/National Severe Storms Laboratory (NSSL))

In addition to all this, water is one of our world's most mobile items, travelling impressive distances in its function as part of our ecology. It flows thousands of miles along our rivers and around our seas. As vapor, it travels miles up through the atmosphere, and as liquid it trickles and plunges miles down into caves and subterranean streams.

These incredible abilities – to travel ceaselessly and to change shape and appearance – are highlighted in one of the Psalms:

> [God] sends His utterance to the Earth; His word runs very swiftly. He gives snow like wool, and scatters frost like ashes. He throws His ice like crumbs – who can stand before His cold? He sends out His word and it melts them; He makes His wind blow, and they flow along as water. He tells His word to Jacob, and His statutes and judgments to Israel.[1]

Why does the text digress from a meditation on God's word to

---

1   Psalms 147:14-19.

the various forms of water – snow, frost and ice – and then back again?

In his commentary on this verse, Rabbi Samson Raphael Hirsch explained that this is not a digression. On the contrary, the meditation on water is deliberately introduced into the analysis of God's word as an illustration of the effect that God's word should have upon us. We see the power of God's decrees in the backdrop of creation, where every part of nature performs its task unquestioningly. Even water, which must metamorphose into so many shapes, shades, textures and densities, fulfills its task reliably and promptly, again and again.

We humans have our own way of listening to God's word. Rather than reacting to it without question, we have the gift of free will, which allows us to choose how we respond to God: with defiance or acceptance, grudgingly or enthusiastically, in fear or in love. The

The edge of the Greenland ice sheet. (Hannes Grober, Alfred Wegener Institute for Polar and Marine Research)

Psalmist invites us to look at the wonders of water as a guide to how much we can adapt ourselves to God's word. We are reminded of its diverse manifestations as fluid, vapor, granule, spheroid, prism, column, needle, flower, plate, star, flake and block. We think about the huge distances that it travels, and its responses to the vagaries of landscape and climate. We are challenged to live up to the example of water by our own free will.

Just as water travels thousands of miles across the world as rivers, seas, glaciers and clouds, we, too, should be prepared to uproot ourselves – psychologically as well as geographically – in order to do what God demands of us. No distance is too great when it comes to divine service. We should be ready to travel the world, touch the skies and descend to the darkest depths in our quest to do God's will.

Just as water is malleable, appearing in manifold forms, we, too,

The Niagara River rapids. (Maureen)

should be ready to change ourselves according to God's will. As people who aspire to be servants of God and the bearers of His word in this world, we can discard our prejudices about what we can and cannot do, and be ready to find ourselves developing in unimaginable ways.

Finally, water can be breathtakingly beautiful in its many shapes and forms. Its glitter, colors, shapes and motion combine to make stunning backdrops to our environment. This is, perhaps, a trace of the spiritual beauty of our work with God.

Icicles on a house in Oslo, Norway. (Hans A Rosbach)

THE BIG CONVERSATION

HILE WE ARE STILL ON EARTH, WE HAVE ANOTHER phenomenon to examine: the extraordinary profusion of living creatures with which we share our planet.

Relative to the hostile extraterrestrial environments in our vicinity, even the most inhospitable corner of our world is a positive paradise, with life blossoming in almost every environment. As we survey the vast range of animals in our world, we find that the sheer number of species is mind-boggling.

Cindaria and *ctenophora* escape our attention most of the time. These creatures blur the difference between solid and liquid or between plant and stone. Jellyfish consist almost entirely of water, so much so that if they are left out in the Sun, they die of evaporation. Coral grows into enormous living reefs, producing strange growths shaped like trees, cones, or nothing

A ctenophore looking for food. (NOAA/OAR/NURP)

else on Earth; but if it is taken out of the sea, it dies and becomes as hard as stone. There are nine thousand varieties of these strange creatures.

Relative to this massive group of creatures, the life forms that are familiar to us seem positively conservative. Mammals – creatures that give birth to live young who drink their mothers' milk – only exist in four thousand variations. There are only four thousand two hundred types of amphibians, and six thousand three hundred kinds of reptiles.

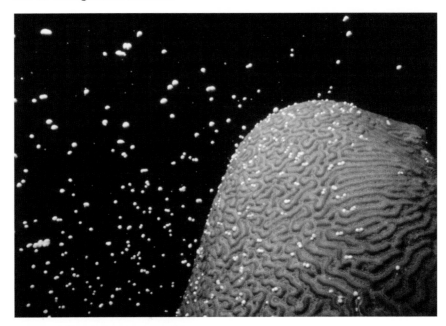

Brain coral spawning. (Emma Hickerson/NOAA)

As we return to the domain of creatures that inhabit environments different from ours – in the sea, underground, inside other creatures and in the air – the numbers rise again. There are six thousand one hundred known kinds of echinodermata (starfish and their relatives), nine thousand different kinds of birds, twelve thousand species each of earthworms, flatworms and roundworms, and eighteen thousand types of fish. There are fifty thousand kinds of mollusk.

But all this is nothing compared to two other groups. There are more than one hundred and twenty-three thousand types of noninsectan arthropods (such as spiders, crabs and lobsters).

The insect world alone has over *a million* different classes of life. In a few square miles of an average North American deciduous forest, one can find centipedes, flies, wasps, weevils, beetles, termites, cockroaches, ants, ticks, wasps, aphids, earwigs, mites, and more.

These figures are necessarily approximate because biologists are constantly discovering new species. Rainforests provide a steady

A giraffe in the wild. (Klaus F)

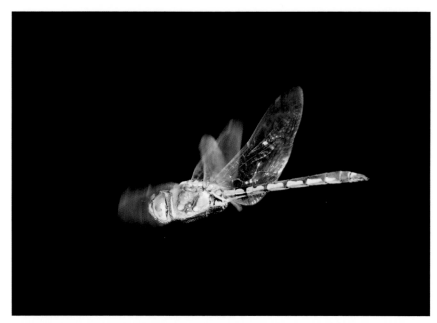

A dragonfly in mid-air. (FIR0002/Flagstaffotos)

stream of new finds, and bacteria evolve and mutate to ensure their own survival.

We can safely assume that, despite the ruin brought to the ecology by the industrial revolution, there are well over a million different kinds of moving living things on the planet, in addition to the multitude of immobile life-forms such as plants, fungi, microorganisms and algae.

A 4 pound lobster. (J S Derwin)

It would be interesting to calculate how many individual living and moving things exist in the world. The numbers would be astronomical. Let us take a very conservative estimate, and assume that there is an average of just a thousand examples of each species at any one time. This would still mean that, as you read this, our planet is home to well over a billion things that hop, slither, crawl, swim, wave, grow, writhe, fly or walk at, just above or just below its surface.

This helps us to appreciate a fascinating Midrash that describes what happened just before God gave the Torah to the Jewish people:

> When the Holy One, blessed be He, gave the Torah, no fowl twittered, no bird flew, no ox bellowed, the Ophan angels did not fly, the Seraphim did not say, 'Holy, holy, holy!' The tides on the sea ceased their tumult, no people spoke. *The whole world was totally still and quiet,* and the voice came out, proclaiming, 'I am the Lord your God.'[1]

Everything stopped in its tracks. The fact that the world was about to experience a direct revelation of God's majesty was so momentous that everything fell silent. All the mollusks, earthworms, mammals, fish and birds and crustaceans and millions of insects – all were frozen, transfixed, at the prospect of hearing the word of their Creator.

Although this interpretation of the Torah is Midrashic, there is an explicit scriptural reference to all the creatures of the world paying attention to God in a much more active way. The very last verse in Psalms exhorts,

An elephant in Tanzania. (Nick and Mel)

'Let every soul praise the Lord!'[2] In his commentary on Psalms (*Tefillot David*), the Malbim says that this is a reference to every living thing praising God: 'The praise of God will spread from His holy lofty realm until it includes every creature.'

We can take this to mean that not just people but every living

1 Shemot Rabbah 29:9.
2 Psalms 150:6.

thing will praise God in its own way. Indeed, the 'Nishmat' prayer that we recite on Sabbaths and festivals begins with a similar sentiment: 'Let the soul of every living thing bless Your name, and let the spirit of all flesh constantly glorify and exalt Your remembrance, our King!'

An Indian peacock.
(Vidhya Narayanan)

Perek Shira, attributed to King David, takes this further, detailing the different songs sung to God by the frog, the crane, the lion and so on.

We can perhaps understand this last verse of Psalms as a counterpoint to the awestruck silence of the Mount Sinai moment, especially since the five books of the Psalms are traditionally associated with the five books of the Torah.

Maybe what we see here is a progression. When God gave the Torah, everything was silent, listening. But God does not wish His universe to be silent forever. He wishes His handiwork to be sentient, to experience and acknowledge the wondrous splendor of His presence, and sing a response to Him. So whereas the Torah was given to a silent world, the Psalms point us forward to a world that reverberates with an awesome and joyous answer to God, a choral symphony in which every living creature will join. History is, in essence, a conversation: God spoke to His creation when He gave the Torah, and one day creation will answer Him.

Here again, the biologists' tally of the world's living creatures gives us a small insight into the praise that is fitting for God at the end of time, when billions of life forms will unite in a hymn of glory to their Creator.

Until that time, we can remember that when we hear someone speak, or see a creature going about its daily business of survival, we are actually experiencing a scrap of that cosmic conversation

We look forward with the Psalmist to the time when every creature will praise God in its own way. (Mila Zinkova)

between God and His creation. However ingenious, endearing or awesome our encounters with our fellow creatures may be, the biologists' data remind us that they are only whispers along the road of history, building towards a mighty, unanimous answer to God's call at Sinai.

FIRE IN THE SKIES

O F ALL THE CREATURES WITH WHOM WE SHARE OUR planet, the toughest are barely known and hardly noticed. They are the extremophiles – microscopic life forms thriving in environments that, by human standards, are extremely hostile. The first to be discovered was *Deinococcus radiodurans*. It was found in 1956 by A W Anderson, a researcher at the Oregon Agricultural Experiment Station, who subjected meat to high doses of gamma radiation in order to see whether this would sterilize it. He found that the radiation did not have the desired effect: some of the meat spoiled, and it was found that a strain of bacteria – *Deinococcus radiodurans* – had taken up residence in the meat since this strain was resistant to radiation. When the bacterium's DNA was shattered by gamma rays, it simply mended itself within twenty-four hours and carried on living.

Deinococcus radiodurans was the first of a whole range of extremophiles that scientists have since discovered.

Strain 121 was the name given to a bacterium found in a hydrothermal vent in Puget Sound off the coast of the USA. Seawater that has leaked down into the Earth's crust is heated and ejected back up on to the seabed. Temperatures in this environment approach boiling point, and the pressure is enough to crush a submarine. Strain 121 was so called because it survives at 121 degrees centigrade, which is the temperature at which many medical and dental instruments are sterilized.

There are many more such creatures. Lithoautotrophs, which can be found on the seabed, live partly off volcanic glass, which they eat in order to digest the silica it contains. The *Ralstonia metallidurans* bacillus thrives in solutions that contain a high concentration of dissolved metal. Halophiles grow where there is a heavy concentration of salt.

These recent discoveries have changed our view of our planet. We have found that even its most inhospitable corners teem with life. This is true of environments far below the Earth's surface as well. Miners have come across bacteria in water that has been trapped for centuries miles down in the Earth's crust.

What of life beyond our world? In his *Pensées*, the seventeenth-century French philosopher Blaise Pascal wrote of the space beyond our world, 'Le silence éternel de ces espaces infinis m'effraie' – 'The

The dry Judean Desert – a sympathetic environment for xerophiles. (David Shankbone)

eternal silence of these infinite spaces fills me with dread.'

But is it silent? Recent discoveries have shown that there may be life out there after all. One of the most significant milestones in extremophile research has been the discovery of cyanobacteria, which thrive in very cold conditions. Cyanobacteria have been found living inside rocks on Devon Island in the Canadian Arctic, where winter temperatures fall as low as minus 50 degrees centigrade. It is thought that cracks in the edges of the rocks, caused by repeated freezing and thawing, have enabled some light to penetrate, and the bacteria use energy from this light to convert carbon dioxide in the air into organic compounds.

This process, combined with traces of moisture trapped in the rocks, makes life possible in an environment similar to the surface of Mars, on which rocks exist in an environment with extremes of heat and cold and some light.

This is the significance of cyanobacteria. If water exists beneath the surface of Mars, perhaps in an underground sea or trapped in tiny pockets beneath the surfaces of rocks, then that water might harbor life. On a larger scale, cyanobacteria indicate that life may exist elsewhere in the universe.

The same significance attaches to the water bear, a tiny (1mm) long creature with more than a passing resemblance to a teddy bear.

A hydrothermal vent: boiling liquid carbon dioxide emerges from a submarine volcano in the Pacific Ocean. (NOAA)

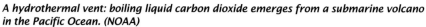

A bleak vista on Devon Island, located deep inside the Arctic Circle. Despite the hostile climate, microscopic living creatures have been found here. (Anthony Kendall)

Some water bears can withstand temperatures up to a hundred and fifty degrees Centigrade, and others can manage down to two hundred degrees below freezing. They can also survive prolonged exposure to the vacuum of space, and a thousand times as much radiation as other creatures can tolerate. In an environment without water, their metabolism slows to a thousandth of its normal rate, and they can last up to a decade in this state, reviving within a few hours when they come into contact with water. Such a robust constitution would enable water bears to withstand the pressures of environments that would be lethal to humans.

Extremophiles in general also raise the possibility of life forms flourishing in extraterrestrial environments formerly thought of as being too radioactive, saline, acidic or otherwise hostile for anything to survive.

In fact, there is a suggestion that life existed on the Moon in the recent past. When Apollo 12 took Pete Conrad and Alan Bean to the Moon in November 1969, Conrad recovered the camera from

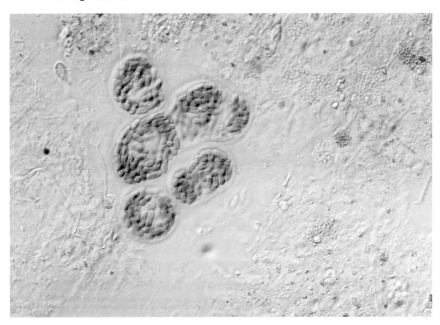

Cyanobacteria discovered in Mexico. (NASA)

Surveyor 3, an unmanned lander that had been there since April 1967. Surveyor 3 had not been sterilized before take-off, and one of its components – a piece of foam inside its camera – was found to contain *Streptococcus mitis* bacteria. This was taken to indicate that the bacteria had survived on the Moon – with virtually no atmosphere or atmospheric pressure, no nutrients, prolonged exposure to radiation and night time temperature averages approaching absolute zero at minus 153 degrees Centigrade – for two and a half years!

Since this sensational discovery, doubt has been cast on the results' validity. The camera was not brought back to Earth in a sealed, airtight container, so it might have been exposed to the bacteria on the return flight. Besides, a breach of sterile procedure was reported in the laboratory where the camera was analyzed, so the bacteria could have come from there as well.

Other hints of life beyond our world have since come to light. The Soviet landers *Luna 16* (launched September 1970) and *Luna*

20 (launched February 1972) brought back samples of lunar dust which, when analyzed, revealed microscopic shapes reminiscent of *Sulfolobus* and *Siderococcus* bacteria.

Furthermore, traces of bacteria were found by an Indian Space Research Organisation balloon released into the stratosphere twelve to twenty-five miles above the surface of the Earth. ISRO announced in March 2009 that the samples included three bacterial colonies that resembled nothing previously discovered, fueling speculation that they might have drifted into our atmosphere from outer space, perhaps carried by a comet from a distant planet.

In 2009, NASA published pictures of what might be fossilized microbes found inside meteorites. NASA used a scanning electron microscope to create new images of meteorites, including chips from the Nakhla meteorite, which landed in Nakhla, Egypt, in 1911, and of Yamato 953, a meteorite discovered in Antarctica by the Japanese polar team.

The Surveyor 3 lander, whose camera may have harboured life on the Moon for over two years. (Apollo 12 astronauts, NASA)

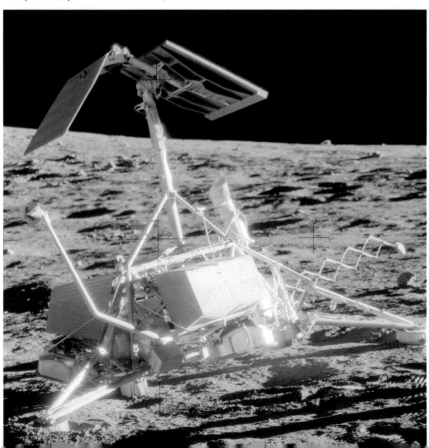

These pictures revealed collections of bumps in cracks which might be fossilized colonies of primitive life forms. NASA also found tiny, partly filled depressions in meteorite surfaces which might have been formed by acid generated by microbes. The debris in the pits may be the remains of the microbes themselves.

Sunrise in the stratosphere, as seen from a space shuttle. The blue layer is made by clouds, while the red layer is formed by particles suspended in the stratosphere. (NASA)

When we extrapolate these findings across the universe, we suddenly gain a new perspective. Wherever there are planets with conditions that are remotely similar to our own, there may be life.

There is a Jewish view of life that gives us further insight into this understanding of the universe. One of the Hebrew words for an animal is *b'ir*.[1] The Hebrew root for this word is the Hebrew root *bet-ayin-resh*, which is more often used to mean fire.[2] This pair of meanings gives us a fascinating insight into the Torah view of animals: they are, in a sense, ablaze!

Rabbi Samson Raphael Hirsch makes this link explicit in his commentary on the Torah, writing, '[Animals] cannot withdraw themselves from Divine Will; in [them], every impulse and every action is an involuntary product of the Divine Fire of Life which had given them life, whose whole lives are accordingly a "burning."' Since animals can only do what they are divinely ordained to do, they serve as primitive representations of devotion to carrying out the will of God.[3]

Granted, animals have no free will, and their merit is not comparable to that of humans, who may choose to serve God out of fear or love. Yet on the other hand, as they go about the tasks that God allotted to them – procreation and survival – they can serve as an illustration of unwavering obedience to divine law.

If we take the meaning of the word in this way, then we can apply it equally to small and large creatures alike. The tiniest insects

---

1   Genesis 45:17; Exodus 22:4; Numbers 20:4.
2   Genesis 45:5; Leviticus 6:5; Numbers 11:1; Isaiah 43:2; Jeremiah 20:9.
3   Commentary on Genesis 45:17.

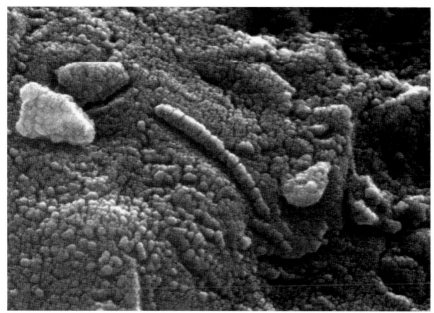

A microscopic image of the interior of ALH84001, a meteorite from Mars discovered in Antarctica. The elongated shape in the center may be a fossilized life form. (NASA)

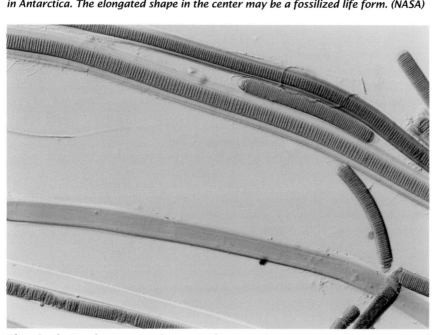

The microbe Lyngbya sp uses nitrogen in the atmosphere to survive. Some planets and moons in our own Solar System have atmospheres containing nitrogen, raising hopes that microbes could be found living beyond our Earth. (NASA)

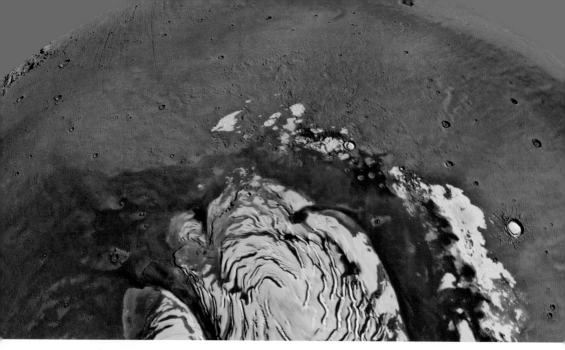

The Martian north polar ice cap contains frozen water; the presence of liquid water would make it easier for life to exist on Mars. (NASA/Goddard Space Flight Center Scientific Visualization Studio)

and bacteria are no less engaged in survival than elephants and camels. Extremophiles, with their tenacity and ruggedness, are also expressions of the divine will.

As we look up at the heavens and imagine the vast assortment of unlikely life forms that may colonize its most obscure regions, we can extrapolate the *b'ir* phenomenon to every corner of the cosmos. Increasing numbers of planets are being discovered orbiting other stars, and it is thought that most of them may be rocky planets like Mars, Venus and Earth, rather than uninhabitable gas giants like Jupiter. We can see the whole of creation in spiritual terms as a panorama of flames, burning with the fierce light of uncompromising adherence to and realization of God's will.

So it is possible that Pascal was wrong. Maybe we are not the sole possessor of life in the center of an immense and barren void. We need not be daunted by the thought of vast stretches of lifeless, sterile space surrounding us on all sides. Rather, it is more likely that we are only one player in a cosmic symphony of obedience to God.

Artist's impression of the Huygens *probe on Titan, with a drizzle of methane in the background. (ESA)*

This image takes on new piquancy in the context of a description of Mount Sinai at the time of the giving of the Ten Commandments. Moses reminds the Jewish people that they stood at the foot of the mountain while the mountain was burning up to the heart of the heavens.[4] The purpose of this was not only to impress the Jewish people. Perhaps it expressed a link between the fire of unhesitating devotion to God in that location and sparks inherent in life forms everywhere in the cosmos. Perhaps this was God's way of saying that the whole universe was incandescent with obedience to its Creator, and that the core of this heavenly inferno was Mount Sinai, where the Jewish people joyously proclaimed, 'All that God has said we will perform and obey!'[5]

We are part of this blaze of divine service. The Torah, the heritage of the Jewish people,[6] was addressed to us in the present day

---

4   Deuteronomy 4:11.
5   Exodus 24:7.
6   Deuteronomy 33:4.

The Hubble Space Telescope was trained on these stars in Sagittarius. Because they are so bright, the telescope picked up small variations in their brightness when a planet passed in front of them. In just over a week, sixteen stars with orbiting planets were identified. (NASA, ESA, K. Sahu (STScI) and the SWEEPS science team)

as well, and we can also shine and burn as we obey its dictates. As we look up at the heavens and imagine them as a colossal blaze of obedience to God, we might also be inspired to contribute our own glimmers of goodness, so that we, too, can contribute to this mighty fire that may well grace the cosmos.

LIFE ON THE OUTSIDE

A S THE ISRAELITES ENTERED THE PROMISED LAND, GOD gave them a stern warning regarding their prospects for a peacful and enduring life in their new home:

> Beware lest your heart be seduced and you turn aside and worship other gods and bow down to them. Then God's anger will burn against you . . . and you will quickly be lost from upon the good land that God is giving to you.[1]

This warning about the grim ordeal of exile is chilling at first reading, but there is *double entendre* in this text which gives us an additional insight into the condition of exile. The Hebrew word for 'land' in this verse is *aretz*, referring to Israel, our national homeland. Elsewhere, the same Hebrew word is also used to indicate the Earth as a whole. For instance, the opening verse of the Torah says, 'In the beginning, God created the Heavens and the Earth.'[2] The word for 'Earth' in this verse is also *aretz*.

Thus, the punishment of exile is conveyed to us in such a way that it can be translated to mean that we will be forced off our home planet. Although the context shows that this is not the verse's primary meaning, we need not ignore the additional nuance in the text. Perhaps there is a suggestion in this secondary meaning that our being forced out of the land of Israel would be as traumatic and perilous as being forced off the planet altogether.

Modern space exploration has shown that it takes a great deal of work to keep a human being alive in space for any length of time, no matter how brief. It requires intricate engineering and entails coping with many ongoing and acute risks simultaneously.

---

1   Deuteronomy 11:16-17.
2   Genesis 1:1.

The sun's light on the Moon is very harsh as there is no atmosphere to filter it. (NASA)

This picture shows the lunar terminator, the boundary between the sunlit and dark parts of the Moon. Sunlit parts of the Moon can be as hot as 123 degrees Centigrade, whereas in shaded areas surface temperatures plunge to -233 degrees Centigrade. (NASA)

Human life is not sustainable in the vacuum of space. Exposure to the space vacuum results in an immediate depletion of oxygen in blood and body tissues, leading to loss of consciousness after about fifteen seconds. This can be followed by circulatory failure and lung collapse within thirty seconds. Anyone subjected to this would have to be placed in a pressurized environment within two minutes in order to have any hope of survival.

Space travelers must also reckon with massive variations in temperature. Outside Earth's atmosphere, temperatures in the sun exceed 150 degrees centigrade, while shaded places may be hundreds of degrees centigrade below zero. Most life forms cannot withstand such temperatures even for a short time.

The Earth's atmosphere also serves as a shield against ultraviolet light and particle radiation from the Sun. In space, beyond the protection of our atmosphere, the Sun can cause blindness, radiation burns and multiple organ failure. Solar flares, which generate occasional bursts of extremely high radiation within our Solar System, are so intense that it is impossible to withstand them. It has been calculated that if a solar flare had occurred during the *Apollo 11* moonwalk in July 1969, it would have sent out a blast of radiation so powerful that the astronauts' spacesuits would not have been sufficient protection, and the astronauts would have been killed.

Micrometeoroid impact on the window of the space shuttle. (NASA)

Addressing all these threats would not be enough to keep astronauts safe. Many areas of space are constantly crisscrossed by micrometeoroids, pieces of rock or metal measuring up to a few millimeters across. We are used to thinking of such tiny things as inconsequential, but their speed makes them lethal. Micrometeoroids travel through space at some sixteen thousand miles per hour (about five times faster than a bullet shot from a hunting rifle), and care must be taken in constructing spacecraft and space suits such that they can withstand such impacts.

Besides all this, it is extremely difficult to move safely through space outside a spacecraft. Because there is almost no gravity away from planets, moons and stars, an astronaut outside a spacecraft risks drifting off into space and being lost forever.

To cope with all these risks, astronauts who leave their spacecraft wear spacesuits that are extremely robust. The suits contain oxygen and are pressurized so that astronauts can breathe and be

Artist's impression of astronauts living on a lunar base. Their rugged spacesuits help them to survive in the harsh lunar environment. (NASA)

protected from the vacuum of space. To guard against extreme temperatures, the suits are heavily insulated. A spacesuit's outer layer must be strong enough to withstand impacts from micrometeoroids. Suits incorporate a cooling system to prevent the astronauts' trapped body heat from accumulating and causing them to overheat. In addition, visors are plated with an extremely thin layer of gold to protect astronauts' eyes from sunlight that is not filtered by the Earth's atmosphere. Spacesuits provide multiple layers of protection, all within a shell that allows astronauts to walk, pick up and hold items, and perform tasks while out in space.

Astronauts tether themselves to their spacecraft or carry jet packs that they can use to move around in space for a limited time. This prevents them from drifting off into space.

Life in a spacecraft is somewhat safer. The body of the spacecraft serves as an airtight, pressurized environment for astronauts, and provides more protection from radiation, micrometeoroids and extremes of temperature. But if a spacecraft's protection were breached, its occupants would die within minutes.

We recall that there is a hint in the Torah that life in exile is as difficult as living outside the Earth. Now that we understand just how dangerous it is to live outside the Earth, we can also understand how precarious life in exile is.

There have been innumerable times when mere survival in exile has been our greatest challenge. The Torah does predict that exile will threaten our very lives:

> I will scatter you among the nations and I will draw the sword after you .... You will be lost among the nations, and the land of the enemies will consume you.[3]
>
> Just as God rejoiced to do good to you and to multiply you, so will He cause people to rejoice over destroying and exterminating you, and you will be lost from upon the land that you are inheriting .... Among those nations you will not be tranquil, and there will be no rest for the sole of your foot.[4]

---

3   Leviticus 26:38.
4   Deuteronomy 28:63, 65.

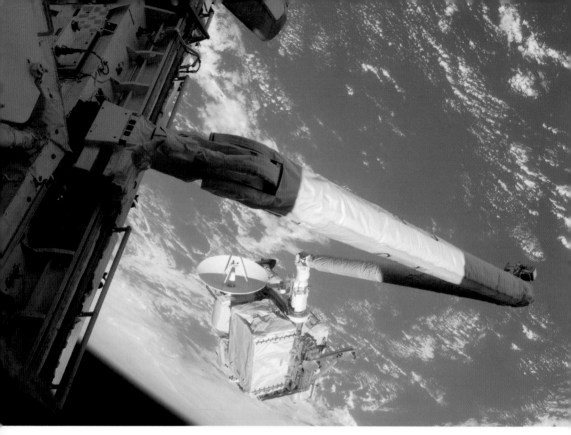

Ingenious methods are used to move objects through space without risking astronauts' lives. Here, a robotic arm is used to install equipment on the International Space Station. (NASA)

In fact life in exile, like life in space, presents us with several challenges at once.

Even as we must cope with repeated threats to our physical existence while we are in exile, we must also protect ourselves spiritually. Away from our homeland, deprived of our Temple, scattered across many lands and harried from place to place, it is difficult to maintain Torah observance. As the Torah predicts, 'God will scatter you among the nations . . . . There you will serve false gods of wood and stone that cannot see, hear, eat or smell.'⁵

The Torah also warns us that exile compromises effective transmission of the Torah to subsequent generations. A cross-generational dislocation develops as children drift away from Jewish

---

5   Deuteronomy 4:27-28.

ways and their parents are powerless to stop them. 'Your sons and daughters will be given over to another people before your very eyes, and you will yearn to bring them back. But you will be powerless to do anything about it.'[6]

Astronauts in space have spacesuits, with their eighteen thousand components, to keep them alive. Spacecraft are designed, constructed and maintained by huge workforces at enormous expense. How do Jews stay alive in exile?

Perhaps the answer may be found in Psalm 91, which contains a detailed account of the protection that God can offer us: '[God] will cover you with His wings. His truth is an encircling shield.'[7]

We can take 'God's truth' to be a reference to the Torah. In another Psalm, the Psalmist places Torah and falsehood in opposition and explicitly links Torah and truth: 'Remove from me the way of falsehood and bestow your Torah graciously upon me. Do not withhold from my mouth a word that is very true, for I have yearned for your ordinances.'[8]

Indeed, after a man has been called to the Torah and the reading

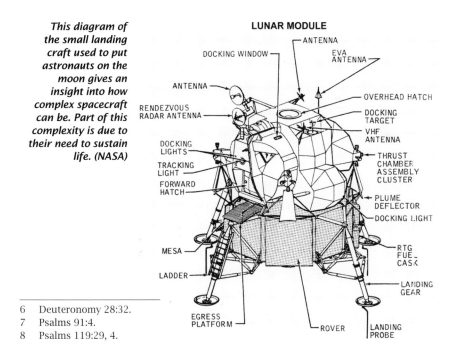

This diagram of the small landing craft used to put astronauts on the moon gives an insight into how complex spacecraft can be. Part of this complexity is due to their need to sustain life. (NASA)

LUNAR MODULE

ANTENNA
DOCKING WINDOW
EVA ANTENNA
ANTENNA
OVERHEAD HATCH
RENDEZVOUS RADAR ANTENNA
DOCKING TARGET
VHF ANTENNA
DOCKING LIGHTS
THRUST CHAMBER ASSEMBLY CLUSTER
TRACKING LIGHT
FORWARD HATCH
PLUME DEFLECTOR
DOCKING LIGHT
MESA
RTG FUEL CASK
LADDER
LANDING GEAR
EGRESS PLATFORM
ROVER
LANDING PROBE

---

6 Deuteronomy 28:32.
7 Psalms 91:4.
8 Psalms 119:29, 4.

has been completed, he recites a concluding blessing celebrating the Torah as the ultimate life-giving truth: 'Blessed are You, Lord our God, Ruler of the universe, who has given us the Torah of truth and planted within us eternal life.'

Bearing this in mind, we might understand that when Psalm 91 describes God's truth as an encircling shield, it refers to the Torah. Torah is a shield that can defend us in difficult situations, just as a spacesuit and spacecraft help astronauts to survive outside the Earth.

Perhaps we can understand this to mean that those who study and observe the Torah will be less susceptible to the ravages of assimilation and will continue to exist as Jews.

And there may be a deeper message here. Perhaps Torah study somehow serves as a protection for the Jewish people as a whole without our being aware of it. Although we have often suffered terribly during our long exile, our ordeals might have been worse had it not been for those brave, loyal and visionary Jews who devoted themselves to encouraging and engaging in Torah observance even when other, more fashionable options were available to them. Rabban Gamliel used to say: 'The more Torah, the more life.'[9]

We can take this a step further still. Perhaps our verse hints that just as an astronaut cannot survive in space without protection, so we cannot withstand exile without the Torah. Whenever exile does present us with a problem, be it anti-Semitism, assimilation or distortion of Torah teaching, we can turn to the Torah itself to help us through. Just as an astronaut hovers outside the world but can continue to breathe and function in the protective bubble of a spacesuit or spacecraft, protected from many harmful forces, so the Torah can protect us through the long years of exile, teaching us, cheering us, inspiring and protecting us.

We should not think, however, that the Torah will no longer be relevant in the Messianic Era when we are all back in Israel.

Whereas astronauts can manage without their spacecraft and spacesuits once they are back on Earth, the Torah will take on a whole new dimension when the Jewish people live in Israel. As well

---

9 Pirkei Avot 2:7.

as cementing our bond with the land[10], it will help us to fulfill our mission to the world, uniting the whole of humanity in the service of God:

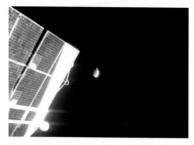

> It will be at the end of days that many peoples will go, and they will say, 'Come! Let us go up to the mountain of the Lord, to the temple of the God of Jacob, so that He may teach us about His ways.' For the Torah will go out from Zion, and the word of the Lord will come from Jerusalem.[11]

The risk of untethered walking in space is demonstrated by this chilling picture of a bag of tools drifting away from the International Space Station during mission STS-126. An astronaut was cleaning away some grease that had leaked inside the bag when it popped loose and drifted away. Valued at $100,000, the tools drifted towards the Earth for months before finally entering the atmosphere and burning up as they plunged down towards the ground. (NASA)

We have not yet attained this goal. Conflict still scars the news as it has scarred all of human history, and we Jews are still scattered across the whole world. But there will come a time when we will return to the land of Israel, united around God, and universal peace will be established.

Here is God's message to Isaiah regarding the ultimate ingathering of the Jewish people:

> And it shall come to pass in that day, that the LORD shall make a harvest from the channel of the river unto the stream of Egypt, and you shall be gathered one by one, O children of Israel.
>
> And it shall come to pass in that day, that the great trumpet shall be blown, and those who were about to perish in the land of Assyria will come, together with the outcasts in the land of Egypt, and they shall worship the Lord in the holy mount at Jerusalem.[12]

We can even use the saga of space exploration to understand the joy of this glorious denouement to human history. As we have

---

10 Deuteronomy 4:40.
11 Isaiah 2:2 - 3.
12 Isaiah 27:12 - 13.

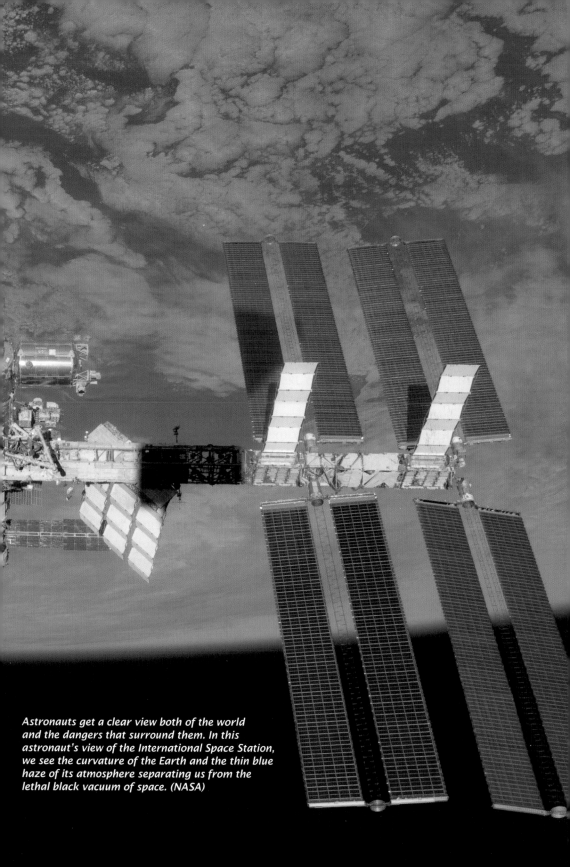

Astronauts get a clear view both of the world and the dangers that surround them. In this astronaut's view of the International Space Station, we see the curvature of the Earth and the thin blue haze of its atmosphere separating us from the lethal black vacuum of space. (NASA)

Artist's impression of a binary star system in the Cygnus constellation. The disk on the right has a black hole at its center which is ripping material off the supergiant star on the left. (ESA/Hubble)

our moods and mental resilience. He is aware of our anguish, and He supports us through dark times. Thus, the reassurances that God binds our wounds and encourages the humble are interrupted by the central phrase depicting God counting and naming the stars to show how much He knows and cares about us.

There is in fact an ancient Midrashic source for this. The third paragraph of Shmot Rabbah refers to this passage in Psalms and says specifically that God names and counts us just as He names and counts the stars.

But this theme has a sequel. There is a still deeper dimension to this comparison of people to stars – a notion of reciprocity. As God reaches out to us, we can also reach out to Him. This is made clear in the very next Psalm: 'Praise [God] all you stars of light!'[7]

If the previous Psalm used stars as a metaphor for human beings, perhaps this succeeding one also refers to us when it calls on stars to praise God. We are to praise God like radiant stars. What does this comparison teach us about our worship?

The stars themselves give us an answer.

Our perception of the stars is that they twinkle silently in the sky. But they are anything but silent. Astronomers discovered in the 1970s that seismic events that emanate from the cores of stars actually do make a kind of noise.

We have already seen[8] that sounds are actually waves of energy traveling through the air. Similar pulses of energy can shoot out from the nuclear reactions in the cores of stars to the surface and then escape into space. By artificially boosting these bursts of energy, we can make them audible as sounds.

Different stars produce different sounds. It has been shown that a neutron star in the star cluster known as Terzan 5 near the center of our Milky Way experienced a huge quake that has set it vibrating like a bell that has been struck. The vibration corresponds to what we think of as F-sharp. Other stars have been found to whistle, hum or rumble. Xi-hydrae, an intensely bright star located 130 light

---

7   Psalms 148:3.
8   *Quick as a flash*, above.

years away from us, sounds like a beating drum and has been set to music.

How, then, do we praise God?

Perhaps we are to understand the sounds made by stars as a metaphor for our own prayers. The first thing that we can learn from this is about where our prayers should come from. The common factor uniting the different voices of the various kinds of stars is that they originate at their cores as mighty pulses of energy that surge outward to the surface and then into space. Likewise, our praise of God is at its best when it wells us from our hearts to our lips with irresistible power and passion.

We can also learn that, like the output of the stars, our prayers can literally span the universe. There is no such thing as a prayer that is not heard, or a person who is too remote for their heartfelt prayer to be audible.

Furthermore, we can learn from the stars about the durability of a prayer. Radio signals emitted by stars can be detected over long distances, even long after the star itself has died. This teaches us perhaps that God does not only hear the prayers of our own time. The prayers of our deceased ancestors are still audible and precious before God even though the people who uttered them are no longer alive. Likewise, our prayers will endure spiritually even after we have left this life. We pray not just for ourselves but for posterity.

In addition, we should not strive to imitate others' form of prayer. Just as the stars produce a wide variety of sounds, so we pray in different ways. Different people find different passages especially moving or difficult. We naturally pray at varying speeds. It is our duty to find a mode of prayer that works for us within the framework of the liturgy that our forebears bequeathed to us and to develop our connection with God in our own God-given way.

And finally, let us not feel frustrated or dissatisfied with ourselves if we find it difficult to pray. Just as a star changes in size and brightness over time, emitting different amounts and types of energy in the course of its life, so we can expect our prayers to change as we mature and our perspectives on life grow broader and deeper. Prayer is the work of a lifetime, and if we start now, we might attain star status.

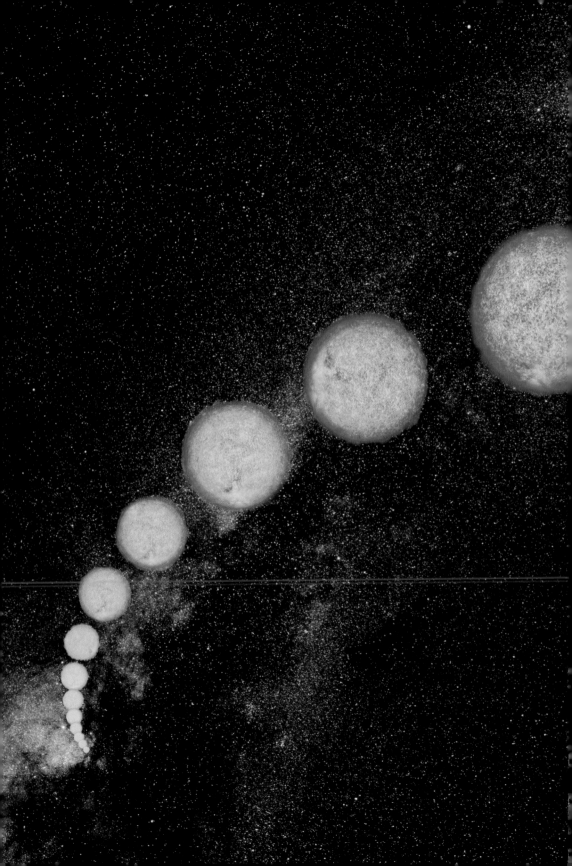

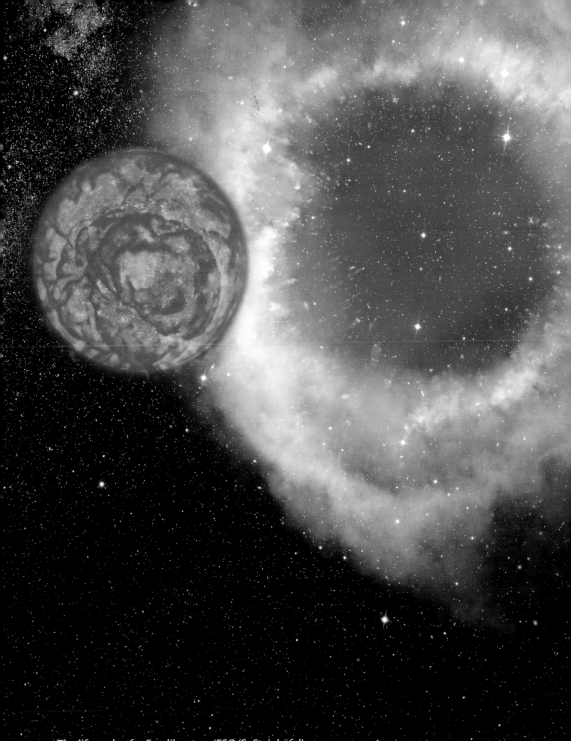

The life cycle of a Sun-like star. (ESO/S. Steinhöfel)

An artist's impression of a magnetar (a neutron star with a magnetic field) which flared in December 2004, releasing as much energy in a tenth of a second as our Sun has generated in 100,000 years. The star's magnetic field is trillions of times more powerful than the one around Earth, so strong that it actually buckles the star's surface, causing it to emit massive amounts of energy. (NASA)

DISTANCE NO OBJECT

E HAVE SEEN ON MANY OCCASIONS THAT THE DIS-
tances covered by modern space probes are almost unimaginable. *Mariner 10*, which flew past Mercury in 1974,
traveled thirty-six million miles before reaching its destination.
The *New Horizons* mission to Pluto entails a journey of three and
a half billion miles.

We also know that such distances are very short compared with
the vastness of space. As we near the end of our tour of the cosmos, let us give our imagination free rein and consider how we
might travel as far as possible – across galaxies, to the other end
of the universe.

The most orthodox method of travel would be one using Newton's third law of motion: that for every action, there is an equal
and opposite reaction.

If something is forced out of a body at great speed, the body will
hurtle off in the opposite direction. This is the principle behind jet
aircraft and modern spaceships. Hot gases are expelled out of the
back of the craft, and it accelerates forwards. To slow down, it fires
the gases forwards through retro rockets, and an equal braking
reaction is exerted backwards on the craft, halting its progress.

Another method which one might use to power a spacecraft is
nuclear fission, harnessing the energy released when a radioactive
nucleus splits into two smaller nuclei.

The problem with both these methods of propulsion is simply
the magnitude of the distances involved in space travel. The nearest star to us is Proxima Centauri, a red dwarf close to the twin
stars Alpha Centauri A & B, some 4.2 light years away from Earth.
Light travels one hundred and eighty-six thousand miles in one
second, which works out as 5,865,696,000,000 miles in one year.
That puts Proxima Centauri a huge 24,635,923,200,000 miles away,

NASA engineers work on Mariner 10 which flew to Venus and Mercury. (NASA)

compared to the Moon, which is less than a quarter of a million miles from Earth. To travel such a long way would require an unmanageable amount of fuel. And Proxima Centauri, as its name suggests, is just next door in terms of galactic travel.

Back to the drawing board.

Nuclear fusion is far more powerful than nuclear fission. It involves fusing atomic nuclei together, a process that also releases large amounts of energy.

The problem of finding fuel might not be totally insurmountable. Hydrogen could be used as the raw material for the fusion process (just like in our own Sun), and hydrogen exists all over space. A craft travelling fast enough could scoop up interstellar hydrogen atoms en route and fuse them on board.

But there are several disadvantages to this as well. Fusion takes place at approximately ten million degrees centigrade, and the logistics involved in generating such temperatures in a spaceship are prohibitive. The plasma (ionized gas) that would be generated would burn through any container in a matter of seconds unless it were contained in strong magnetic fields, so there would also be a difficulty in designing fuel tanks.

And there would still be the problem of speed. Travelling to

NASA's New Horiz
mission blasts off from C
Canaveral bound for Plu
(NA

different stars would be extraordinarily time-consuming. The only way it could be done would be to put a whole village on the ship and hope that new generations would keep being born to perpetuate life on board for the thousands of years required for any kind of serious trip.

It would be possible to introduce a variation on this theme and thrust a spaceship forward with controlled nuclear explosions. In the 1970s, the British Planetary Society worked on Project Daedalus, a spaceship that could travel at twelve percent of the speed of light by triggering two hundred and fifty nuclear explosions every

NASA's massive F-1 rocket engine produced 1,500,000 pounds of thrust and shattered windows in nearby buildings during its test firing (shown here). Five such engines were used to power NASA's Saturn V rocket, but the rocket was not sufficiently powerful to take humans to the next star in our galaxy. (NASA)

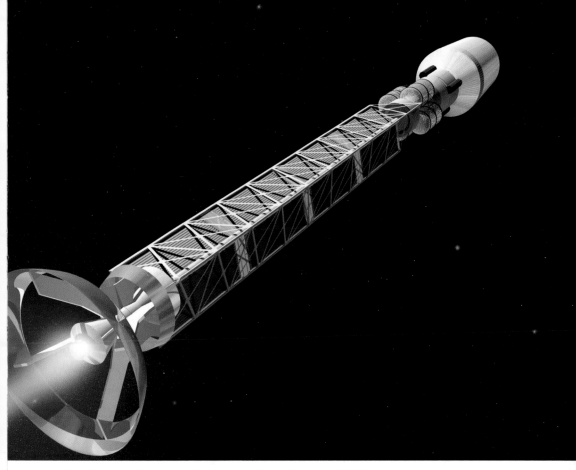

Artist's impression of a rocket powered by antimatter. (NASA)

second. But, here again, the problem of fuel capacity makes the idea unworkable.

Yet although conventional physics may have let us down, there are some more exotic ideas out there that might do the trick. Like antimatter, for example.

The physicist Paul Dirac formulated the concept of antimatter in 1929. He predicted that each of the particles that make up atoms has a counterpart known as an antiparticle. Whenever antimatter and matter meet, they join, annihilating each other and releasing energy. A relatively small quantity of antimatter would be enough to heat hydrogen that could be used as the propulsion to send a spacecraft off at a speed that would be useful for travelling vast distances.

An artist's impression of the effect of a Black Hole on its immediate environment. (Alain R)

It will happen . . . that you will reflect in your heart in the midst of all the nations to which God will banish you. You will return to the Lord your God and you will listen to His voice . . . with all your heart and soul. God will restore your fortunes, and He will have mercy upon you. He will return and gather you from among all the nations where God scattered you.

Even if you have been banished to the end of the heavens, God will gather you in and take you from there. God will bring you to the land that your ancestors inherited, and you will inherit it . . . . He will liberate your heart . . . and you will love Him with all your heart and soul, so that you may live.[2]

In ancient times, it may not have been clear how far away the heavens were. The Talmud says that the people who built the tower of Babel thought that they could use it to climb up into the sky to pierce it or to fight against God.[3] But in our own time we have discovered just how fantastically vast the heavens are, and we have found that travel across a significant part of the universe is and always has been impossible.

A Jewish person may be incredibly remote from God, cut off from all aspects of Jewish life and society, to such an extent that just as we cannot cross the universe, no amount of human effort can restore their soul, and no amount of persuasion or urging will do the slightest bit of good. A soul can be so lost that no human endeavor will have any effect upon it.

But God promises that He can work miracles in the hardest of hearts and that He can help anyone to return no matter how far away that soul may be. There is no such thing in Judaism as a lost soul because God can trigger a Messianic Age in anyone. If we allow Him to do that for us, then we will witness the global Messianic Age when the world will be united in the service of God.

---

2   Deuteronomy 30:1–6.
3   Sanhedrin 109a.

THE DEATH OF THE UNIVERSE

THERE IS BROAD AGREEMENT IN SCIENTIFIC CIRCLES THAT although our universe is going to last for a very long time, it will not last forever in the way that it exists now.

Before investigating this, we should remember that in divine terms, this is not a major problem. We know that we are not wholly subject to the laws of nature. God loves us and can provide for us, changing the course of history and the laws of nature as He wishes in order to allow us to survive. His infinite and eternal plan does not depend on the limitations of the physical universe.

But the universe is set up in such a way that, when one looks at it from a purely mechanistic point of view, one finds that it is a system facing doom. Astrophysicists Fred Adams and Gregory Laughlin divided the history of the universe into various eras. We are currently in the Stelliferous Era: new stars are being born, many stars shine as they reach their mature phase, others are exploding as supernovae, collapsing into black holes or neutron stars, or fading away. Even though some of the material thrown out by supernovae may reform into new stars, there will normally be some remnant that will stay inert. This means that over time, there will be less and less material available to create new stars, and ultimately no new stars will form.

Supernova: a star explodes into a vast cloud of dust and gas. (NASA, ESA and the Hubble SM4 ERO team)

In the mechanistic view of the universe, the Degenerate Era will follow in approximately a hundred trillion years from now, with all stars having ceased to shine because their fuel is exhausted. Some significant bodies will still exist at this point. Black holes will suck in anything within

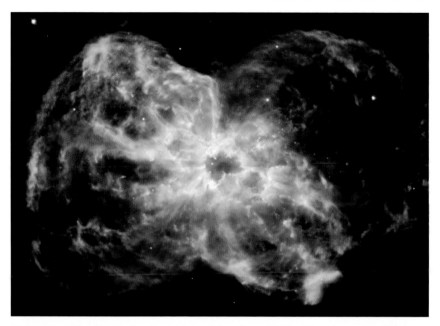

This spectacular image shows a star reaching the end of its life. It has cast off its outer layers of gas which form a nebula around it. The star itself has become a white dwarf, a burnt out relic with a surface temperature of some 200,000 degrees Celsius, seen here as a white dot in the centre of the nebula. (ESA, K. Noll (STScI), Hubble Heritage Team (STScI, Hubble Heritage Team, AURA))

their reach and neutron stars will maintain their immense density. There will be a faint glow emitted by white dwarfs – dead stars that give out a dull light as their stored heat gradually leaks away.

Some stellar remnants – the bodies that are left over once stars have burnt out – will accelerate through space, speeding up as a result of close encounters with other drifting bodies, and will eventually be ejected from their galaxy altogether. Stellar remnants that do not escape their galaxy will draw closer to its center, contributing to a massive black hole that will absorb all the material in its vicinity. This is the Black Hole Era. Black holes, the only large structures left, will dominate the universe.

But ultimately, even black holes die. They emit radiation and gradually evaporate, shining briefly as their temperature rises towards the end of their lives before emitting major particles such as electrons and protons.

Artist's impression of the debris disk left by a comet being torn apart in the gravitational field around a white dwarf. (NASA/JPL-Caltech/T. Pyle (SSC))

This is the start of the Dark Era, in which certain subatomic particles (photons, electrons and others) fly around and only occasionally encounter one another. There is now very little energy density, and the universe decays further as some of the remaining particles pair up to form short-lived structures that will ultimately disin-

tegrate. According to the scientific model, this is predicted to happen when the universe is around 10^{100} (1 followed by one hundred zeroes) years old.

Thus, the universe that we think of as an eternal entity is actually a massive demonstration not of the infinite, but of the finite. It is intriguing to think of the cosmos as something that, left to its own devices, will eventually die. All its unimaginably vast distances, enormous energy and the trillions of years of its life expectancy are not proof against the ravages of time. The very fact that the universe functions and interacts with itself means that it is doomed to end.

This is a sobering notion. Next to infinity, nothing material is sacred!

Kohelet (Ecclesiastes) can be understood to be saying something similar in his comments on the futility of things of this life. 'Utterly worthless!' is the normal translation of the opening passage. 'Utterly worthless, all is worthless!'[1]

The Hebrew word *hevel*, translated as 'worthless' or 'vanity,' has an underlying meaning of 'transient.' Rabbi Samson Raphael Hirsch translates the word to mean this in his commentary on the Torah's account of the birth and naming of Abel – *Hevel* in Hebrew.[2] Abel, he says, was so called because he was named after the expulsion

1   Ecclesiastes 1:2.
2   Rabbi Samson Raphael Hirsch's commentary on Genesis 4:1.

from the Garden of Eden when his parents Adam and Eve understood that life was going to be difficult and that everything in the
world would now be cursed with transience.

If we take the opening remark of Kohelet at face value and
understand it as referring to all that exists, it takes on a new reso-
nance. The entire cosmos, says Kohelet, is transitory. Inexorable
laws of nature doom the mightiest galaxies to extinction. True, the
lifespan of our universe is measured by numbers so large that we
can hardly imagine them. Yet compared to the eternal timeframe
in which God lives and by which we try to judge our lives, all these
trillions of years do not amount to the blink of an eye.

Is Kohelet really talking about literally everything when he says
'All is transient'? After all, he is writing about the human condition.
Is he perhaps referring to all human endeavor and ambition? The
book does not make that clear.

Perhaps the lament, 'All is transient!' deliberately combines the
view of the universe with the view of humanity. The ambiguity
in the term *all* leads us to apply it both to the whole of creation
and to the whole of human life because, Kohelet tells us, they are
variations on the same theme. Kohelet tells us that the transience
of the physical universe is actually a commentary on our own lives.

As we look around the universe and reflect on the fact that,
in the normal run of things, all of its colossal mass, complexity,
light, energy, and color are set to disappear, we are actually contemplating a parable of the mortality and vanity of all the physical
things in our own lives. The death sentence for the cosmos, albeit
suspended for the foreseeable future, is a death sentence for us
all and for much of what we hold dear. Kohelet brings this to our
attention. The death of the universe, which mirrors the transience
of human endeavor, prompts us to reconsider our priorities.

But we should remember that, in addition to the burden of mortality, humans have the key to eternity. Towards the end of the
book of Kohelet,[3] we read: 'Remember your Creator in the days of
your youth, before the days of evil come about which you will say,
"I have no wish for them."' There follows what the Talmudic sage

---

3   12:1-7.

Rabbi Gamliel bar Rabbi[4] takes as a poetic account of the decline of the bodily faculties, culminating with the verse, 'The dust will return to the ground as it was, but the spirit will return to the Lord who gave it.'

We carry the magic of immortality within ourselves. Our bodies grow and wither in a flash by nature's standards; but the spark of God within us will never die.

The Torah enables us to develop this precious dimension of our being. Each commandment is an opportunity to build the soul, developing it in the same way that physical exercise develops the body. Surmounting spiritual challenges adds something immortal and indestructible to us.

When we engage with God, we can even triumph over time. (S Sepp)

A lifetime devoted to charity, Torah study or family is a precious jewel set in God's throne, and its luster will never fade. The angelic component of a human being, blessed with the gift of eternal life, can outlive the cosmos itself.

---

4   Shabbat 151b.

HYPERSPATIAL JUDAISM

I N THIS CHAPTER, WE TRAVEL TO SOMEWHERE BEYOND SPACE as we know it – the fourth dimension.

We perceive space in three dimensions: up/down, right/left and forward/backward. All directions in which something might travel are combinations of these three dimensions. But scientists, mathematicians and philosophers have posited the existence of other spatial dimensions as close to ours as up/down is to left/ right.

It is almost impossible for us to imagine a fourth dimension. But we can imagine what it would be like for us to meet a being from the fourth dimension by putting ourselves in the shoes of someone who only has two dimensions.

Let us imagine the experiences of people living in a two-dimensional world, such as a piece of paper lying flat on a table. (Technically, a piece of paper is three-dimensional because it has thickness, but we can ignore this for the purposes of this thought experiment.) Our Paperworld friends can go forward, backward, left and right, but they have no conception of up and down. For them, the vertical plane does not exist, and if we were to try to explain it to them they would not have the mental capacity to visualize it.

Now let us intervene in their world. We track a group of inhabitants walking along the paper and put a fingertip down on the paper in front of them. They are

We can view a banana in many different ways because we live in three dimensions. But a two-dimensional being would only perceive a banana passing through their plane as a fluctuating yellow line. (Fir0002/Flagstaffotos)

A literary exploration of multiple dimensions written by an English schoolmaster, Edwin Abbott Abbott, in 1884.

astonished. For them, the fingertip is only visible inasmuch as it touches their two-dimensional plane, and the rest of it is *up* – in a plane beyond their conception. A pink circle has appeared from out of nowhere right in front of them. As the finger is lifted off the page, it suddenly disappears from view again.

We decide to try a different experiment. We raise the paper off the table, pick up a banana, and plunge the banana right through the paper. This time, the people of Paperworld are paralyzed with fright. A fluctuating yellow circle appears in front of them as the banana makes its way through the paper, and as it disappears it leaves a big hole in their world. They have no idea what has hit them.

For us, living in three dimensions, what has happened is perfectly comprehensible. But because the people of Paperworld have one less dimension than we have, they only perceive and understand a small part of what goes on in a three-dimensional world, and it cannot make sense to them.

When it comes to us understanding life in four spatial dimensions, we experience as much difficulty as the people of Paperworld have when they try to understand how we live. We are simply locked into three dimensions, and visualizing or understanding a fourth spatial dimension is almost beyond us.

We can gain indirect insights into the fourth dimension by understanding the relationship between a three-dimensional solid and the two-dimensional shadow it casts on to a flat surface. This can then be extrapolated up into four dimensions, such that

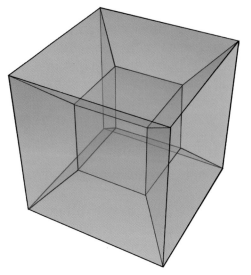

A four-dimensional cube would cast a three dimensional shadow like this. (Goffrie, Mouagip)

If we could unfold a tesseract (a four-dimensional cube), it would look like this. (DMN, Stannered)

computers can generate pictures of three-dimensional shadows of four-dimensional objects. One can go further and create three-dimensional shadows of four-dimensional shadows of five-dimensional objects, and so on. But it takes great effort to begin to visualize anything beyond our own world of three dimensions.

We should bear in mind that this is not just an academic exercise. Certain scientific models about the development of the universe only work if we treat space as hyperspace, having more than three dimensions. It might be that our universe is actually hyperspatial, but we can only perceive three of its dimensions.

These recent investigations into higher-dimensional physics and geometry help us to understand a passage in the Torah in a new, more coherent way.

Shortly after the sin of the Golden Calf, Moses asks to be allowed to see God's full glory. God answered, 'Behold, [there is a] place with Me, and you will stand on the rock . . . . I will put you in a cleft in the rock, and you will see My back, but My face may not be seen.'[1]

---

1   Exodus 33:21.

A Midrashic opinion quoted in Rashi's commentary on this verse takes God's opening phrase to mean 'Behold, [the notion of] place is next to Me.' God is the place in which the world exists and the world is not a place in which He exists. In other words, God is beyond the notion of place as we understand it.[2]

Of course, we are in no way supposed to imagine that God lives in a fourth spatial dimension, since God has no physical form or location whatever. But we can understand this verse as an illustration of how little we can comprehend God's interaction with the world. Based on this Talmudic interpretation, we can take this verse to mean that God was telling Moses - and us - that we understand Him so little that it is *as if* He were living in a higher spatial dimension.

Thus, since we are locked in our physical world, we can only perceive God in a derived, shadowy way, just as we can only understand a four-dimensional figure indirectly and imperfectly. It takes great effort on our part even to begin to comprehend God's view of the world, let alone how He exists and acts. Thus, God sums up His explanation of His nature by telling Moses, 'You will see My back, but My face cannot be seen.'[3] Just as the hyperspatial world is beyond our ken, says God, so is the heavenly realm and its workings. Just as the people of Paperworld misunderstand a finger as a mysterious fluctuating pink circle, so our perception of God is fragmentary and incomplete, as if we were trying to see His face but can only see His back.

The very next passage in the Torah[4] is a remarkable demonstration of divine mercy. God instructs Moses to hew a second set of tablets to be engraved with the Ten Commandments. The relationship between God and His people is repaired. It is going to be all right.

We can and should see this as a demonstration of God's forgiveness and love. He was able to sweep away the sin of the Golden Calf to such an extent that He could still regard us as His own

---

2   Beraishit Rabbah 68:9.
3   Exodus 33:23
4   Exodus 34:1.

people, His treasure on Earth.[5]

However, in view of what came immediately before this passage, we can understand this episode in a new and more dramatic light. To be sure, the carving of the stone for the second Ten Commandments is a powerful and concrete indication of God's mercy. But we have just learned from

We encounter an approximation of the relationship between two and three dimensional views with shadows, as in this view of the shadow cast by a vase of flowers. Shadows can give us a sense of shape and size, but reveal very little about depth, substance, texture and color. Similarly, we can have a glimpse of God's kindness and mercy without fully understanding how He interacts with us. (Nevit Dilmen)

God's preceding words to Moses that what we see of God is but a tiny, indirect shadow of what is really going on.

The love and forgiveness that shine forth from this passage, with God granting a second chance to the Jewish people, are only shadows of the true extent of God's feelings for us. God's love for us is incomprehensible in its depth, strength and permanence. His forgiveness is mightier and more complete than anything we could imagine. He aches with love for us, and will quell His rage for the sake of that love.

It is the same for any quality that we perceive in God: however He is depicted, however He appears to us, we are only seeing flat, indirect shadows of the real thing.

This metaphor can teach us a further lesson. The Paperworld creatures cannot perceive the third dimension however close it is to them. We might wave a finger one millimeter above them, but because they have no perception of "up", our finger is invisible to them.

Similarly, God reminds us, just because we cannot see Him does

---

5   Exodus 19:5.

not mean that He is far away. He may be breathtakingly close, as close and as imperceptible as an object in the fourth dimension can be to a three-dimensional person. His invisibility is not because of Him, but because of us.

We need not be depressed by our inadequacy in this regard. After all, we are only human and God understands that. But we can remember that whenever we think we have seen the end of God's love and mercy, we have actually hardly reached the beginning. And when He seems remote, He may actually be right there with us.

could predict how the system would react over the long term. One could work the mathematics through for as long as one liked, calculating what might happen at each second, but without any precise repeating cycle being established. Although the system had clear rules, it was still unpredictable.

Ruelle and Takens were not the first to encounter this phenom-

Colored smoke pours into the air as an aeroplane lands next to it. The smoke makes the complex air turbulence visible and enables scientists to study it. This complexity is used as a metaphor for the unfathomable nature of divine justice. (NASA Langley Research Centre)

enon. Some ten years earlier, MIT scientist Edward Lorenz had been working on a similar problem with convection currents in water. In an effort to learn how to predict weather patterns, Lorenz studied what happened to water when it was heated from below, since its behavior is similar to warm air currents rising from the ground and interacting with colder air higher up.

As the water at the bottom of the container became warmer, it expanded and became less dense, causing it to rise. When it reached the top of the container, it cooled and began to fall, while water that had arrived at the bottom of the container began to expand and rise in its turn.

But this did not create a smooth circular motion like a Ferris wheel because the system was much more complex than one might think. As hot water rose, it interacted with cooler water on the way, heating it and delaying its fall. Sometimes, water that had reached the top and cooled continued its circular motion because of its momentum, going down and then up again even though it was now so cold that its temperature alone would not cause it to rise. Sometimes, however, the cooler water might lose momentum sufficiently for other hot water to rise and reverse its flow.

Lorenz discovered that the motion of the water kept changing and never settled down into a smooth pattern. But it only moved according to the motion prescribed by the laws of turbulence.

Let us be clear. Turbulence in a liquid can look random, and might never settle down into a predictable pattern. But it is in fact created by a system with rules. Like many naturally occurring phenomena, it is order that looks like chaos.

Predicting the exact progress of a drop of water in a turbulent system such as a waterfall can be very difficult. (Stoatbringer)

Lorenz went a stage further in his analysis of unpredictable order. He devised three equations to describe and calculate unpredictable flow in convection, yielding three figures at each point in the convection to describe where the convection current in the liquid would travel next. He then plotted the motion of the liquid on a graph based on three axes, revealing the progression of the liquid's flow in a three-dimensional diagram.

The resulting image became an icon in chaos theory. Lorenz calculated more than five hundred points for the convection of the liquid, and found an ordered shape appearing on his graph. The line never repeated itself, developing instead into a pair of concentric rings. The line crossed over from one set to the other when the flow changed direction.

This shape, showing the order underpinning an apparently disorderly system, led the system to be called a *strange attractor* because the sets of three figures generated by Lorenz were always attracted to certain areas and patterns on the graph. Since then, thousands of strange attractors have been identified or generated in computer simulations, and the images created by people tracking them are as much art as science.

Now we can better understand the comparison of God's judgment to turbulence. Although the movement of liquid is governed by rules, it looks random. Similarly, God's judgment is governed by His own divine wisdom. But, like turbulence, it cannot be predicted. Random and chaotic though it seems, it is actually perfect and consistent.

Like Lorenz, we have something to help us see the order beneath the apparent chaos of our world – the Torah. Events that seem disjointed and random are shown to have an underlying justice and

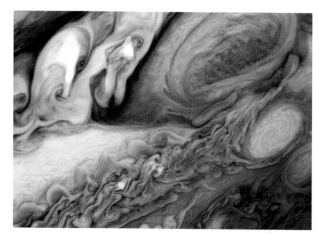

Turbulence exists beyond our world as well. This picture taken by the Voyager 1 space probe shows turbulence among the clouds of Jupiter around the famous Great Red Spot. (NASA/JPL)

symmetry, affording us a glimpse of the wisdom and justice with which God rules His world.

The book of Esther gives us a glimpse into the divine plan. Toward the beginning of the story, we read that the wicked Haman sent out a decree announcing the annihilation of the Jewish people throughout the Persian Empire.[5]

---

5   Esther 3:13.

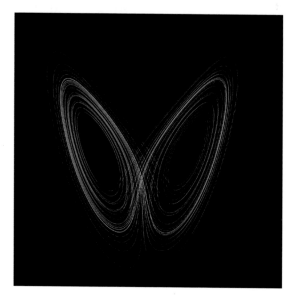

The Lorenz attractor. (Wikimol)

Turbulence in water flowing around an obstacle.
(Aarchiba)

The Jewish people were bewildered and horrified. Mordechai, Queen Esther's cousin, typified their reaction: 'Mordechai tore his clothes and put on sackcloth and ashes. He went out into the midst of the city and cried out with a loud and a bitter cry.'[6]

We can imagine that Mordechai would not have understood how there could be any justice behind Haman's savagery. Yet it is said that Mordechai's 'great and very bitter cry' was actually expiation for a similar cry that occurred earlier in Scripture. Here are the words of Esther Rabbah, a Midrashic exposition of the book of Esther:

> Rabbi Chanin said, 'Jacob made Esau cry one cry [when he procured the blessing from their father Isaac], as it is written:[7] '[Esau] cried a great and bitter cry.' [So in retribution, Esau's descendant Haman made Jacob's descendant Mordechai cry a great and bitter cry.][8]

This is just one instance of the plot behind the plot, demonstrating that what looks unfair may in fact be the expression of a higher divine justice.

Our voyage into the ethereal realm of divine wisdom has taken us a little step further. The verse in Psalms does not help us understand God's interaction with the world. Quite the contrary. It warns

---

6   Esther 4:1.
7   Genesis 27:34.
8   Esther Rabbah 8:1.

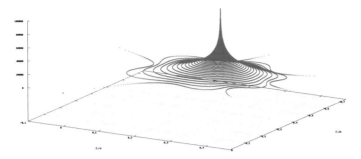

Strange attractors can have an abstract beauty of their own. (Adam Majewski)

us that His governance will seem mysterious and incomprehensible. If we try to second-guess how God drives history, we will get it wrong again and again.

But at the same time, it is reassuring. We are not to allow the random appearance of history to mislead us into thinking that it is random in fact. Like a turbulent liquid, human history is order masquerading as chaos. Deep beneath the surface of the human experience lies a plan, created and nurtured by God.

Perhaps this idea underpins another passage featuring the word *t'hom,* in Psalm 42, where the sons of Korach teach, 'Turbulent water ("t'hom") calls to turbulent water ("t'hom") to obey [God's] guidance.'[9]

---

9   Psalms 42:8.

The rules are universal and simple but the results can be fiendishly complicated. The complex turbulence pattern in a stream of water is replicated on a massive scale by Mira, a star hurtling through the Cetus constellation and ejecting mass as it travels along. The star's tail is thirteen light years long. (NASA)

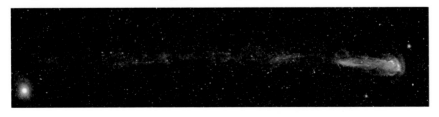

On this verse Rabbi Hirsch wrote:

> The great, billowy deep appears like an uncontrolled, overpowering mass of water, but nevertheless the ocean moves with clock-like regularity. God's almighty Law guides the mighty mass of waves just as man directs small quantities of water to form man-made channels. So too, it would appear to the superficial eye that the waves of suffering, following one upon the other with ever-growing force, overwhelm [one] with uncontrolled violence, but actually it is the Lord who guides and channels them all.

'An uncontrolled, overpowering mass of water'. (Tewy)

THE STAR OF THE SHOW

J EWISH TRADITION INVESTS THE FIGURE OF THE MESSIAH with great importance. In Maimonides' *Mishneh Torah*,[1] the Messiah is defined as the herald of a new age on Earth, a man so holy that he will be able to bring the whole world to acknowledge God, establish enduring and equitable peace on Earth, and bring about the building of the Third Temple in Jerusalem. The Messianic Era will be characterized by a clear awareness of God, such that the notion of defying or neglecting a divine decree will be as unthinkable as forgetting to breathe. The prophet Isaiah said, 'The Earth will be full of the knowledge of God as the waters cover the sea.'[2]

The Messiah will have such an acute awareness of right and wrong that he will have a supernatural perception of what conforms to Torah statutes:

> The spirit of the Lord will rest upon him, a spirit of wisdom and understanding, a spirit of advice and might, a spirit of knowledge and fear of the Lord . . . . He will not judge according to what his eyes see, and he will not decide according to what his ears hear. And he will judge the poor with righteousness . . . .[3]

The timeline of our religious experience focuses on the arrival of the Messiah and the sacred, harmonious epoch that he will introduce. Every Jewish set of prayers concludes with the recital of *Aleynu*, a prayer which looks forward to the time when 'God will be One and His name will be One.'[4]. This means there will be no ambiguity or equivocation in the universal homage that creation pays to its Creator in the new global golden age. The ritual Passover

---

1   Hilchot Melachim 11:4.
2   Isaiah 11:9.
3   Isaiah 11:2-4.
4   Zechariah 14:9.

Artist's impression of the asteroid belt. (NASA/JPL-Caltech/T. Pyle (SSC))

assurance on a verse in Psalms: 'We are His people and the sheep of His pasture; this very day [would the Messiah come] if you would but listen to His voice!'[8]

The Messianic era, then, is as close as the next meteorite. It is ready for the asking, always poised to come into the world when we have risen to the challenge.

Perhaps we can also learn something from the number of asteroids out there. There are twenty-six large asteroids in the belt, together with millions more that measure up to a mile across.

This reminds us that there is not only one person who could be the Messiah. Rather, there is a potential Messiah in each generation, and if both that person and the world are ready, then the Messianic plan will begin to unfold. In fact, there is a view that everyone should look to be their own Messiah, setting spiritual goals, accomplishing them and becoming a better person.

Finally, meteorites travel at great speed. We have already seen from the account of the Tunguska Event that a meteorite can fly at half a million miles per hour, enough to compromise its own

8   Psalms 95:17.

existence. Similarly, the Messiah will not be tardy in his arrival. God will dispatch him in great haste, and he will spare nothing – not even himself – to accomplish his sacred mission with the greatest possible vigor and speed.

Looking at it in human terms, this shows how much God wants us to be closer to Him. He looks for us to earn this closeness so that, when the time comes, there will be no delay. The prolonged Jewish exile is so dark and painful that some no longer look for the Messiah, while others are unaware of the very concept. But it is something for us to look to as an expression of our own spiritual challenge. If we rise to the occasion and release the spirituality that is inherent within us, we will have to wait no longer. God will send His Messiah as soon as we are ready.

A meteor streaks towards the ground. (Navicore)

the universe, they might have had some inkling of God's boundless might and wisdom, and felt both humbled and honored to be there.

King Solomon addressed God in prayer at the dedication of his Temple in Jerusalem: 'Behold, the highest heavens cannot contain You! How much more so is this Temple too small for You?!'[17] With these wise words, Solomon made people realize that any human attempt to grasp the divine must ultimately fail, and that any insight that we might gain into God's greatness would only be a blurred glimpse of the truth. The immensity of the cosmos and the divine majesty that the Temple conveyed are only fragments of a reality that is simply too big for us to grasp.

But the link between the Temple and the universe can be developed further. We have seen that there is, as it were, a physical representation of an echo of God's voice pervading the whole universe, manifested as cosmic microwave background radiation. Similarly, when people entered the Temple, their awareness of God's greatness will have been accompanied by a perception of His original commandment, 'Be!' To enter the Temple was to be overwhelmed by symbols of life.

Thus, the ritual bathing that one had to carry out before entering the Temple conveyed a sense of entering into a new life, since in Judaism, water symbolizes life:

> For as the rain comes down, and the snow from heaven, and they do not return there, but water the earth, and make it bring forth and bud, that it may give seed to the sower, and bread to the eater, so shall My word be that goes forth out of my mouth: it shall not return to Me empty. Rather, it shall accomplish that which I please, and it shall prosper in the thing that I sent it to do.[18]

The table with twelve loaves or 'shewbread' on it opposite the seven flames of the menorah ('candlestick') indicated God's gifts to us, whether physical ones such as food or sacred ones like the light of the Torah.

The Hebrew word for 'sacrifice,' *korban*, does not come from a

---

17 I Kings 8:27.
18 Isaiah 55:10-11.

The fire on the altar was a symbol not of death but of rebirth. (Pavel Ševela /Wikipedia Commons)

root that means 'renunciation.' Instead, it comes from the root that means 'to draw near.' The animal giving its lifeblood to be poured upon the altar in the Temple's outer courtyard and its flesh to be consumed by its flame symbolized not human death but human rebirth, life given over to be hallowed upon the altar and to be fuel for God's light in the world.[19]

In sum, everything about the Temple, properly understood, was an echo of God's original call to life in the very first verse of the Torah.[20] This call resounded throughout the Temple as it resounds throughout the universe.

At the heart of the Temple stood the Ark of the Covenant. The presence of the Ark dominated the Temple in the desert and, later, King Solomon's Temple in Jerusalem. It was situated at, and signified, the heart of both structures.

Here again, at the very center of the whole Temple complex, we find the word of God pervading consciousness as it pervades the universe. It was the place from which God's voice issued to speak to Moses.[21] It was the context for the holiest ceremony of the Jewish year when the High Priest, dressed in white linen clothing made specifically for this occasion, would offer incense to God before the Ark on Yom Kippur.[22]

The Ark contained the original Ten Commandments that had been carved by God and broken by Moses. It also contained the second set of the Ten Commandments and a Torah scroll written by Moses himself.[23] In fact, one of the names for the Holy of Holies, the room where the Ark stood, was *D'vir*,[24] which is based on the Hebrew word *davar*, meaning 'word,' since this was the home of the word of God.

Finally, we recall that most of the universe consists of matter and energy that are immensely powerful but almost incomprehensible, and certainly nothing like anything we experience in our daily

---

19 See Rabbi Samson Raphael Hirsch's commentary on Leviticus 1:7.
20 Genesis 1:1.
21 Exodus 25:22.
22 Leviticus 16.
23 Deuteronomy 31:24-25.
24 I Kings 8:6.

Artist's impression of the Ark of the covenant containing the Ten Commandments and a Torah scroll dictated by God to Moses. God's voice emanated from between the two cherubim, which symbolised the Jewish people's dedication to the Torah and their readiness to welcome the Divine Presence. (Ben Schumin/The George Washington Masonic National Memorial)

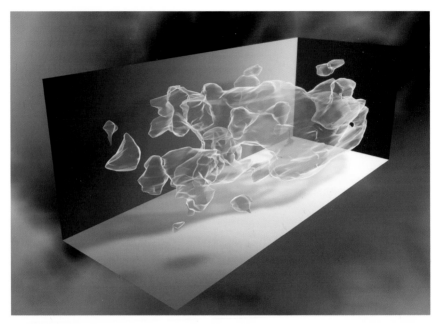

A map of dark matter in a small section of space. The bright spots represent galaxies that have been grouped under the influence of dark matter. (Copyright © NASA, ESA and R. Massey (California Institute of Technology))

lives. Similarly, when we enter the Temple, we are in alien territory, surrounded by concepts and energies that we can barely perceive and far less grasp. This is God's world, not ours, and the rules are otherworldly.

But we must not think that this composite metaphor of the Temple representing the universe only worked for Temple times. It is well known that the synagogues of today represent and, in some way, are temporary substitutes for the Temple.

The Torah and later prophetic writings hint at this. In the list of curses at the end of the book of Leviticus, God warned, 'I will turn your cities into ruins and I will lay waste your sanctuaries.'[25] Torat Kohanim deduces from the plural 'sanctuaries' that the Jews were expected to have synagogues for prayer as well as the Temple, and synagogues are also considered holy places.

This means that, in a smaller way, the synagogue enables us to

25 Leviticus 26:31.

access the same kind of spirituality as we could find in the Temple itself. When we enter a synagogue, we can also have an awareness that we are approaching a Presence so vast that the entire universe cannot contain it. We can look beyond the walls of the room and feel disoriented by God's limitless and awesome majesty, which our prayers mention in loving detail.

Here, for example, is a passage that we recite every morning. It is clear that we are straining the limits of thought and language in an attempt to express fully God's greatness:

> Sing to the Lord, everyone on Earth. Recount His salvation every day. Recount His glory among the nations, His wonders among all the peoples. The Lord is great and exceedingly praised, and He is awesome above all other gods . . . . Glory and splendor are before Him, might and delight in His abode. You families of nations, give glory and strength to the Lord. Give to the Lord the glory of His name. Bring a gift and come before Him, prostrate yourselves before the Lord in the splendor of holiness.[26]

We can also understand the metaphor of the echo of God's word in the context of a synagogue. A synagogue, like the Temple, has a feeling of life about it, and is an echo of the Temple echo of God's word. How is this?

Even though we cannot offer sacrifices as long as we do not have the Temple in Jerusalem, we recall and re-enact them in our prayers. Like the priests entering the Temple, we are supposed to wash our hands before we pray[27]. The first part of every morning service includes an account of the daily sacrifices, and we recite extra prayers on days, such as the Sabbath and the festivals, when extra offerings were made in the Temple. The prophet Hosea said, 'We will replace bulls with our lips,'[28] indicating that prayer may be counted as if we had offered sacrifices ourselves. Thus, the symbolic transition from old life to new life enacted by the sacrificial ritual can also take place through our prayers, especially if

---

26 I Chronicles 16:23-29.
27 Orach Chaim 233:2.
28 Hosea 14:3.

our words guide our hearts to renewed life in God. To plunge into prayer is to plunge into new life.

As we enter the synagogue, we can also understand that we are engaged in an activity which, though very powerful, contains aspects that we do not understand. It seems inconceivable that an infinite, omnipotent, omniscient God should be interested in our prayers, which come from our less-than-perfect minds, lips and hearts. Yet according to Jewish tradition, God cares very much about our prayers in a way that we cannot comprehend. Thus, the *Mishnah Berurah* quotes a mystical account from *Sefer Hechalot* of how God receives our prayers:

> Blessed are you by God . . . if you tell My sons what I do when they proclaim My holiness and say 'Holy! Holy! Holy!' Teach them that their eyes should be raised heavenward in their house of prayer and that they should raise themselves up, for I have no enjoyment in this world like that time when their eyes are raised to Mine. At that time, I grasp My glorious throne at the place where it has an image of Jacob, and I embrace and kiss it and cause their merits to be remembered, and I hasten their redemption.[29]

Rather like dark matter and dark energy, which dominate the universe but stay just out of our sight, prayer in the synagogue has more to it than meets the eye. We are in an environment with awesome forces that interact with us and that we can unleash even though we barely comprehend them.

We can push this metaphor even further, since a Jewish home is also considered a kind of Temple. This point is made in the story of Jacob, who had a dream in which God appeared to him in the humblest of homes – a row of stones stacked around his head – and made a momentous promise to him:

> Then God said . . . 'I will give the land that you are lying on to you and to your descendants. And your descendants shall be as the dust of the Earth, and you will spread to the west, and to the east, and to the north, and to the south. All the families of the world will be blessed through you.'

---

29 Orach Chaim 125:5.

APPENDIX 3 – FURTHER BIBLICAL SOURCES

THERE ARE MANY BIBLICAL METAPHORS THAT BECOME more emphatic or take on new meaning when we understand them in the light of modern science. Here are several:

'My thoughts are not your thoughts, and My ways are not your ways' says the Lord. 'Just as the heavens are high above the Earth, so My ways are high above your ways, and My thoughts are high above your thoughts.' (Isaiah 55:8-9)

Thus says the Lord to Edom . . . 'The arrogance of your heart has seduced you, you who sit in the cleft in the rock, in a lofty habitation, saying in your heart, 'Who will bring me down to Earth?'

If you are as high up as an eagle, or if you put your home in the stars, I will bring you down from there,' says the Lord. (Obadiah, vv. 1-4).

The wise will shine as brightly as the radiance of the heavens, and those that turn the multitudes to righteousness will be like the stars for all eternity. (Daniel 12:3)

The book of Job abounds with references to the natural world. It begins with the story of Job, a righteous man whom God tests by allowing calamities to befall him. Job and his friends have a long debate about the nature of divine justice, and Job, initially resigned to his lot, comes to the conclusion (chapter 31) that he is righteous, implying that God is unjust. Finally, God appears and rebukes Job, using the wonders of the natural world as a proof that He is much wiser than humans, and that His ways not to be questioned:

Then Job answered and said, '. . . How can a man justify Himself before God? If one wishes to argue with Him, one could not answer one of a thousand questions that He might ask.

'He is wise and mighty . . . He takes the mountains unawares when He overturns them in His wrath. He shakes the Earth from its place, and

tations of heavenly bodies at all when one's intent is to use them to learn or teach Jewish law.

There is a view that such imagery can also be used to encourage and facilitate observance and study of the Torah. In his commentary on the book of Joshua,[5] Rashi quotes a tradition that a sculpture of the Sun was placed upon Joshua's grave in order to remind people that he had been so righteous that he was able to ordain the miracle of the stopping of the Sun.[6]

The Shulchan Aruch makes this point explicitly:

> It is forbidden to form representations of things in the heavenly realm such as . . . the ministering angels . . . even if they are just decorative . . . and models of the Sun and Moon and stars are forbidden whether they are in relief or carved into a surface.
>
> However, if they are reproduced for educational purposes, in order to understand and teach, they are all permitted even if they are in relief.[7]

Since this book is intended to educate and inspire about Judaism, it is permitted to include pictures that illustrate and clarify the text.

(A fuller exposition of this and other Jewish laws associated with art can be found in Rabbi Yoel Schwartz's *Madrich Torani La-umanut* ['Torah Guide to Art'], Dvar Yerushalayim: 1992.)

---

5   Joshua 24:30.
6   Ibid. 10:12-13.
7   Yoreh De'ah 141:4.

to make such an image, since one has not made it oneself. Never-theless, Shmuel suggested that the image be disfigured since keep-ing it intact might lead people to suspect Rabbi Yehudah of idol-atry.

Generally speaking, we might suspect people of idolatry if they have some kind of idolatrous form which is not publicly visible, but we do not suspect them if they have the image in a public place. In fact the Talmud cites the story of Avuha de-Shmuel and Levi who prayed in a synagogue with a statue of the king in it. Since there was no question of the synagogue hosting an image dedicated to idolatry, there was no problem with praying in the presence of such an image.

So Rabbi Yehudah had done nothing wrong in having his ring made, but keeping it laid him open to a suspicion of idolatry, which was why Shmuel recommended that he deface it. Rabban Gamliel, on the other hand, had done nothing wrong at all in having the pictures of the Moon. Because the pictures had been made by other people, he had not transgressed the prohibition against making them. Since he was the head of the rabbinical court, he was a public figure, and the room where the pictures were kept was comparable to the synagogue with the statue of the king. It was obvious that they were not there to be worshipped.

The Talmud gives two other possible explanations as to why it was permitted for Rabban Gamliel to have images of the Moon.

One explanation is that the images were made up of various pieces like jigsaw puzzles, and he would only assemble them for the interrogation of witnesses. This meant that he could even have kept them in a private place when he was interviewing witnesses. His keeping the pieces did not raise a suspicion of his being idol-atrous because they were not normally left around in the shape of the Moon. The Shulchan Aruch,[3] the basic code of Jewish law, quotes this reasoning as a minority view, but commentaries on the Shulchan Aruch[4] recommend not relying on this leniency.

Another explanation is that the Torah does not forbid represen-

---

3   Yoreh De'ah 141:7.
4   Ibid, Taz 15 and Shach 32.

what it is like to feel a different amount of gravity. Of course, I was experiencing gravity just like anyone else, but I was falling, along with the Space Station, as we orbited the Earth.

It doesn't feel that way, however. It feels more like there is a 'gravity switch' on the wall, and someone flipped the switch. When you arrive in orbit, and the engines cut off, suddenly you are weightless and it stays that way the entire time you are there. At some point I recall thinking, 'I can hardly imagine what it will feel like to live with gravity again every day'. I won't ever forget that feeling, and I'm reminded of it quite often when I feel the pressure of my body against a surface. I didn't 'sit down' for all that time, and sitting down actually hurt for a few weeks when I came back.

The strength of gravity on Earth felt enormous when I returned. I couldn't believe how persistent and forceful it was for quite some time. On my first night back I recall feeling like I couldn't get all my body parts against the ground firmly enough to satisfy the Earth's gravity. I fell down even while crawling on all fours! I could lean my head to the side and feel the wash of acceleration through my head as if I was making a steep turn in an aircraft. It was amazing to sense gravity like that upon my return.

After many months, life on Earth felt normal again, but I can watch a video from my mission and easily recall the feeling of living without gravity. There was a special freedom and superman-like feeling that is very addictive. You get used to thinking in 3D – not limiting yourself to one orientation. So many tasks are easier if you can do them 'upside down' or in some other orientation, and you never need a ladder!

Sleeping is pure luxury in Space. I would fall asleep in one position and wake up floating in that same position hours later. There is no back pain, twisted sheets, pressure points, tossing and turning . . . . nothing. Interestingly, it took many months before I started to dream onboard of doing things while floating. Usually in my dreams up there I was back on the ground. It took even longer on the ground to start dreaming about being in Zero-G, but I hoped I finally would. I had dreams of flying all my life, but now those dreams are a reflection of a reality that my mind really knows.

Aside from gravity, there is, of course, a transformation in how makes its pillars tremble. He gives a command to the Sun, and it does not rise. He blocks out the stars. He alone stretches out the heavens, and treads on the waves of the sea. He makes the Bear, Orion and the Pleiades . . . '

'He does great things beyond our comprehension, an infinite number of wonderful things . . . How could I answer Him back or argue with Him?' (Job 9:1-14)

Then Bildad the Shuhite answered and said, '. . . Dominion and dread are with Him; He makes peace in His high places. Can anyone count His armies? Is there anyone upon whom His light does not shine?'

'How, then, can man be justified before God? How can he that is born of woman be clean before Him?'

'Behold, even the Moon has no brightness, and the stars are not pure in His sight! How much less so man, who is a worm! How much less so the son of man, who is a maggot!' (Job, chapter 25)

Then Job answered and said, '. . . God stretches out the north over empty space, and suspends the Earth in a void. He binds water in His thick clouds, and the cloud is not ripped underneath them. . . . He has drawn a boundary on the waters between light and darkness . . . He stirs up the sea with His power . . . '

'Indeed, these are just a fraction of His ways. How small a whisper is heard of Him! Who can understand the thunder of His mighty deeds?' (Job, chapter 26)

Then God answered Job out of a whirlwind, and He said, 'Who darkens counsel with ignorant words? Gird your loins like a man, for I will ask you questions, and you must answer Me.'

'Where were you when I laid the foundations of the Earth? . . . Who determined its measure, and who stretched the line over it? How were its foundations made firm, and who laid its corner stone, when the morning stars sang in unison, and all the sons of God shouted for joy?'

'Who shut up the sea with doors when it broke out . . . when I laid down a decree for it, and set up bars and doors, and said, "You may come this far, but no further, and your proud waves will stay here'"? . . .'

'Have you entered the springs of the sea, or walked in the recesses of the deep? Have you surveyed the breadth of the whole Earth? . . .'

'Have you entered the treasuries of the snow, or seen the treasuries of the hail?'

'How does light part, and how is the east wind scattered on the Earth? Who hollowed out a channel for the flood, and who made a path for the lightning?'

'Who makes it rain on the desolate, abandoned wilderness, satisfying the deserted and wasted Earth and bringing out the buds of tender herbs?'

'Does the rain have a father? Who gave birth to drops of dew? From whose womb came forth ice, and who made the hoarfrost?'

'Can you bind the chains of the Pleiades, or loosen the bonds of Orion? Can you lead out the constellations in their right time, and guide the Bear with her sons? Do you know the decrees of the heavens, and can you establish their dominion on Earth? Can you call out to the clouds and make them cover you with floods of water? Can you send out lightning bolts that go out and stand ready for your command?'

'Who put wisdom into the recesses of the body, and who gave understanding to the mind? Who can count the clouds with wisdom? . . .'

Then the Lord spoke to Job again, saying, '. . . Will you dismiss My judgment? Will you condemn Me in order that you may be justified?'

'Or do you have an arm like God? Can you thunder with a voice like Him? Put on majesty and supremacy, and array yourself with glory and beauty! Send out your wrath, and look upon every proud person and humiliate them! Look on everyone who is arrogant, and bring them down. Tread the wicked down where they are. Hide them in the dust together . . . Then I will admit to you that your own right hand can save you.'

(Job 38–40)

BIBLIOGRAPHY

Here is a list of some of the books I used to research *Intergalactic Judaism*:

Barzovski, Rabbi Shalom Noach (The Slonimer Rebbe) (1997): *Netivot Shalom*. Yeshivas Beis Avraham Slonim Jerusalem.

Capra, Fritjof (1976): *The Tao of Physics*. Fontana.

Clark, Rabbi Matityahu (1999): Etymological Dictionary of Biblical Hebrew based on the commentaries of Rabbi Samson Raphael Hirsch. Feldheim.

Gleick, James (1998): *Chaos*. Vintage. London.

Gribbin, John 1998: *In Search of Schrodinger's Cat*. Black Swan, London.

Gribbin, John (2001): *Space - our final frontier*. BBC London.

Hirsch, Rabbi Samson Raphael (1984-1995): *The Collected Writings*. Feldheim (for the Rabbi Dr Joseph Breuer Foundation and the Samson Raphael Hirsch Publications Society), Jerusalem, New York.

Hirsch S R (1978) - The Hirsch Siddur: the order of prayers for the whole year. Translation and Commentary by Samson Raphael Hirsch Feldheim Publishers, Jerusalem, New York.

Hirsch, Rabbi Samson Raphael (1989): *The Pentateuch Translated and Explained*. Judaica Press, Gateshead.

Kaku, Michio (1995): Hyperspace: A Scientific Odyssey through Parallel Universes, Time Warps and the Tenth Dimension. Oxford University Press, Oxford.

Kaplan, Rabbi: 'On Extraterrestrial Life.' (1983) First published in *Intercom* in December 1972 and since incorporated into *The Aryeh Kaplan Reader* (Mesorah Publications).

Luzzatto, Rabbi Moshe Chaim (1983): *Derech Hashem* ('The Way of God'). Translated by Rabbi Aryeh Kaplan. Feldheim. Jerusalem, New York.

Luzzatto, Rabbi Moshe Chaim (2005): *Mesillat Yesharim* ('The Path of the Just'). Translated by Yosef Leibler. Feldheim, Jerusalem, New York.

McNab, David and Younger, James (1999): *The Planets*. BBC, London.

Midrash Rabbah HaShalem (1994). Avida Da'at Umeyda Ltd, Jerusalem.

Sperling, Rabbi Avraham Yitzchak (1982): *Ta'amei ha-minhagim -u-mekorei ha-dinim* (The Reasons for Customs and the Sources of the Laws). Eshkol. Jerusalem.

Volozhin, Rabbi Chaim (1989): *Nefesh HaChaim*. Yissachar Dov Rubin, Bnei Brak.

I also used the Tanach (the Jewish Bible), the Babylonian Talmud and the Shulchan Aruch, all of which are published by various organizations.

GLOSSARY AND BIOGRAPHIES

Gaon of Vilna (1720-1797): Lithuanian commentator on halacha, Talmud and mysticism.

Halacha: Jewish law (adjective: *halachic*).

Hirsch, Rabbi Samson Raphael (1808-1888): German advocate of 'Torah Im Derech Eretz' ('Torah with the way of the world') focussing on constructive engagement with the wider world through Judaism.

Luzzatto, Rabbi Moshe Chaim (1707-1746): Italian mystic, author of *Mesillat Yesharim* and *Derech Hashem*.

Magen Avraham (c. 1633-1683): Polish rabbi and halachic authority.

Maimonides (1135-1204): Jewish philosopher, halachic authority and physician in Spain, Morocco and Egypt.

Midrash: collection of stories, elaborations and halachic rulings based on the Bible written around the second century, presenting mystical and thought-provoking perspectives on the text.

Mishnah (written by Rabbi Yehudah HaNassi, c.200): brief encyclopaedic summary of the Torah laws conveyed by oral tradition since the time of Moses.

Mishnah Berurah (by Rabbi Yisroel Meir Kagan (Poland, 1838-1933)): encyclopaedic commentary on Orach Chaim.

Mishneh Torah (written by Maimonides): summary of the halacha derived from the Talmud.

Mitzvah: commandment.

Nachmanides (1194-1270): Spanish Jewish philosopher, mystic and commentator on the Bible and Talmud.

Ohr HaChaim (1696-1743): Moroccan mystic, philosopher and commentator on the Bible and Talmud.

Orach Chaim: one of the four parts of the Shulchan Aruch.

Pirkei Avot ('Ethics of the Fathers'): a part of the Mishnah dealing with ethical matters.

Rabbenu Tam (1100-1171): grandson of Rashi; halachic authority and Talmud commentator from Ramerupt, France.

Radak (Rabbi David Kimchi from Narbonne in Provence (1160-1235)): Bible commentator and grammarian.

Rashba (Rabbi Shlomo ben Aderet (1235-1310)): commentator on the Talmud and halacha. Leader of Spanish Jewry.

Rashi (Rabbi Shlomo Yitzchaki of France (1040-1105)): commentator on the Bible and Talmud.

Sefer Chassidim (by Rabbi Yehudah ben Shmuel of Regensburg (1140-1217)): a book on prayer and moral conduct.

Shulchan Aruch: a halachic summary of the laws derived from the Mishneh Torah and other major halachic works, written by Rabbi Yosef Karo in the sixteenth century.

Slonimer Rebbe (Rabbi Sholom Noach Berezovsky (1911-2000)): born in Belarus; wrote *Netivot Shalom*, Chassidic insights into Torah, the Jewish calendar and Jewish philosophy.

Talmud: a collective term designating both the Mishnah and the Gemara - discussions on the Mishnah which were compiled c. 500 by Ravina and Rav Ashi.

Tiferet Yisrael (written by Rabbi Yisrael Lipschitz of Dessau, Germany (1782-1860)): commentary on the Mishnah.

Tishri: a month in the Jewish calendar, falling in September and/or October.

Torah: can refer to either the entire corpus of the Jewish Bible and all traditionally based commentaries on it including the Talmud, Midrash, Mishneh Torah, Shulchan Aruch, Kabbala (Jewish mysticism) etc, or the Pentateuch: Genesis, Exodus, Leviticus, Numbers and Deuteronomy.

Volozhin, Rabbi Chaim (1749-1821): disciple of the Gaon of Vilna, author of *Nefesh HaChaim* and founder of a famous yeshiva school (Talmudic school) in Volozhin, now in Belarus.

Ch is pronounced as in *loch*.

PICTURE CREDITS, LEGAL AND COPYRIGHT NOTICES

Front cover

Back cover

Foreword

Introduction

Performing under Pressure

Ultra-violet picture of cloud cover on Venus (NASA); Infrared picture of clouds on Venus (NASA); How Venus looks beneath the clouds (NASA/JPL); Venus probe opens its parachute and is struck by lightning (NASA); Magellan radar image of the surface of Venus (NASA); Artist's impression of surface of Venus (ESA); NASA's Magellan probe being prepared for take-off (NASA/JPL).

Divine brilliance

A beam of white light broken in a prism (NASA, ESA, A Feild, STScI); Diagram of electromagnetic spectrum (Copyright © Zouaveman le Zouave 2007; published under the Creative Commons Attribution ShareAlike 3.0 Unported License: http://en.wikipedia.org/wiki/File:Light_shining2.JPG; cropped from original); Iridescent clouds breaking sunlight into different colours (Copyright © Mila Zinkova 2007; published under the Free Documentation License version 1.2 or any later version: http://en.wikipedia.org/wiki/File:Irid_clouds1.jpg; cropped from original); Cloud in sunlight (Copyright © Ibrahim Iujaz 2006; published under the Creative Commons Attribution 2.0 Generic License: http://www.flickr.com/photos/49512158@N00/770557316/; cropped from original); Coffee maker in visible and infrared light (Torsten Henning); Greenwich Park laser (Copyright © RJP 2005; published under the Creative Commons Attribution Share Alike 2.0 Generic License: http://www.flickr.com/photos/12708857@N00/60371186/; cropped from original).

Moonstruck!

Total eclipse seen from Hacibetkas, Turkey (Copyright © Cactus 26 2006; published under Creative Commons Attribution Sharealike 3.0 Unported, 2.5 Generic, 2.0 Generic and 1.0 Generic licenses: http://commons.wikimedia.org/wiki/File:SolarEclipse20060329tr01.jpg; cropped from original); The Moon's shadow over Antarctica during a solar eclipse (Jacques Descloitres, MODIS Land Rapid Response Team, NASA/GSFC); Diamond ring effect during an eclipse (John Walker); Total eclipse (John Walker); Map of eclipses from Biblical times (Courtesy Fred Espenak, GSFC, NASA. For more information on solar and lunar eclipses, see Fred Espenak's Eclipse Web Site: www.sunearth.gsfc.nasa.gov/eclipse/eclipse.html); The Moon pushes in front of the Sun (John Walker); Geometry of solar eclipse (Sagredo); Total lunar eclipse (NASA).

Earthshine

Diagram showing how the Sun's light reflects off the Earth on to the Moon (NASA); Sunlight reflecting off the Earth as seen from the International Space Station (STS 129 crew, NASA); Fire fighters attend to a blazing car (Copyright © A Magill; published under Creative Common Attribution ShareAlike 2.0 Generic License: http://www.flickr.com/photos/amagill/3225245640/); Picture of Earthshine (Copyright © Steve Jurvetson, 2007; published under the Creative Commons Attribution 2.0 Generic License: http://www.flickr.com/photos/44124348109@N01/364086029/); Earthrise (NASA).

To life!

Diagram of Earth's tilt relative to its orbital plane (Picture of Earth by NASA; Concept and annotations to picture copyright © Dennis Nilsson 2007; published under Creative Commons Attribution 3.0 Unported License; captions made clearer for ease of legibility: http://en.wikipedia.org/wiki/File:AxialTiltObliquity.png); Diagram of Solar System (NASA, JPL); Martian landscape (NSSDC/NASA/JPL); Hurricane Katrina seen from space (NOAA); Palm trees in a typhoon (FEMA/NOAA); Moon seen from Earth (Copyright © Wing Chi Poon 2007; published under the Creative Commons Attribution ShareAlike 2.5 Generic License: http://commons.wikimedia.org/wiki/File:Lunar_Corona.jpg).

The lens of Torah

Diagram of gravitational lensing (NASA, ESA, Andrew Fruchter (STScI), and the ERO team (STScI + ST-ECF); Gravitational lensing imaged by Hubble (NASA, Andrew Fruchter and the ERO Team [Sylvia Baggett (STScI), Richard Hook (ST-ECF), Zoltan Levay (STScI)] (STScI)); Einstein cross (NASA/ESA/STScI); Starry night sky (Copyright © Roberto Mura 2008; published under the GNU Free Documentation License 1.2 or any later version: http://commons.wikimedia.org/wiki/File:Milky_way_-_southern_hemisphere_contrast.jpg).

The celestial clock

Lichen growing on a rock (Copyright © Barbara Page 2007; published under the Creative Commons Attributions ShareAlike 3.0 Unported License: http://en.wikipedia.org/wiki/File:Plants_flowers_ice_rocks_lichens_230.jpg; rotated and cropped from original); Footprint in the lunar dust (NASA); Sun orbiting galaxy (NASA/JPL-Caltech/R.Hurt; Survey credit: GLIMPSE team); Two interacting galaxies ((NASA, ESA, and the Hubble Heritage Team (STScI/AURA)-ESA/Hubble Collaboration, B. Whitmore (STScI), James Long (ESA/Hubble)).

Quick as a flash!

Lightning flashes on Jupiter (Galileo Project, JPL, NASA); Lightning brightens the night sky (Copyright © John R Southern 2003; published under the Creative Commons Attribution ShareAlike 2.0 Generic License: http://www.flickr.com/photos/krunkwerke/267608325/sizes/o/in/photostream/; cropped from original); Lightning strike in Toronto (Copyright © Raul Heinrich 2008; published under the GNU Free Documentation License version 1.2 or any later version: http://commons.wikimedia.org/wiki/File:CN_Tower_struck_by_lightning.jpg; cropped from original); Lightning seen from above (Copyright © 350z33 2010; published under the GNU Free Documentation License version 1.2 or any later version: http://en.wikipedia.org/wiki/File:LightningAboveCloudsView.JPG); Rare lightning forms in upper atmosphere (Copyright © Abestrobi 2008; published under Creative Commons Attribution ShareAlike License Unported: http://en.wikipedia.org/wiki/File:Upperatmoslight1.jpg; captions rewritten for ease of legibility); Cloud to cloud lightning (Copyright © Fir0002/Flagstaffotos 2007; published under GNU Free Documentation License version 1.2 only: http://en.wikipedia.org/wiki/File:Cloud_to_cloud_lightning_strike.jpg); A tree struck by lightning in a forest in Greece (Copyright © Iaberis 2009; published under the Creative Commons Attribution ShareAlike 3.0 Unported License: http://en.wikipedia.org/wiki/File:Tree_struck_by_lightning.JPG; cropped from original).

All fired up!

Stromboli eruption (Copyright © Wolfgang Beyer 1980; published under the GNU Free Documentation License version 1.2 or any later version: http://en.wikipedia.org/wiki/File:Stromboli_Eruption.jpg); Map of the Earth's tectonic plates (USGS); Mount St Helens before the eruption (Harry Glicken, USGS); Mount St Helens after the eruption (Lyn Topinka, USGS); Pyroclastic flows on Mt St Helens (Peter W Lipman, USGS); Lightning generated by a volcanic eruption (Copyright © Oliver Spalt 1995; published under GNU License version 1.2 or any later version and Creative Commons Attribution ShareAlike 2.0 Generic and 3.0 Unported Licenses: http://en.wikipedia.org/wiki/File:Rinjani_1994.jpg); Olympus Mons swathed in carbon dioxide clouds (Mariner 9/NASA/JPL/Caltech); Volcano on Io, one of the moons orbiting Jupiter, photographed by Voyager 1. (NASA); Ground ripped apart in San Francisco earthquake 1906 (G K Gilbert, USGS); Smoke plume from Mt St Helens (USGS, Matt Logan); Erupting volcano seen from space (NASA); Blowdown at Obscurity Lake (Rick Hoblitt, USGS); View down on to Mount Helens (John Pallister, USGS).

Weight loss

Airplane parabola pictures (NASA); Greg Chamitoff plays chess (NASA); Greg Chamitoff carries an instrument rack (NASA).

Our Master's Voice

Trinitite (Copyright © Shaddack 2009; published under the Creative Commons Attribution ShareAlike 3.0 Unported License: http://commons.wikimedia.org/wiki/File:Trinitite-detail5.jpg; cropped from original); House destroyed by nuclear blast (courtesy of National Nuclear Security Administration/Nevada Site Office); Operation Teapot fireball (courtesy of National Nuclear Security Administration/Nevada Site Office); Characteristic mushroom cloud rises to 40,000 feet two minutes after the Ivy Mike detonation (courtesy of National Nuclear Security Administration/Nevada Site Office); The mushroom cloud from the Ivy Mike test rose to a height of twenty-five miles and broadened until it measured a hundred miles across (courtesy of National Nuclear Security Administration/Nevada Site Office); Cedars (Copyright © Peripitus 2009; published under the GNU Free Documentation License version 1.2 or any later version: http://commons.wikimedia.org/wiki/File:The_Cedars_road_view.jpg).

A sunny disposition

Space shuttle Atlantis silhouetted against the Sun (Copyright © Thierry Legault 2009); Sunspots (Copyright © SiriusB) 2004; published under the GNU Free Documentation License version 1.2 or any later version: http://en.wikipedia.org/wiki/File:Sun_projection_with_spotting-scope.jpg); Aurora on Saturn (NASA/JPL/J T Trauger); Comet P1 McNaught (Copyright © Fir0002/Flagstaffotos 2007; published under GNU Free Documentation License version 1.2 only: http://en.wikipedia.org/wiki/File:Comet_P1_McNaught02_-_23-01-07.jpg); Voyager 2 studying the limits of solar influence (Walt Feimer, NASA); The Sun photographed by Skylab 4. (NASA/Skylab 4).

Manpower?

Smash like the one that made the Caloris Basin (T Pyle, SSC); The Valhalla Crater on Callisto (NASA, JPL); Valles Marineris, the 1,500 mile long canyon on Mars (NASA); Close-up of nucleus of Halley's comet (Halley

Multicolor Camera Team, Giotto project, ESA); Fragments of Shoemaker-Levy 9 on their collision course with Jupiter. (NASA, ESA, and H. Weaver and E. Smith (STScI)); View of Jupiter showing brown marks where fragments of the Shoemaker Levy comet ripped into the planet's atmosphere. (Hubble Space Telescope Comet Team/NASA); Clouds on Neptune formed by 700 mph winds (NASA).

Human greatness

Oort Cloud diagram (Donald K Yeomans, NASA and A Feild (STScI)); The Carina Nebula (NASA/ESA/M Livio and the Hubble Twentieth Anniversary Team); Diagram of the Milky Way (NASA/JPL-Caltech); Omega Centauri (ESO); Map of the universe (Copyright © Richard Powell 2006; published under the Creative Commons Attribution ShareAlike 2.5 License: captions rewritten and scale line redrawn for ease of legibility: http://www.atlasoftheuniverse.com/universe.html).

The Great Variety Show

Rosy Martian sunset seen from Mars (IMP/JPL/NASA); Deimos (NASA/ JPL Viking Project); A montage comparing the relative sizes of Jupiter and Earth (NASA/Brian0918/Herbee); Saturn and moons (NASA); Uranus (Voyager 2/NASA); Miranda (NASA); Diamond (Copyright © Steve Jurvetson; published under the Creative Commons Attribution 2.0 Generic License: http://www.flickr.com/photos/jurvetson/156830367/; cropped from original); Comet Hale-Bopp (Copyright © Hans Bernhard 2009; published under Creative Commons Attribution ShareAlike 3.0 Unported License: http://commons.wikimedia.org/wiki/File:Comet_over_Munich_1.jpg; cropped from original); LL Pegasi (ESA, Hubble, R. Sahai (JPL), NASA)

Solid facts?

Lithium-7 atom (Copyright © Halfdan/Indolences; published under the GNU Free Documentation License version 1.2 or any later version); Coal in fireplace (Copyright © Stahlkocher 2004; published under the GNU Free Documentation License version 1.2 or any later version: http://commons.wikimedia.org/wiki/File:Steinkohle_aus_dem_Bergbau.jpg); Eiffel Tower (Brian Tibbets, 2007); Tower block (Copyright © Simon Grubb 2007; published under the Creative Commons Attribution ShareAlike 2.0 Generic Licenses: http://www.flickr.com/photos/mrgrubb/1313952926/; cropped from original); Interference pattern in water drawn by Thomas Young (Thomas Young); Light patterns through single slit and double slit (Copyright © Patrick Edwin Moran 2007; published under the GNU Free Documentation License version 1.2 or any later version: http://commons.wikimedia.org/wiki/File:Single_%26_double_slit_experiment.jpg); Flag blowing in the wind (Copyright © Per Palmkvist Knudsen, 2006; published under Creative Commons Attribution ShareAlike 2.5 Generic License: http://en.wikipedia.org/wiki/File:Dannebrog.jpg); Gold bar (Szaaman 2009); Bread (Copyright © Yoninah 2006; published under GNU Free Documentation License version 1.2 or any later version: http://commons.wikimedia.org/wiki/File:Challah_Braiding.jpg; cropped from original)

Nothing doing

Overview of subatomic particles (Copyright © Gaetan Landry 2009; published under the GNU Free Documentation License version 1.2 or any later version: http://en.wikipedia.org/wiki/File:Particle_overview.svg); Neptune and Triton (NASA/JPL); Casimir effect diagram (Copyright © Emok 2008; published under the Creative Commons Attribution ShareAlike 3.0 Unported License: http://en.wikipedia.org/wiki/File:Casimir_plates.svg; letters closer together than in original).

Making the world go round

Aurora australis seen from space (Crew of STS 39/NASA); Solar wind and the Earth's magnetosphere (NASA); Dust storm in Kansas (NWS, NOAA); Asteroid Gaspra (Galileo Orbiter/NASA/JPL/USGS); Asteroid impact on Earth (NASA/Don Davis); Meteor Crater (Dave Rodd, USGS).

Expanding our horizons

Mercury (NASA/JPL); Carbon dioxide frost on the surface of Mars (NASA); Artist's impression of the landing sequence of the Huygens probe on Titan (NASA/ESA/JPL); Triton's pink nitrogen ice cap (NASA); Triple sunset on a hypothetical moon orbiting HD 188753 Ab (NASA/JPL-Caltech); Torah scroll (Copyright © Willy Horsch 2007; published under GNU Free Documentation License version 1.2 or any later version; cropped from original version).

Go with the flow

A large hailstone (NOAA Photo Library, NWS Wichita, Kansas); A storm cloud gathers over Chaparral, New Mexico (Greg Lundeen, NOAA); Snowflakes under a microscope (Wilson Bentley); Microscopic view of a single snowflake. (Erbe, Pooley: USDA, ARS, EMU); Sunbeams visible in mist over lake (Copyright © Mila Zinkova 2008; published under GNU Free Documentation License version 1.2 or any later version: http://en.wikipedia.org/wiki/File:Crepuscular_rays_in_ggp_2.jpg; cropped from original); Wall cloud with tail cloud (NOAA Photo Library, NOAA Central Library; OAR/ERL/National Severe Storms Laboratory (NSSL)); Rime on a tree (Richardfabi); Edge of the Greenland ice sheet (Copyright © Hannes Grobe, Alfred Wegener Institute for Polar and Marine Research, 1992; published under Creative Commons Attribution Share Alike 2.5 Generic License: http://commons.wikimedia.org/wiki/File:Greenland_ice-sheet_hg.jpg; cropped from original); Niagara River Rapids (Copyright © Maureen 2009; published under the Creative Commons Attribution ShareAlike 2.0 Generic License: http://www.flickr.com/photos/72511054@N00/16412745); Icicles on a house in Oslo, Norway (Copyright © Hans A Rosbach 2009; published under the Creative Commons Attribution ShareAlike 3.0 Unported License: http://en.wikipedia.org/wiki/File:Tidemandsgate_20090222-1.jpg; cropped from original).

The big conversation

A ctenophore (OAR/NOAA/ NURP); Coral spawning (Emma Hickerson/NOAA); A giraffe in the wild (Copyright © KlausF 2004: published under the GNU Free Documentation License version 1.2 or any later version: http://en.wikipedia.org/wiki/File:Giraffe_Kruger.jpg; cropped from original); Dragonfly in midair (Copyright © Fir0002/Flagstaffotos 2006; published under GNU Free Documentation License version 1.2 only: http://en.wikipedia.org/wiki/File:Dragonfly_midair.jpg); A 4 pound lobster (J S Derwin); Elephant in Tanzania (Copyright © Nick and Mel 2006; published under Creative Commons Attribution ShareAlike 2.0 Generic License: http://www.flickr.com/photos/nickandmel/419810995/in/set-7215760005104260/; cropped from original); Indian peacock (Vidhya Narayanan 2011: published under the Creative Commons Attribution ShareAlike 3.0 License: http://upload.wikimedia.org/wikipedia/en/b/b4/Indian_Peacock_Plumage.jpg; cropped from original); School of Goldband Fusiliers (Pterocaesio chrysozona) in Papua New Guinea (Copyright © Mila Zinkova 2004; published under the GNU Free Documentation License version 1.2 or any later version: http://en.wikipedia.org/wiki/File:School_of_Pterocaesio_chrysozona_in_Papua_New_Guinea_1.jpg; cropped from original).

Fire in the skies

The Judean Desert (Copyright © David Shankbone 2007, published under Creative Commons Attribution ShareAlike 3.0 Unported License and GNU License version 1.2 or any later version: http://en.wikipedia.org/wiki/File:Judea_2_by_David_Shankbone.jpg; cropped from original); Hydrothermal vent (NOAA); Devon Island (Anthony Kendall); Cyanobacteria found in Mexico (NASA); The Surveyor 3 lander on the Moon (NASA); Sunrise in the stratosphere (NASA); Microscopic view of the interior of meteorite ALH84001 (NASA); Martian north polar ice cap (NASA/Goddard Space Flight Center Scientific Visualization Studio); Artist's impression of the surface of Titan (NASA); Stars around which planets orbit (NASA, ESA, K Sahu (STScI) and SWEEPS ('Sagittarius Window Eclipsing Extrasolar Planet Search') team).

Life on the outside

Sunlight on the Moon (NASA); The lunar terminator (NASA); Micrometeoroid impact on space shuttle window (NASA); Artist's impression of astronauts on the Moon (NASA); Robotic arm on International Space Station (NASA); Diagram of lunar module (NASA); Tool bag lost in space (NASA); The International Space Station with the Earth in the background (NASA).

All star cast

V838 Monocerotis (NASA, ESA, H E Bond (STScI)); Artist's impression of binary star system (NASA, JPL/CalTech); Binary star system in Cygnus (ESA, Hubble); The Life of Sun-like stars (Copyright © ESO/S. Steinhöfel; published under the Creative Commons Attribution 3.0 Unported License); Flaring magnetar (NASA).

Distance no object

NASA engineers work on Mariner 10 (NASA); NASA's *New Horizons* mission blasts off from Cape Canaveral bound for Pluto (NASA); Test firing F-1 engine (NASA); Artist's rendition of a rocket powered by antimatter (NASA); Deep Space 1 (NASA); Simulation of Black Hole in front of Large Magellanic Cloud (Copyright © Alain R 2006; published under Creative Commons Attribution ShareAlike 2.5 Generic License: http://commons.wikimedia.org/wiki/File:BH_LMC.png; cropped from original).

The Death of the Universe

Artist's impression of a dust cloud from a supernova explosion (Hubble SM4 ERO team, NASA, ESA); NGC 2440, an exploding planetary nebula (ESA/NASA/K Noll (STScI)/Hubble Heritage Team, AURA); Artist's impression of a disk of debris around a white dwarf (T Pyle/SSC/NASA/JPL-Caltech); Sand timer (Copyright © S Sepp 2007; published under the GNU Free Documentation License version 1.2 or any later version: http://en.wikipedia.org/wiki/File:Wooden_hourglass_3.jpg).

Hyperspatial Judaism

Banana pictures (Copyright © Fir0002/Flagstaffotos 2009; published under the GNU Free Documentation License version 1.2 only: http://en.wikipedia.org/wiki/File:Banana_and_cross_section.jpg); Cover of Flatland book (Edwin Abbott Abbott); Three-dimensional shadow cast by four-dimensional cube (Copyright © Goffrie, 2006 modified by Mouagip 2010; published under the GNU Free Documentation License version 1.2 or any later version: http://en.wikipedia.org/wiki/File:Hypercube.svg); Unfolded tesseract (DMN, modified by Stannered); Shadow of flowers in a vase (Copyright © Nevit Dilmen 2006; published under the GNU Free Documentation License version 1.2 or any later version: http://commons.wikimedia.org/wiki/File:Shadow_2752.jpg)

Old world order

Turbulence generated by aircraft (NASA Langley Research Centre); High Force waterfall, Teesdale, UK (Stoatbringer); Turbulence on Jupiter (NASA/JPL/Caltech); The Lorenz attractor (Copyright © Wikimol 2006; published under GNU Free Documentation License Version 1.2 or any later version and Creative Commons Attribution ShareAlike 3.0 Unported License and Creative Commons Attribution ShareAlike 1.0, 2.0 and 2.5 Generic Licenses: http://en.wikipedia.org/wiki/File:Lorenz_attractor_yb.svg); Turbulence in water (Aarchiba); Strange attractor's abstract beauty (Copyright © Adam Majewski 2009; published under the Creative Commons Attribution ShareAlike 3.0 Unported License); Mira (NASA); Wave breaking (Copyright © Tewy 2006; published under the GNU Free Documentation License Version 1.2 or any later version: http://commons.wikimedia.org/wiki/File:Asilomar_State_Beach_(Breaking_wave)_03.jpg).

The star of the show

Fragment from the Sikhote-Alin meteorite (Copyright © Doug Bowman 2004; published under the Creative Commons Attribution 2.0 Generic License: http://www.flickr.com/photos/16533652@N00/2506852); Artist's impression of an asteroid belt (T Pyle, SSC, NASA); A meteor streaking towards the ground (Copyright © Navicore 2009; published under Creative Commons Attribution 3.0 Unported License: http://commons.wikimedia.org/wiki/File:Leonid_Meteor.jpg; cropped from original).

The universal temple

Temple Mount, site of the Temple built by King Solomon (Copyright © Asaf Ts 2007; published under the GNU Free Documentation License version 1.2 or any later version: http://en.wikipedia.org/wiki/File:Temple_mount.JPG); Diagram of Temple (Copyright © Gabriel Fink 2009; published under GNU Free Documentation License version 1.2 or any later version: http://en.wikipedia.org/wiki/File:Tabernacle_Schematic.jpg. Captions rewritten for ease of legibility); COBE satellite (COBE science team/NASA); Cosmic microwave background radiation map (WMAP/NASA); Rainfall (Copyright © Malene Thyssen http://commons.wikimedia.org/wiki/User:Malene; published under the GNU Free Documentation License version 1.2 or any later version and Creative Commons Attribution ShareAlike 2.5 Generic License: http://en.wikipedia.org/wiki/File:Regnbyge.jpg; cropped from original); Fire (Copyright © Pavel Sevela 2007; published under Creative Commons Attribution ShareAlike 3.0 Unported License: http://commons.wikimedia.org/wiki/File:Fire_from_loppings.JPG; cropped from original); Artist's impression of the ark of the covenant (Copyright © Ben Schumin 2006; published under the Creative Commons Attribution ShareAlike 2.5 Generic License: http://commons.wikimedia.org/wiki/File:Royal_Arch_Room_Ark_replica_2.jpg); Map of dark matter (Copyright © NASA/ESA/R Massey (Caltech)); Shabbat table (Gila Brand; Licensed under the Creative Commons Attribution 2.5 Generic License: http://en.wikipedia.org/wiki/File:ShabbatableS.jpg; cropped from original and reshaped into a oval).

Appendix 1

Greg Chamitoff floating in the International Space Station (NASA).

TEXT OF THE GNU FREE DOCUMENTATION LICENSE

0.   PREAMBLE

The purpose of this License is to make a manual, textbook, or other functional and useful document "free" in the sense of freedom: to assure everyone the effective freedom to copy and redistribute it, with or without modifying it, either commercially or noncommercially. Secondarily, this License preserves for the author and publisher a way to get credit for their work, while not being considered responsible for modifications made by others.

This License is a kind of "copyleft", which means that derivative works of the document must themselves be free in the same sense. It complements the GNU General Public License, which is a copyleft license designed for free software.

We have designed this License in order to use it for manuals for free software, because free software needs free documentation: a free program should come with manuals providing the same freedoms that the software does. But this License is not limited to software manuals; it can be used for any textual work, regardless of subject matter or whether it is published as a printed book. We recommend this License principally for works whose purpose is instruction or reference.

1.   APPLICABILITY AND DEFINITIONS

This License applies to any manual or other work, in any medium, that contains a notice placed by the copyright holder saying it can be distributed under the terms of this License. Such a notice grants a world-wide, royalty-free license, unlimited in duration, to use that work under the conditions stated herein. The "Document", below, refers to any such manual or work. Any member of the public is a licensee, and is addressed as "you". You accept the license if you copy, modify or distribute the work in a way requiring permission under copyright law.

A "Modified Version" of the Document means any work containing the Document or a portion of it, either copied verbatim, or with modifications and/or translated into another language.

A "Secondary Section" is a named appendix or a front-matter section of the Document that deals exclusively with the relationship of the publishers or authors of the Document to the Document's overall subject (or to related matters) and contains nothing that could fall directly within that overall subject. (Thus, if the Document is in part a textbook of mathematics, a Secondary Section may not explain any mathematics.) The relationship could be a matter of historical connection with the subject or with related matters, or of legal, commercial, philosophical, ethical or political position regarding them.

The "Invariant Sections" are certain Secondary Sections whose titles are designated, as being those of Invariant Sections, in the notice that says that the Document is released under this License. If a section does not fit the above definition of Secondary then it is not allowed to be designated as Invariant. The Document may contain zero Invariant Sections. If the Document does not identify any Invariant Sections then there are none.

The "Cover Texts" are certain short passages of text that are listed, as Front-Cover Texts or Back-Cover Texts, in the notice that says that the Document is released under this License. A Front-Cover Text may be at most 5 words, and a Back-Cover Text may be at most 25 words.

A "Transparent" copy of the Document means a machine-readable copy, represented in a format whose specification is available to the general public, that is suitable for revising the document straightforwardly with generic text editors or (for images composed of pixels) generic paint programs or (for drawings) some widely available drawing editor, and that is suitable for input to text formatters or for automatic translation to a variety of formats suitable for input to text formatters. A copy made in an otherwise Transparent file format whose markup, or absence of markup, has been arranged to thwart or discourage subsequent modification by readers is not Transparent. An image format is not Transparent if used for any substantial amount of text. A copy that is not "Transparent" is called "Opaque".

Examples of suitable formats for Transparent copies include plain ASCII without markup, Texinfo input format, LaTeX input format, SGML or XML using a publicly available DTD, and standard-conforming simple HTML, PostScript or PDF designed for human modification. Examples of transparent image formats include PNG, XCF and JPG. Opaque formats include proprietary formats that can be read and edited only by proprietary word processors, SGML or XML for which the DTD and/or processing tools are not generally available, and the machine-generated HTML, PostScript or PDF produced by some word processors for output purposes only.

The "Title Page" means, for a printed book, the title page itself, plus such following pages as are needed to hold, legibly, the material this License requires to appear in the title page. For works in formats which do not have any title page as such, "Title Page" means the text near the most prominent appearance of the work's title, preceding the beginning of the body of the text.

The "publisher" means any person or entity that distributes copies of the Document to the public.

A section "Entitled XYZ" means a named subunit of the Document whose title either is precisely XYZ or contains XYZ in parentheses following text that translates XYZ in another language. (Here XYZ stands for a specific section name mentioned below, such as "Acknowledgements", "Dedications", "Endorsements", or "History".) To "Preserve the Title" of such a section when you modify the Document means that it remains a section "Entitled XYZ" according to this definition.

The Document may include Warranty Disclaimers next to the notice which states that this License applies to the Document. These Warranty Disclaimers are considered to be included by reference in this License, but only as regards disclaiming warranties: any other implication that these Warranty Disclaimers may have is void and has no effect on the meaning of this License.

2. VERBATIM COPYING

You may copy and distribute the Document in any medium, either commercially or noncommercially, provided that this License, the copyright notices, and the license notice saying this License applies to the Document are reproduced in all copies, and that you add no other conditions whatsoever to those of this License. You may not use technical measures to obstruct or control the reading or further copying of the copies you make or distribute. However, you may accept compensation in exchange for copies. If you distribute a large enough number of copies you must also follow the conditions in section 3.

You may also lend copies, under the same conditions stated above, and you may publicly display copies.

3. COPYING IN QUANTITY

If you publish printed copies (or copies in media that commonly have printed covers) of the Document, numbering more than 100, and the Document's license notice requires Cover Texts, you must enclose the copies in covers that carry, clearly and legibly, all these Cover Texts: Front-Cover Texts on the front cover, and Back-Cover Texts on the back cover. Both covers must also clearly and legibly identify you as the publisher of these copies. The front cover must present the full title with all words of the title equally prominent and visible. You may add other material on the covers in addition. Copying with changes limited to the covers, as long as they preserve the title of the Document and satisfy these conditions, can be treated as verbatim copying in other respects.

If the required texts for either cover are too voluminous to fit legibly, you should put the first ones listed (as many as fit reasonably) on the actual cover, and continue the rest onto adjacent pages.

If you publish or distribute Opaque copies of the Document numbering more than 100, you must either include a machine-readable Transparent copy along with each Opaque copy, or state in or with each Opaque copy a computer-network location from which the general network-using public has access to download using public-standard network protocols a complete Transparent copy of the Document, free of added material. If you use the latter option, you must take reasonably prudent steps, when you begin distribution of Opaque copies in quantity, to ensure that this Transparent copy will remain thus accessible at the stated location until at least one year after the last time you distribute an Opaque copy (directly or through your agents or retailers) of that edition to the public.

It is requested, but not required, that you contact the authors of the Document well before redistributing any large number of copies, to give them a chance to provide you with an updated version of the Document.

4. MODIFICATIONS

You may copy and distribute a Modified Version of the Document under the conditions of sections 2 and 3 above, provided that you release the Modified Version under precisely this License, with the Modified Version filling the role of the Document, thus licensing distribution and modification of the Modified Version to whoever possesses a copy of it. In addition, you must do these things in the Modified Version:

A. Use in the Title Page (and on the covers, if any) a title distinct from that of the Document, and from those of previous versions (which should, if there were any, be listed in the History section of the Document). You may use the same title as a previous version if the original publisher of that version gives permission.

B. List on the Title Page, as authors, one or more persons or entities responsible for authorship of the modifications in the Modified Version, together with at least five of the principal authors of the Document (all of its principal authors, if it has fewer than five), unless they release you from this requirement.

C. State on the Title page the name of the publisher of the Modified Version, as the publisher.

D. Preserve all the copyright notices of the Document.

E. Add an appropriate copyright notice for your modifications adjacent to the other copyright notices.

F. Include, immediately after the copyright notices, a license notice giving the public permission to use the Modified Version under the terms of this License, in the form shown in the Addendum below.

G. Preserve in that license notice the full lists of Invariant Sections and required Cover Texts given in the Document's license notice.

H. Include an unaltered copy of this License.

I. Preserve the section Entitled "History", Preserve its Title, and add to it an item stating at least the title, year, new authors, and publisher of the Modified Version as given on the Title Page. If there is no section Entitled "History" in the Document, create one stating the title, year, authors, and publisher of the Document as given on its Title Page, then add an item describing the Modified Version as stated in the previous sentence.

J. Preserve the network location, if any, given in the Document for public access to a Transparent copy of the Document, and likewise the network locations given in the Document for previous versions it was based on. These may be placed in the "History" section. You may omit a network location for a work that was published at least four years before the Document itself, or if the original publisher of the version it refers to gives permission.

K.   For any section Entitled "Acknowledgements" or "Dedications", Preserve the Title of the section, and preserve in the section all the substance and tone of each of the contributor acknowledgements and/or dedications given therein.

L.   Preserve all the Invariant Sections of the Document, unaltered in their text and in their titles. Section numbers or the equivalent are not considered part of the section titles.

M.   Delete any section Entitled "Endorsements". Such a section may not be included in the Modified version.

N.   Do not retitle any existing section to be Entitled "Endorsements" or to conflict in title with any Invariant Section.

O.   Preserve any Warranty Disclaimers.

If the Modified Version includes new front-matter sections or appendices that qualify as Secondary Sections and contain no material copied from the Document, you may at your option designate some or all of these sections as invariant. To do this, add their titles to the list of Invariant Sections in the Modified Version's license notice. These titles must be distinct from any other section titles.

You may add a section Entitled "Endorsements", provided it contains nothing but endorsements of your Modified Version by various parties—for example, statements of peer review or that the text has been approved by an organization as the authoritative definition of a standard.

You may add a passage of up to five words as a Front-Cover Text, and a passage of up to 25 words as a Back-Cover Text, to the end of the list of Cover Texts in the Modified Version. Only one passage of Front-Cover Text and one of Back-Cover Text may be added by (or through arrangements made by) any one entity. If the Document already includes a cover text for the same cover, previously added by you or by arrangement made by the same entity you are acting on behalf of, you may not add another; but you may replace the old one, on explicit permission from the previous publisher that added the old one.

The author(s) and publisher(s) of the Document do not by this License give permission to use their names for publicity for or to assert or imply endorsement of any Modified Version.

5.   COMBINING DOCUMENTS

You may combine the Document with other documents released under this License, under the terms defined in section 4 above for modified versions, provided that you include in the combination all of the Invariant Sections of all of the original documents, unmodified, and list them all as Invariant Sections of your combined work in its license notice, and that you preserve all their Warranty Disclaimers.

The combined work need only contain one copy of this License, and multiple identical Invariant Sections may be replaced with a single copy. If there are multiple Invariant Sections with the same name but different contents, make the title of each such section unique by adding at the end of it, in parentheses, the name of the original author or publisher of that section if known, or else a unique number. Make the same adjustment to the section titles in the list of Invariant Sections in the license notice of the combined work.

In the combination, you must combine any sections Entitled "History" in the various original documents, forming one section Entitled "History"; likewise combine any sections Entitled "Acknowledgements", and any sections Entitled "Dedications". You must delete all sections Entitled "Endorsements".

6.   COLLECTIONS OF DOCUMENTS

You may make a collection consisting of the Document and other documents released under this License, and replace the individual copies of this License in the various documents with a single copy that is included in the collection, provided that you follow the rules of this License for verbatim copying of each of the documents in all other respects.

You may extract a single document from such a collection, and distribute it individually under this License, provided you insert a copy of this License into the extracted document, and follow this License in all other respects regarding verbatim copying of that document.

7.   AGGREGATION WITH INDEPENDENT WORKS

A compilation of the Document or its derivatives with other separate and independent documents or works, in or on a volume of a storage or distribution medium, is called an "aggregate" if the copyright resulting from the compilation is not used to limit the legal rights of the compilation's users beyond what the individual works permit. When the Document is included in an aggregate, this License does not apply to the other works in the aggregate which are not themselves derivative works of the Document.

If the Cover Text requirement of section 3 is applicable to these copies of the Document, then if the Document is less than one half of the entire aggregate, the Document's Cover Texts may be placed on covers that bracket the Document within the aggregate, or the electronic equivalent of covers if the Document is in electronic form. Otherwise they must appear on printed covers that bracket the whole aggregate.

8.   TRANSLATION

Translation is considered a kind of modification, so you may distribute translations of the Document under the terms of section 4. Replacing Invariant Sections with translations requires special permission from their copyright holders, but you may include translations of some or all Invariant Sections in addition to the original versions of these Invariant Sections. You may include a translation of this License, and all the license notices in the Document, and any Warranty Disclaimers, provided that you also include the original English version of this License and the original versions of those notices and disclaimers. In case of a disagreement between the translation and the original version of this License or a notice or disclaimer, the original version will prevail.

If a section in the Document is Entitled "Acknowledgements", "Dedications", or "History", the require-ment (section 4) to Preserve its Title (section 1) will typically require changing the actual title.

9.   TERMINATION

You may not copy, modify, sublicense, or distribute the Document except as expressly provided under this License. Any attempt otherwise to copy, modify, sublicense, or distribute it is void, and will automatically terminate your rights under this License.

However, if you cease all violation of this License, then your license from a particular copyright holder is reinstated (a) provisionally, unless and until the copyright holder explicitly and finally terminates your license, and (b) permanently, if the copyright holder fails to notify you of the violation by some reasonable means prior to 60 days after the cessation.

Moreover, your license from a particular copyright holder is reinstated permanently if the copyright holder notifies you of the violation by some reasonable means, this is the first time you have received notice of violation of this License (for any work) from that copyright holder, and you cure the violation prior to 30 days after your receipt of the notice.

Termination of your rights under this section does not terminate the licenses of parties who have received copies or rights from you under this License. If your rights have been terminated and not permanently reinstated, receipt of a copy of some or all of the same material does not give you any rights to use it.

10.   FUTURE REVISIONS OF THIS LICENSE

The Free Software Foundation may publish new, revised versions of the GNU Free Documentation License from time to time. Such new versions will be similar in spirit to the present version, but may differ in detail to address new problems or concerns. See http://www.gnu.org/copyleft/.

Each version of the License is given a distinguishing version number. If the Document specifies that a particular numbered version of this License "or any later version" applies to it, you have the option of following the terms and conditions either of that specified version or of any later version that has been published (not as a draft) by the Free Software Foundation. If the Document does not specify a version number of this License, you may choose any version ever published (not as a draft) by the Free Software Foundation. If the Document specifies that a proxy can decide which future versions of this License can be used, that proxy's public statement of acceptance of a version permanently authorizes you to choose that version for the Document.

11.   RELICENSING

"Massive Multiauthor Collaboration Site" (or "MMC Site") means any World Wide Web server that publishes copyrightable works and also provides prominent facilities for anybody to edit those works. A public wiki that anybody can edit is an example of such a server. A "Massive Multiauthor Collaboration" (or "MMC") contained in the site means any set of copyrightable works thus published on the MMC site.

"CC-BY-SA" means the Creative Commons Attribution-Share Alike 3.0 license published by Creative Commons Corporation, a not-for-profit corporation with a principal place of business in San Francisco, California, as well as future copyleft versions of that license published by that same organization.

"Incorporate" means to publish or republish a Document, in whole or in part, as part of another Document.

An MMC is "eligible for relicensing" if it is licensed under this License, and if all works that were first published under this License somewhere other than this MMC, and subsequently incorporated in whole or in part into the MMC, (1) had no cover texts or invariant sections, and (2) were thus incorporated prior to November 1, 2008.

The operator of an MMC Site may republish an MMC contained in the site under CC-BY-SA on the same site at any time before August 1, 2009, provided the MMC is eligible for relicensing.

HOW TO USE THIS LICENSE FOR YOUR DOCUMENTS

To use this License in a document you have written, include a copy of the License in the document and put the following copyright and license notices just after the title page:

Copyright (c) YEAR YOUR NAME.

Permission is granted to copy, distribute and/or modify this document under the terms of the GNU Free Documentation License, Version 1.3 or any later version published by the Free Software Foundation; with no Invariant Sections, no Front-Cover Texts, and no Back-Cover Texts.

A copy of the license is included in the section entitled "GNU Free Documentation License".

If you have Invariant Sections, Front-Cover Texts and Back-Cover Texts, replace the "with . . . Texts." line with this:

with the Invariant Sections being LIST THEIR TITLES, with the Front-Cover Texts being LIST, and with the Back-Cover Texts being LIST.

If you have Invariant Sections without Cover Texts, or some other combination of the three, merge those two alternatives to suit the situation.

If your document contains nontrivial examples of program code, we recommend releasing these examples in parallel under your choice of free software license, such as the GNU General Public License, to permit their use in free software.

CREATIVE COMMONS LICENSE

The Creative Commons Licenses can be viewed as follows:

Creative Commons Attribution ShareAlike 1.0 Generic License:
   http://creativecommons.org/Licenses/by-sa/1.0/

Creative Commons Attribution 2.0 Generic License:
   http://creativecommons.org/Licenses/by-sa/2.0/

Creative Commons Attribution ShareAlike 2.5 Generic License:
   http://creativecommons.org/Licenses/by-sa/2.5/

Creative Commons Attribution ShareAlike 3.0 Unported License:
   http://creativecommons.org/Licenses/by-sa/3.0/